T5-BPZ-152

NATIONAL WELFARE AND ECONOMIC INTERDEPENDENCE

National Welfare and Economic Interdependence

The Case of Sweden's Foreign Trade Policy

EBBA DOHLMAN

CLARENDON PRESS · OXFORD
1989

382.3
D655n

Oxford University Press, Walton Street, Oxford OX2 6DP
Oxford New York Toronto
Delhi Bombay Calcutta Madras Karachi
Petaling Jaya Singapore Hong Kong Tokyo
Nairobi Dar es Salaam Cape Town
Melbourne Auckland
and associated companies in
Berlin Ibadan

Oxford is a trade mark of Oxford University Press

Published in the United States
by Oxford University Press, New York

©Ebba Dohlman 1989

All rights reserved. No part of this publication may be reproduced,
stored in a retrieval system, or transmitted, in any form or by any means,
electronic, mechanical, photocopying, recording, or otherwise, without
the prior permission of Oxford University Press

British Library Cataloguing in Publication Data
Dohlman, Ebba
National welfare and economic
interdependence : the case of Sweden's foreign
trade policy.
1. Sweden. Foreign trade. Policies of
government
I. Title
382.3' 09485
ISBN 0-19-827558-7

Library of Congress Cataloging in Publication Data
Dohlman, Ebba.
National welfare and economic interdependence : the case of
Sweden's foreign trade policy/Ebba Dohlman.
p. cm.
Bibliography: p. Includes index.
1. Sweden—Commercial policy. 2. Sweden—Nonalignment.
3. Textile industry—Government policy—Sweden. 4. Sweden—Foreign
economic relations. I. Title.
HF1567.D65 1989   382'.3' 09485—dc19   88-39860
ISBN 0-19-827558-7

Phototypeset by Dobbie Typesetting Limited

Printed in Great Britain
by Biddles Ltd.
Guildford and King's Lynn

90-2028

Library of
Davidson College

Acknowledgements

The writing of this book would not have been possible without the inspiration and support given by a number of individuals and institutions. For generous financial support, I am grateful for the University of London Central Research Fund grant; the Stiftelsen Siamon grant from G. Grönberg's Advokatbyrå; the Nordic Cooperation Committee award for International Politics including Peace and Conflict Research; and the European Free Trade Association scholarship in the area of European trade and trade policy for postgraduate research.

Those individuals who stimulated my interest in textile trade policy, and who inspired me particularly in the initial stages of the work, include the former Chairman, Textiles Surveillance Body, and Ambassador to Switzerland, Paul Wurth, as well as other members of GATT, Peter Tulloch, Triptee Jenkins, Åke Lindén, Sanjoy Bagchi, David Hartridge, and Andrée Jost. I am indebted also to Nicolas Marian of the International Textiles and Clothing Bureau.

I have also benefited from discussions and suggestions from Swedish academics and officials including Carl Hamilton of the Institute for International Economics; Gunnar Sjöstedt of the Swedish Institute of International Affairs; Ambassador Odevall and Torsten Westlund of the Swedish Ministry for Foreign Affairs; Magnus Vahlquist and Lars Karlberg formerly of EFTA; Peter Kleen of the Swedish Board of Commerce and Åke Weyler of Textilimportörerna.

I should not neglect to mention all my friends and staff from the London School of Economics who have, in one way or another, given me valuable advice and endless support. Of these, I am particularly indebted to James Mayall and to Diana Tussie. They have borne with me through all my moments of doubt and have generously shared with me their time, their wisdom and their enthusiasm.

Amongst all those women who have sacrificed their free time to decipher and type my hieroglyphics, I am particularly grateful to Lynne Broadley and Avril Ellis. They have ultimately done much more for me than just type.

Last but not least, I would like to extend special thanks to all the Dohlmans and to my husband, Andrew Dean. They have provided me with an endless stream of encouragement and it is from them that I have learned the importance of patience and tenacity.

E.D.

Author's Note

As this book goes to press, it appears that some major reforms in Swedish textile policies are in prospect. In a statement on the economy on 20 October 1988, the Government announced its intention to allow all its current bilateral textile trade agreements with 'low-cost' countries to lapse by 31 July 1991, at the time when MFA 4 expires. Within the new round of multilateral trade negotiations, Sweden would also strive to bring back her textile and clothing trade within GATT rules. The statement declared that import restrictions lead to higher prices for consumers and can result in a net welfare loss for the country. A deregulation would be beneficial to consumers and help prevent inflation. It might also have positive effects for developing countries.

The statement noted that following a long-standing and intensive structural adjustment the textile and clothing industries had achieved greater stability and improved their profitability in recent years. Despite proposals to continue certain support measures to confront the anticipated hardening of competition in 1991, these substantial reforms seem to indicate that the force of the arguments against protectionism which this book had dealt with has now been acknowledged.

Contents

Tables and Figure

Tables

Figure

Abbreviations

BTN	Brussels Nomenclature
CCN	Customs Co-operation Nomenclature
COCOM	the Coordinating Committee on Export Controls
ECSC	European Coal and Steel Community
EEC	European Economic Community
EFTA	European Free Trade Association
FBU	Försörjningsberedskapsutredningen
GATT	General Agreement on Tariffs and Trade
GNP	gross national product
GSP	generalized system of preferences
IBRD	International Bank for Reconstruction and Development
IMF	International Monetary Fund
ITO	International Trade Organization
LDC	less-developed countries
LO	Landsorganisation (Federation of Trade Unions)
LTA	Long-Term Arrangement on Cotton Textiles
MFA	Multi-Fibre Arrangement
MFN	most-favoured-nation
MTN	Multilateral Trade Negotiations
MVP	minimum viable production
NATO	North Atlantic Treaty Organization
NICs	newly-industrialized countries
NIEO	new international economic order
NTB	non-tariff barriers
ÖCB	Överstyrelsen för civil beredskap (the National Board for Civil Preparedness)
OECD	Organization for Economic Co-operation and Development
OEEC	Organization for European Economic Co-operation
ÖEF	Överstyrelsen för ekonomiskt försvar (the National Board of Economic Defence)
OMA	orderly marketing arrangements
OPEC	Organization of Petroleum Exporting Countries

RKE	Riks-Kommissionen för ekonomisk försvarsberedskap
SITC	Standard International Trade Classification
SOU	Statens Offentliga Utredningar (Swedish Official Studies)
STA	Short-Term Arrangement on Cotton Textiles
TSB	Textiles Surveillance Body
UN	United Nations
UNCTAD	United Nations Conference on Trade and Development
VER	voluntary export restraints

Introduction

Economic liberalism is a fair-weather philosophy. It assumes that welfare will be maximized if government interference is kept to a minimum and the allocation of resources is decided by market forces. After 1945, under American leadership, this economic philosophy was elevated to become one of the major supports of the Western political, as well as its economic, order. For most of the Western states which embraced this philosophy, and joined the new international institutions which were created to protect it, there was no conflict between this economic strategy and their security policies: they were members of the Western Alliance and did not therefore have to have an elaborate system of economic contingency planning. In the case of Sweden as a neutral, however, there was from the start a tension between the economic implications of the country's traditional policy of neutrality, which required such contingency planning, and the authorities' enthusiastic support for liberal trade policies as the best way of providing for economic growth and prosperity. This study examines the way in which this tension, which was at first concealed by the dynamism of the Western economy in general, has gradually embroiled the Swedish government in an economic-defence policy which is both internally inconsistent and, in important respects, ineffective.

This study then explores two particular themes in contemporary international economic relations. The first concerns the general relationship between national security and the international trading order; the second, the particular problems posed by this relationship for neutral countries.

Both themes are addressed primarily as they arise for one such country, Sweden. But, because the relationship between Sweden's economic security and foreign trade policies cannot be understood in isolation, several chapters are devoted to exploring the two themes in their wider international context. The main argument, moreover, is that this context has undergone a major change since 1945: the conception of security employed by modern states, above all by neutrals, has been progressively widened to include welfare and the defence of the national economy generally. As a result of this enlarging of the states' responsibilities it has become increasingly difficult to reconcile the requirements of economic security for individual states with the multilateral trade rules of the GATT. This problem is illustrated in the second part of the study by means of a case study of international trade in textiles, the sector in which it has arisen most sharply.

The extent to which foreign trade and trade policy had a bearing on the problem of war and peace was considered by political and economic thinkers even in the ancient world, and more particularly since the rise of the modern centralized state. Those who perceived this link were concerned with the following questions: What are the economic causes and effects of war? In what ways should the problems of security and war industries be handled in economic policy? Which economic conditions and policies are most conducive to international peace and co-operation? Is peace possible, and if so, can it be maintained through international institutions? This study is primarily concerned with the changing conception of the relationship between trade policy and security in the context of post-war interdependence. But, although as we shall see, conceptions of security have changed, modern writers have none the less taken over many earlier positions, just as contemporary governments use many traditional economic policy measures.

This problem of change and continuity in both the literature and in government policy will be illustrated in summary form here and then elaborated in Chapter 1. Ancient economic and political thought addressed some of these questions in terms of the benefits of self-sufficiency versus specialization. Economic self-reliance was characteristic of primitive or isolated societies and, indeed, predates the modern state. Classical Greece was a world which aspired towards self-sufficient city-states. In his writings, Aristotle showed little inclination towards specialization: 'everyone would agree in praising the territory which is most entirely self-sufficing, and that must be the territory which is all-producing, for to have all things and to want nothing is sufficiency'.[1]

---

[1] Aristotle, *Politics*, 1326^b, 26–30, tr. Ernest Barker, *The Politics of Aristotle* (Oxford, 1946).

Economic self-reliance in classical philosophy was considered as an end in itself and a means of obtaining or preserving an identity.

The mercantilists, whose doctrines appeared during the demise of the feudal economy and growth of commercial capitalism, were also concerned with the national unification and identity of the state but viewed economic policy and, more specifically, protectionist devices as mere instruments for increasing the wealth and power of the state.

The objectives of increasing profits and power at the expense of rival states were seen as one and the same interest, which could be achieved by maintaining a favourable balance of trade. But, although power rather than security was the dominating concern of mercantilist governments, several small states were able to develop a policy of security based on neutrality as a way of protecting their trading rights during a period of virtually permanent economic warfare.

The view of exchange contained in traditional mercantilist thought was zero-sum: in any trade, one's gain was the other's loss. Although, as we shall see, one consequence of liberal thought has been to undermine this assumption with respect to 'normal' economic relationships, and hence to deflect attention away from the special trade problems of small neutral states, there is a strong mercantilist legacy in much of the realist and even some of the modernist literature on international relations.

The work of Albert Hirschman is an example of contemporary 'realism'. In *National Power and the Structure of Foreign Trade* (1945) he addresses the question of why and how foreign trade may be used consciously as an instrument of national power policy. The main example he uses is the foreign trade policy of the Third Reich. A parallel post-war example would be the periodic attempts by the Western powers, particularly the United States, to impose a general trade embargo against the Soviet Union and Eastern Europe.

Two influential contemporary authors who may be classified as neo-mercantilists are Keohane and Nye. In *Power and Interdependence* (1977) they adopt an eclectic approach to analysing economic interdependence in the context of national security. They are particularly concerned with the vulnerability of states in terms of the costs associated with interdependence among industrialized countries. As states become increasingly interdependent, they expose themselves to the danger of manipulation by other states having greater resources in a military and economic sense.

The phase in the history of economic thought that has remained the strongest influence on international trade policy to the present day is classical liberalism. Adam Smith, Malthus, and Ricardo all attached considerable importance explicitly or implicitly to the relationship between free trade and national defence. Although many liberals conceded that agriculture or war industries should be protected in case of a blockade in wartime, they generally believed that free trade would benefit all countries and therefore obviate the inevitability of war and conflicts. Thus, the pursuit of prosperity rather than power dominated their perceptions of how international relations would evolve and peace prevail.

Since the alleged relationship between peace and prosperity in liberal economic thought is central to the themes discussed in this study I shall return to it in more detail. The important point to make here is that the modern 'neo-liberal' view of international relations has adopted many of the ideas originating in classical and neo-classical economic thought. Although such authors as Haas, Young, Bergsten, and Cooper have recognized both the costs and benefits derived from the increasingly complicated interconnectedness of states, in the last analysis they regard interdependence as conducive to international order.

The benefits that have accrued from economic interdependence since 1945 are often attributed to the international environment and organization created by the Bretton Woods system (the IMF and IBRD) as well as the GATT. Cohen, another neo-liberal, has written, 'The interdependence of the world economy was both a cause and a result of the design of the post-war economic order.'[2] One need only compare the post-war period of world trade, production, and productivity trends—as well as international movements of capital, skills, and technology—with previous periods, to understand why

---

[2] Benjamin Cohen, Introduction to Wolfgang Hager, 'Economic Security', in id. *et al.*, *European Economic Issues*, Praeger Special Studies in International Economics and Development, Atlantic Institute Studies III (New York, 1977).

the freeing of trade in the GATT system was believed to contribute to the wealth and rising standards of living within industrialized countries.

Also evident, however, were the costs of interdependence. Fears about a substantial restriction of national autonomy provoked debates about how to counter these effects. In an important study, *The Economics of Interdependence*, written in 1968 when vulnerability first began to be felt, Cooper drew attention to the costs of the high level of prosperity based on specialization and exchange on each society's particular goals and policies. It 'both enlarges and confines the freedom of countries to act according to their own lights. The central problem of international economic co-operation is *how to keep the manifold benefits of extensive international intercourse free of crippling restrictions while at the same time preserving a maximum degree of freedom for each nation to pursue its legitimate economic objectives.*'[3] In effect, dependence was the price one had to pay for the benefits of a division of labour.

For most of these writers, the contemporary realists as much as the neo-liberals, concern with security has arisen out of reflection on the experience of post-war economic interdependence, although the particular emphasis given by policy-makers to the issue has varied with time and circumstances. But, while in the 1960s their major concern had been with interdependence rather than security *per se*, since the early 1970s the problem of economic security in the context of complex interdependence has emerged as the central issue. This is due primarily to the oil price rises of 1973/74. Initial fears about the security of oil supplies gave rise to a more general concern that the world economy could have entered an era of serious supply shortages for other raw materials as well, whether the shortage was real or induced by 'cartels' such as OPEC.

Although problems of dependence and autonomy had been debated in the 1950s and 1960s with regard to developing countries, the actions by the OPEC cartel in acquiring control over supplies and prices of oil demonstrated that dependence could be a two-way street, in some cases benefiting the

---

[3] Richard Cooper, *The Economics of Interdependence*, Council on Foreign Relations (New York, 1968).

developing countries. For the industrialized countries, which had promoted interdependence among themselves and disregarded the interests of developing countries, this new state of insecurity was viewed as a particularly alarming threat. The neo-liberals reacted to the new situation by redefining economic security. Thus, Cooper discussed it as, 'The capacity of a society (nation) to enjoy and cultivate its culture and values.'[4] Hager, a West German writer, defined economic security as being threatened 'when external economic parameters are changed in such a manner as to produce a strain on the sociopolitical system of a nation which leads to its breakdown'. He wrote further that, 'Most threats to economic security are, in contrast to military threats, diffuse, difficult to diagnose and rarely the result of an overtly hostile act.'[5]

The new perception of vulnerability was not directly related to the international market system or to the GATT. Thus, solutions to the problem of insecurity were not sought in trade-restricting measures. On the contrary, states lacking vital resources were preoccupied in maintaining a steady flow of imports at stable prices. The reason why vulnerability did not immediately lead to general trade restrictions is that the problem arose with respect to raw materials and commodities which had not been a major issue of contention within GATT. Indirectly, there was, of course, a relationship, since it may plausibly be argued that the process of trade liberalization had been made possible by low-cost supplies of energy and other raw materials.

On the basis of this assumption, until recently, no Western government and very few analysts had associated economic security with the need to protect industries in order to secure supplies considered essential for the well-being, or indeed survival, of the population in case of war or serious international crisis. Most arguments defending protectionism since the GATT was created have converged on welfare issues, balance of payments or infant-industry considerations rather than security. Apart from the ready availability of raw

---

[4] Richard Cooper, 'Security and the Energy Crisis', in *The Middle East and the International System*, Part II Adelphi Paper No. 115, Spring 1975.

[5] Wolfgang Hager, 'Economic Security', p. 75.

materials, the most likely reason for this absence is to be found in the theoretical underpinnings of the GATT. As we shall see, implicit in the principles of the GATT is the assumption, based on classical and neo-classical thought, that free trade will mitigate the conflicts that can lead to war. The trouble with this assumption, however, is that it cannot handle the negative consequences of interdependence. And although the system of rules embodied in the GATT, which in theory separated the political aims of states from the commercial affairs of their citizens and thus promoted free trade and interdependence was intended as an instrument of peace, it has, paradoxically, increasingly induced the pressures it was meant to stem, those of economic nationalism—the tendency by states to define 'interest' in narrow national terms and to return to the elusive search for self-sufficiency.

That these pressures have not so far led to a breakdown of the international economic order comparable to that of the 1930s is perhaps best explained by the fact that for the most part the new rivalries are among states which are members of the Western Alliance. By the same token, however, it may plausibly be asked whether the negative costs of interdependence are likely to pose particularly acute problems for those small neutral states which stand outside the system. This certainly appears to be the view of several of their governments which during the 1970s began to call for selective protection as a means of resisting interdependence and to boost domestic production. The fear was that the larger the share of imports in total domestic consumption of a product, the greater the vulnerability to embargoes and external demands. This fear generally arose most sharply as a result of low-cost imports from developing countries. In effect, states began to question arguments for further liberalization of trade and revived, although within a peacetime context, a traditional argument for protecting industries sensitive to disruption during war or serious international crises. One such state which has revived this argument with particular sophistication in the context of textiles trade is Sweden whose case will be looked at in detail.

This, then, is the general scope of the argument within which this study is framed. Before turning to the development of Sweden's foreign economic policy, it will be useful to consider in more detail in Chapter 1 the origins of the two contrasting intellectual traditions on which Swedish policies, like those of the industrial West as a whole, have been built.

The first of these concerns the arguments for the protection of the national economy; the second, the alleged relationship between peace, prosperity, and security.

1 Commercial Policy and State Security: The Intellectual Background

1 Arguments for protection

Within the contemporary order, protection has always been represented as an 'irrational' deviation from the ideal state of affairs. It is important to recall, therefore, that historically there have always been justifications for protecting certain industries in the interest of defence, an exception to the free trade system which was, moreover, not neglected by the founders of the post-war international trade order. In reviewing Western economic thought on the question of protection, one can distinguish between traditional trade protection arguments and defence protection arguments. It is the former with which I am concerned in this section.

Until the Middle Ages national self-sufficiency or autarky was generally the natural, inevitable, and necessary condition of economic life. Once the centralized state began to emerge, transportation facilities increased and costs declined: exchanges of more specialized products were developed. Self-sufficiency was no longer desirable. However, when the period of mercantilism began around the end of the fifteenth century, self-sufficiency became a means of strengthening the influence of one state over other states; it was an economic policy that was, at the same time, the ultimate aim of state policy.

The aim of the mercantilist leaders was more specifically to strengthen the state against both rivals abroad and remnants of the feudal structure at home by using various monetary, protectionist, and other economic devices as instruments to this end. The strengthening of the power of the realm was largely identified with commercial interests, that is, with the merchants' profits in terms of money or precious metals. They then demanded the intervention of the state to protect their trading interest and to break down the many medieval barriers to commercial expansion.

A very important element of mercantilism was the belief that in trade relations one state's gain must be matched by another state's loss: exports were to be encouraged as a means of achieving the inflow of gold and silver while imports were to be restricted in order to maintain a favourable balance of trade. Mutually beneficial trade had no place in mercantilist thought. Protectionism therefore served as a means of enriching the country. Adam Smith later described the system of protection during this period as follows:

The restraints upon importation were of two kinds.

First, restraints upon the importation of such foreign goods for home consumption as could be produced at home, from whatever country they were imported.

Secondly, restraints upon the importation of goods of almost all kinds from those particular countries with which the balance of trade was supposed to be disadvantageous.

These different restraints consisted sometimes in high duties, and sometimes in absolute prohibitions.[6]

The mercantilists never argued in favour of complete self-sufficiency, because, in fact, to acquire wealth through the accumulation of precious metals, foreign trade was indispensable.[7]

Since mercantilism was a system that equated the good of the citizens with the power of the state, and one in which states constantly sought advantages at the expense of others, it was inexorably a system of commercial warfare. The element of security therefore did not enter into mercantilist thought as distinct from other policy goals. Warfare was an inevitable factor of international relations, and trade relations in pursuit of power were not, indeed, antithetical to security considerations; the two policies went hand in hand in complete conformity with one another.

The protectionist aspects of mercantilism were adopted by some later theorists, most notably those of the German romantic school, who provided the modern doctrine of autarky with its classic definition. Fichte and Müller are among the most important in this category. They followed the mercantilist tradition of subordinating all other loyalties

---

[6] Adam Smith, *Wealth of Nations*, Cannon edn., vol. I (London, 1930), 416–17.

[7] Thomas Munn, *England's Treasure by Foreign Trade* (1669), 49; Economic Classics Series, pp. 28–9.

and values to the unity and power of the state. Protectionism was not merely a temporary expedient, but an end in itself. The issue of security was largely irrelevant since no separation was made between economic strength and military strength. Economic power was used for the service of national power.

This was, however, not necessarily the case with later advocates of protectionism. As we shall see in the next section, some of the classical economists made protection for defence the only exception to the doctrine of *laissez-faire* or to what they envisaged as an otherwise completely free trade system. Arguments for protection, originating in the nineteenth and early part of the twentieth centuries, no longer viewed autarky as the ultimate aim of policy to which all else must be subordinated, but rather as a temporary means to create a climate conducive to the opening of trade. The most well-developed of arguments for such temporary restrictions include, first, protecting an infant industry until it achieves a level of development at which it can compete internationally and, second, protecting the economy generally to improve the 'terms of trade' or balance of payments or to achieve more diversified production.

More recently, a third argument has been added, namely protection as a remedy to unemployment. But, even in this case, advocates of protection viewed the policy in terms of a limited and specific aim. It is perhaps because of this difference in motives that Michael Heilperin has distinguished between what he sees as 'old' protectionism and 'new' protectionism. 'Protectionism (in the nineteenth and early twentieth centuries) belonged to a liberal age. It was in conformity—and not in contradiction—with the operations of the price system of the market economy and of individual private enterprise.'[8]

The American Alexander Hamilton developed the theory for the first of these arguments. His rationale for the use of trade protection came to be known as the 'infant industry' argument which was based on the assumption that industries would, with the help of temporary protection, develop their potential to the point of competing internationally. His aim

---

[8] Michael Heilperin, *Studies in Economic Nationalism*, Graduate Institute of International Studies, series No. 35 (Geneva, 1960), p. 17.

was primarily to encourage the creation of new industries in economies that had the potential for industrial growth, but he was equally concerned to promote agricultural growth. Hamilton was mainly preoccupied with the growth of the US economy, which lagged behind that of Great Britain in the latter part of the eighteenth century. More recently this argument has been put forward by the developing countries. But Hamilton was also concerned with protectionism for the sake of security in the event of a future war. To quote from a report he wrote for the House of Representatives in 1791, 'not only the wealth but the independence and security of a country appear to be materially connected with the prosperity of manufactures. Every nation, with a view to these great objects, ought to endeavour to possess within itself all the essentials of national supply'.[9] Unlike the mercantilists, however, Hamilton was not concerned with the pursuit of power for its own sake, but with the defence of a free state.

Friedrich List (1789–1846) developed the infant-industry argument further and also provided a more general defence of protection in the interests of industrial development and diversification. The backward condition of Germany at this time led him to oppose the doctrine of Adam Smith and expound a theory of protection which would ensure the establishment and growth of the manufacturing industry. The government was to intervene with tariffs only if the state had a manufacturing potential, such as Germany did at the time, and protection was to be discontinued as soon as the industries could compete internationally, unless they were threatened with extinction.

In his most important work, *Das nationale System der politischen Ökonomie* (1841), List did not reject the liberal notion that free trade was justified on the assumption that there was a 'universal union' of nations as guarantee of peace, but argued that such an environment did not yet exist, and though it was inevitable that it would evolve in such a way, industry had to be built up starting at the national level. Protection and wars could not yet be renounced, but the development of national industries would

---

[9] Michael Heilperin, *Studies in Economic Nationalism*, Graduate Institute of International Studies, series No. 35 (Geneva, 1960), p. 58.

lead 'to a point at which the free trade system is more advantageous to a nation than a system of restrictions . . .'[10]

The third 'modern' argument for protection relates to the full-employment policies which most Western governments pursued between 1945 and the late 1970s. Experience of high and persistent unemployment in the inter-war period led many liberals to reject the Darwinian aspects of the doctrine, at least on the national level, and to acknowledge that measures urged in the interest of the individual were not necessarily also in the interest of the community at large. Under certain circumstances, protection could be justified therefore as a means of combating what was now perceived as the one major weakness in liberal theory, namely the absence of any provision for social legislation to protect the weak and to effect a more equal distribution of wealth in the community. This welfare argument for protectionism is sometimes associated with mercantilism, but more frequently with the work of John Maynard Keynes.

This aspect of Keynes's thought has been highlighted by one writer as follows:

In turning against the orthodox support for free trade, Keynes challenged not the ideal world of *laissez-faire* which, with modifications, he continued to support, but 'its tacit assumptions which are seldom and never satisfied, with the result that it cannot solve the economic problems of the actual world'. . . . For Adam Smith, the state played a vital but purely regulative role. Keynes endowed it with positive functions designed to check the notoriously heartless and, as he believed, politically dangerous consequences of non-interventionist policies at the state level.[11]

Although Keynes began his career as a devout free trader, he gradually started sympathizing with protectionist policies.

An example of his early orthodoxy was evident in the special supplements that he wrote for the *Manchester Guardian* under the title 'Reconstruction in Europe' (1921). 'We must hold to free trade in its widest interpretation, as

---

[10] Edmund Silberner, *The Problem of War in Nineteenth Century Economic Thought* (Princeton, NJ, 1946) 191.

[11] James Mayall, 'The Liberal Economy', in id. (ed.), *The Community of States* (London, 1982), 100; John Maynard Keynes, *General Theory of Employment, Interest and Money*, 1936.

an inflexible dogma to which no exception is admitted . . .
I include in free trade the abandonment of any attempt to
secure for ourselves exclusive supplies of food and
materials—in spite of what is said below about the pressure
of population on resources'.[12]

Later, as the unemployment and budgetary problems grew
worse, Keynes in 1931 began to advocate the use of the tariff.
In a debate between Keynes and Professor Lionel Robbins
which was conducted in the *New Statesman*, he wrote, 'I do
not believe that a wise and prudent budget can be framed
today without recourse to a revenue tariff. But this is not
its only advantage. In so far as it leads to the substitution
of home-produced goods for goods previously imported, it will
increase employment in this country.'[13]

Keynes further believed that full employment through state
intervention was indeed the only way to prevent economic
warfare.

but if nations can learn to provide themselves with full employment
by their domestic policy . . . there need be no important economic
forces calculated to set the interest of one country against that of
its neighbours. There would still be room for the international
division of labour and for international lending in appropriate
conditions. But there would no longer be a pressing motive why
one country need force its wares on another or repulse the offering
of its neighbour . . . with the express object of upsetting the
equilibrium of payments so as to develop a balance of trade in its
own favour. International trade would cease to be what it is,
namely, a desperate expedient to maintain employment at home
by forcing sales on foreign markets and restricting purchases, . . .
but a willing and unimpeded exchange of goods and services in
conditions of mutual advantage.[14]

Keynes's motives for advocating protection thus appear to
have been purely peaceful and without mercantilist
overtones. If there was any doubt on this score it became
apparent when in the latter part of his life he played one of
the leading roles as advocate of international economic co-
operation at the Bretton Woods' Conference of 1944. His
interest was

---

[12] 4 Jan. 1921   [13] 7 Mar. 1931.
[14] Keynes, *General Theory*, pp. 382–3.

how to protect the Western liberal order, not from a more attractive doctrine, but from the compelling pressures of a self-destructive atavism. The problem in other words was how to achieve by management what the classical and neo-classical economists thought they had demonstrated by argument, the reconciliation of private, national and international interests.[15]

So far we have looked at the three most important arguments for trade protection in the history of Western economic thought. The one aspect omitted above is, of course, the defence argument for protection which is most closely associated with the classical liberals to whose arguments I now turn.

2 Peace, prosperity, and the problem of security in classical liberalism

It was largely in response to the continual warfare during the mercantilist period that the classical system of economics developed in the nineteenth century. The policy of restricting imports in order to maintain a favourable balance of payments at all costs to the disadvantage of other states was in itself a system of belligerency. Liberal economists were unwilling to accept the fatalistic attitude of the mercantilists according to whom war was inevitable. In its place they substituted optimism, elaborating a system based on increasing international exchanges and unshackling barriers to trade in the expectation that their system would lead not only to greater wealth for all, but also to a more peaceful world.

Some classical liberals, for example Richard Cobden, had the utopian vision that if only the economic domain could be separated from the political, and international trade allowed to flow freely without government intervention, there would be no further reason to go to war. International trade represented for Cobden a mutually beneficial relationship among nations fairly equal in wealth and power and one in which the gains from trade would also be distributed evenly. Cobden's views on the relationship between world trade and peace were the opposite of the mercantilists'. In furthering the international division of

[15] Mayall, 'The Liberal Economy', p. 101.

labour, commerce, he said, was 'binding us in abject dependence upon all countries of the earth . . . and freedom of commerce and exemption from warfare will be the inevitable fruits of the future growth of [their] mechanical and chemical improvement, the germ of which has only been planted in our day'.[16] Thus, economic interdependence would undermine the instinct for violence as states came to perceive the dangers of severing such ties to be much greater than those of fostering them.[17]

While, among the Utopian liberals, Cobden developed furthest the inconsistencies between peace and prosperity on the one hand, and protectionism and warfare on the other, his basic position was shared by other liberal thinkers such as James Mill[18] and MacCulloch.[19]

Not all liberals, however, were so optimistic. On the contrary, they conceded that wars were still a possibility which obliged the government to intervene in matters of defence. But although, as we have seen, many writers within the mercantilist tradition advocated economic self-sufficiency as an end in itself, most liberals regarded the defence argument for protection as merely a means of maintaining security. War was a contingency which they recognized but one which was fundamentally subversive of the liberal system. Provided the peace was kept, however, the government's involvement in the defence industry was not seen to contradict the principles of the liberal trade system as a whole.

In the *Wealth of Nations* Adam Smith devoted considerable space to an attack on the mercantile system. He criticized the manipulation of foreign trade in the interests of individual

---

[16] *The Political Writings of Richard Cobden*, i (London, 1868), 190, quoted in Peter Cain, 'Capitalism, War and Internationalism in the Thought of Richard Cobden', *British Journal of International Studies*, Oct. 1979, 234–5.

[17] J. Morley, *The Life of Richard Cobden*, i (London, 1881), 230, quoted in Cain, 'Capitalism, War and Internationalism', p. 240.

[18] James Mill studied the problem of war in a polemic against two other writers, 'Commerce Defended: An Answer to the Arguments by which Mr. Spence, Mr. Cobbett and Others Have Attempted to Prove that Commerce is not a Source of National Wealth' (1807).

[19] MacCulloch devoted considerable time and space to the problem of war in *Discourse on the Rise, Progress, Peculiar Objects and Importance of Political Economy* (1824), and in *Principles of Political Economy* (1825).

countries, the protection and the measures aimed at maintaining a consistently favourable balance of trade as harmful and of no common benefit. All restrictions were to be removed in favour of completely free competition, domestically and internationally.

Smith was aware of the problems posed by overdependence on particular markets or sources of supply. He was convinced, however, as were later liberal economists, that this dependence was primarily a consequence of an unhealthy trading system. Thus a universal free trade system could effectively neutralize the power element which had previously monopolized international commercial relations, by spreading trade so widely over the various markets that an interruption of trade with one or the other country would not cause national damage.

Questions of war and peace did not enter directly into Adam Smith's thought because he assumed that what was good for the community was also good for the individual and for the world. And this good, moreover, was best served by the least amount of government intervention. He did, nevertheless, admit to one exception to the principle of *laissez-faire* in the interest of defence. In foreign commerce he justified taxes in order to develop a national self-sufficiency in such things as saltpetre and in shipping which were considered indispensable for the national defence. The Navigation Acts were promulgated in response to Smith's belief that a merchant marine for the navy should be encouraged to ensure preparedness in case of attack. Such measures were to be taken even if they involved an economic sacrifice.

While Smith conceded the case for industrial protection for war industries, Malthus was one of the first of the liberals to advocate protection in agriculture because of the danger of being cut off in war from foreign grain supplies. This was a natural corollary to his belief that the main cause of war was the inevitable excess of population relative to the means of subsistence. But since Malthus's concern was primarily with a multiplying population rather than protection, free trade was also not seen as a remedy against poverty and war. Nevertheless, he urged that free trade be pursued as much as possible.

One of the clearest expressions of the classical vision of perfect harmony was expressed by David Ricardo:

Under a system of perfectly free commerce, each country naturally devotes its capital and labour to such employments as are most beneficial to each. This pursuit of individual advantage is admirably connected with the universal good of the whole. By stimulating industry, by rewarding ingenuity, and by using most efficaciously the peculiar powers bestowed by nature, it distributes labour most effectively and most economically; while by increasing the general mass of production it diffuses general benefits, and binds together by one common tie of interest and intercourse, the universal society of nations throughout the civilized world.[20]

Yet Ricardo was not the Utopian that the above quotation seems to imply. The reason why, unlike some liberals, Ricardo opposed any protection in anticipation of war was that he believed wars to be accidental. He devoted considerable attention to the relationship between international trade and national defence, and was convinced of the necessity for the nation to be independent in agricultural production. Writing against the background of the Napoleonic wars, he argued that although agricultural production in most circumstances could be adopted to the special needs created during a war, the problem would become more acute at the war's end. At this time, special import duties imposed on corn imports would not contradict free trade providing they were imposed as a temporary expedient only. A tax on imports would give domestic producers the protection required to regain competitiveness. The eventuality of protecting manufactured goods on the other hand did not enter into his discussion at all, most likely for the reason that Great Britain was already the most advanced and powerful nation at that time.

John Stuart Mill's thesis is also worth mentioning. While this may be interpreted as favouring industrial protection for reasons of defence, he was clearly opposed to agricultural protection for that reason.

It is ridiculous to found a general system of policy in so improbable a danger as that of being at war with all the nations of the world

---

[20] P. Sraffa (ed.), *The Works of David Ricardo* (London, 1951), 133–4.

at once; or to suppose that, even if inferior at sea, a whole country could be blockaded like a town, or that the growers of food in other countries would not be as anxious not to lose an advantageous market, as we should be not to be deprived of their corn.[21]

Having now considered in some detail the intellectual foundations of the industrialized West, we have seen that the problem of security in the context of international commercial relations arises as paramount only in the thought of the classical liberals. It is evident that in the period preceding this nineteenth-century pre-occupation, as in the period that succeeded it, the notion of economic security in this context was seldom considered relevant. Not until the very recent past does it reappear among the concerns of statesmen or economic theorists. Since a pre-occupation with security, or more precisely its absence or breakdown, has dominated so much of twentieth-century international relations, the question therefore arises: in what ways have modern liberals dealt with this problem and why has it apparently lost its relevance in their work?

In the modern period of liberalism, few theorists even acknowledge the criteria of economic security as a phenomenon in international relations. One exception to this rule is Professor Lionel Robbins, who, although not contributing anything new to the concept, did at least concede its validity: He wrote that

although it is possible to exaggerate the influence of the idea of self-sufficiency as a means of presenting the characteristic ethos of the national state, it is important not to underestimate the influence of the ideal of economic self-sufficiency, regarded, not as an end in itself, but as a means of military defence. It has always been conceded by free traders that, if the location of any particular form of production within the borders of the national state was regarded as essential to security against outside attacks, then measures designed to foster this industry could not be regarded as contrary to national policy . . . The German agrarian policy was defended on military grounds. Since the war, experience of the difficulties which may arise in case of blockade or widespread interruption of national commerce has led to a vast extension of such measures.

---

[21] *Principles*, bk. V, chap. x, sect. i, pp. 920–1, quoted in Silberner, *The Problem of War*, p. 64.

The extensive protection of industries capable of being used for munition-making has also been defended on this ground.

However, Robbins goes on to demonstrate the costs of such measures and insists that one cannot have both security *and* what he considers the far more preferable wealth that comes with free international commerce.[22]

Other modern liberals neglect to develop ideas on economic security at all, presumably because they either employ a stricter conception of the separation between politics and economics, or because they take economic security for granted. Friedrich Hayek's thoughts on economic security are coloured by his belief in the primacy of the individual rather than the state. In this context he views the problem of economic security in terms of protecting the *individual* only against those uncontrollable factors which would prevent him from maintaining a minimum income and standard of living.[23] Government intervention in the market-place for any other reasons, national or international, is seen as inimical to the liberal values of individual freedom. Thus, Hayek writes, 'It is one of the most fatal illusions that by substituting negotiations by states or organized groups for competition for markets or raw materials, international friction would be reduced.'[24] Although demonstrating his allegiance to the traditional liberal separation of commerce from politics, he is more sceptical regarding the possibility of attaining peace through international trade.

As the economic nationalism of the inter-war period was gradually superceded by a more internationally co-operative spirit after the First World War, the focus of political and economic thought also turned to new issues. The process by which this was accomplished is discussed in the next section. Two underlying reasons for the shift in intellectual focus are worth noting, however. The first concerns the impact of Cold War on the international economy. The major rift in international economic relations was no longer in the market

[22] Lionel Robbins, *The Economic Basis of Class Conflict* (London, 1939), 112–19.

[23] See also Charles F. Frank, Jr., *Foreign Trade and Domestic Aid* (Washington, DC, 1977).

[24] Friedrich A. Hayek, *The Road to Serfdom* (London, 1944), 163–4.

order but across the East–West ideological divide which, amongst other things, separated states according to their adherence to collectivist or market principles. The security of most industrial countries, although not of course of the neutrals, was provided by the Western Alliance under American leadership. A second related reason for this shift in intellectual focus, which emanated from the United States, was connected to the evolution of the social sciences. Liberal political economy gave way to 'economic science', the attempt to imitate as closely as possible the procedures of the physical sciences, which were considered highly successful. This more rigorous approach to the subject provided a useful new start for economists who had partly been blamed for the disastrous period of the Great Depression. But the new 'science' was based on a number of assumptions about the behaviour of individuals and firms and could no longer deal with exogenous factors within its system. They could, of course, deal with the economics of defence if that was a given like any other activity. Rather than study the phenomenon of economic defence *per se*, and its role in the liberal trading system, the emphasis often rested purely on efficiency considerations, that is, measuring the cost versus the benefits of defence industries.

3 The origins of the post-1945 international economic order

The arguments for protection discussed in the previous two sections were, with the exception of the 'welfare' argument, all essentially formulated during the eighteenth and nineteenth centuries. They resurfaced in public debate, however, in the immediate aftermath of the Second World War and during the negotiations of the abortive ITO and of the GATT. Before turning to this debate it is important to recall that the post-war system was constructed against the background of the breakdown of the liberal trading order in the 1930s and represented a deliberate attempt to insure against any repetition of that experience.

Between the end of the First World War and the onset of the Great Depression, there was a concerted attempt to re-establish the pre-war world trading system on approximately its old foundations. An important aspect of President Wilson's programme of international co-operation was an attempt to establish equality in trading conditions and the removal of trade barriers, but the Covenant of the League of Nations contained only a° watered-down version of a pledge of 'equitable treatment' of commerce of other members of the League, to be accorded 'subject to and in accordance with the provisions of international conventions existing or hereafter to be agreed upon by members of the League'.[25]

Between 1920 and 1929 four major conferences were held to consider the problem of international economic problems.[26] The four broad goals at these meetings were 'to improve the legal and administrative basis of international commercial relations; to reduce or eliminate prohibitions and quantitative restrictions on imports and exports; to rehabilitate and generalize the principles of unconditional most-favoured-nation treatment; to reduce the general level of tariffs'.[27]

The resolutions and recommendations that were the result of these conferences, many of which reappeared later in the Havana Charter, marked the culmination of efforts in the pre-depression period to establish a code of conduct for the world trading system.

In practice these conferences led to some progress in the legal and administrative aspects of international co-operation, but had little success in the tariff field. Although clauses existed in these resolutions allowing states to maintain sovereignty over areas they considered vital to national autonomy, they were ultimately considered to be not far-reaching enough. For instance, the Prohibitions Convention reserved to the parties the right to adopt prohibitions and restrictions 'for the purpose of protecting in extraordinary and abnormal circumstances, the vital interests of the country'. With the experience of the First World War still fresh in the minds of statesmen, many governments lacked the political security necessary for such commitments as were called for. They

---

[25] Article 23 of Covenant.

[26] The Brussels Financial Conference of 1920, the Genoa Conference of 1922, the Geneva World Economic Conference of 1927.

[27] William Adams Brown, Jr., *The United States and the Restoration of World Trade* (Washington, DC, 1950) 30.

were [not] prepared to forgo their control over the export of certain products essential for their own national defence and important for the purpose of bargaining with other governments . . . They were not prepared altogether to abandon their power of direct control over the most important lines of trade with each and every country or to renounce completely the most convenient instruments for exercising that control.[28]

For a short period, tariff increases were kept in check, but any further efforts at achieving world-wide reductions were abortive. Already in the late 1920s, moreover, pressures were mounting for an upward revision of tariffs, most notably in the United States. In addition to the political and social insecurity felt by many governments, there was a deep-rooted conviction in the United States, in particular, that high protection was the means to secure its national prosperity. Those pressures increased as time went on and contributed significantly to the Depression of the 1930s. Tariffs began to rise sharply following the decline in agricultural prices in 1929. The Hawley-Smoot Tariff was then enacted in 1930 by the US which increased protection on 900 items. Further impetus to the Depression was given when the United Kingdom, followed by other countries, abandoned the Gold Standard in 1931. By the end of the year twenty-six countries had imposed quantitative restrictions, high tariffs, and control over foreign exchange transactions.

In 1933 one final abortive attempt was made to reconstruct a freer international trading system before widespread economic warfare broke out. During the early 1930s the Western economies experienced a serious crisis of deflation and mass unemployment to which all governments responded in similar ways. Policies were implemented to increase exports, depreciate currencies, and protect domestic industries through high import tariffs and quantitative restrictions. Each government attempted to gain power and advantages over every other government. However, the cumulative effect of nationalistic and internationally anarchic policies was self-defeating and chaotic for all.

---

[28] League of Nations, *Commercial Policy in the Interwar Period: International Proposals and National Policies* (Geneva, 1942), 116–17.

Without elaborating on the various theories that have been advanced to explain the Great Depression, it is worth pointing out some of the major trends during this period.

First, the problem of falling agricultural prices had serious international ramifications. Increasing agricultural output and intervention in favour of domestic production were consequences of First World War shortages and the desire for self-sufficiency in case of a future blockade.

Secondly, a movement towards regional and bilateral arrangements emerged in the smaller European countries,[29] in Eastern Europe, and between the United Kingdom and the Dominions[30] which marked a clear departure from the most-favoured-nation principle.[31]

Thirdly, an extension of international agreements between private industries was agreed upon in 1931 with the hope that such cartel formation might lead to a better organization of production and trade. In practice they were to have a trade restricting effect.[32]

Fourthly, the pressing internal demands of employment and development policies which had been largely ignored in the international conferences began the trend towards greater government intervention at the expense of liberal free trade and non-discrimination. Autarky increasingly became accepted as an objective of trade policy.

Despite a further effort by Britain, France and the United States to realign and maintain the greatest possible equilibrium in the system of international exchanges,[33] government policies were generally already set on a negative and

[29] Oslo Convention, 1930, on economic co-operation was signed by Denmark, Norway, Sweden, and Belgium, in which they undertook not to increase tariff duties or introduce new ones without notifying other countries; Ouchy Convention, 1932, signed by Belgium, Luxemburg and the Netherlands but open to all countries, was aimed at a reciprocal and progressive reduction of economic barriers, based on League of Nations principles.

[30] Ottawa Agreements, 1932, referred to the United Kingdom's expansion of its preference system to all members of the Commonwealth.

[31] Howard P. Whidden, *Preferences and Discriminations in International Trade*, Committee on International Economic Policy in Cooperation with the Carnegie Endowment for International Peace (1945).

[32] Brown, *The United States*, p. 42.

[33] Tripartite Declaration formulated by France, the United States and the United Kingdom, *Federal Reserve Bulletin* (Oct. 1976), 759.

irreversible path, the culmination of which was the outbreak of the Second World War.

Whatever the 'real' causes of the Second World War, the fact that the United States government, especially Secretary of State Cordell Hull, believed that European protection in general, and German and Italian economic nationalism in particular, was partly responsible was to have an enormous influence on United States thinking about post-war political and economic reconstruction.

The first intimation of the future shape of United States trade policy was provided by the Atlantic Charter and Mutual Aid Agreement with the United Kingdom. This was, however, only the first of several initiatives to work out post-war programmes in commercial and related areas. In all of those initiatives the following principles were held to be fundamental. First, under Article IV of the Atlantic Charter the two countries agreed to:

endeavour with due respect for their existing obligations, to further the enjoyment by all states, great or small, victors or vanquished, of access, on equal terms, to the trade and raw materials of the world which are needed for their economic prosperity.

Second, under Article V, they agreed to

bring about the fullest collaboration between all nations in the economic field with the object of securing, for all, improved labour standards, economic advancement and social security.[34]

These fundamental principles reflected the United States' conviction of the imperative need for an institutional legal framework as the basis for international economic co-operation. The intention was to create a framework for rules of conduct in trade relations that would lead not only to greater certainty and predictability in international transactions, but also to a system that would ensure freedom of access to markets and assure the regular and equitable growth of international trade as well as some measure of domestic welfare. This, the American government believed, was fundamental to maintaining peaceful conditions.

[34] *Documents on American Foreign Relations, 1941–42*, World Peace Foundation (1942), quoted in Brown, *The United States*, p. 47.

Against this background, negotiations were initiated to create an International Trade Organization (ITO). In the event, however, the ITO was never ratified by the United States, although in 1947 an important part of the defunct ITO known as the General Agreement became an international contractual agreement and institution. The establishment of the General Agreement on Tariffs and Trade (GATT) was therefore an offshoot of a much broader plan laid down in the Havana Charter to cover all aspects of commercial, financial, and monetary co-operation. In contrast the GATT was to deal mainly with the reduction of tariffs to trade in manufactured and semi-manufactured goods.

The GATT, whose basic principles and exceptions will be discussed in the next section, contained a number of inherent weaknesses but was nevertheless believed to represent a big step forward in creating the appropriate environment in which states could obtain the full benefits of international trade.

The compromises that were made in institutionalizing the GATT, instead of the more ambitious ITO, ultimately involved dropping those issues whose absence was believed to have led partially to failure of negotiations in the inter-war period for international economic co-operation. Such issues also included some of the substantive chapters in the Havana Charter, such as those dealing with 'Employment and Economic Activity' and 'Economic Development and Reconstruction'. Although the basic principles of the GATT acknowledged the necessity for governments to maintain full employment, the Agreement contained no substantive proposals to cope with any potential problems of structural adjustments or the provision of welfare. It should be noted, however, that this failure was not merely the result of compromise, but arose from the underlying philosophy of the founding fathers. While the Keynesian revolution had led to acceptance on the national level that the free play of market forces was not automatically redistributive and that some form of government intervention was therefore required, this proposition was not accepted at the international level. Here the principles of classical liberalism survived much longer.

As we have seen, the aim of the nineteenth-century liberals was to destroy the mercantilist assumptions which equated the wealth of the state with its power. They attempted to do this by drawing a distinct line between the system of economics and the political system. Economics belonged to the realm of market forces which, if left to its own devices, would ultimately cater to the needs of the citizens. The government, on the other hand, was to play a minimal role only in maintaining law and order and providing essential services. At the international level the GATT was in effect a translation of this idea and the need for management was conceded only in so far as to maintain this separation between trade and politics.

Many writers have questioned the validity of this separation. E. H. Carr, for example, argued that

economic forces are in fact political forces. Economics can be treated neither as a minor accessory of history, nor as an independent science in the light of which history can be interpreted. Much confusion would be saved by a general return to the term 'political economy' which was given the new science by Adam Smith himself and not abandoned in favour of the abstract 'economics' even in Great Britain itself, till the closing years of the nineteenth century.[35]

Throughout this study we shall be confronted by the tension between the attempt to organize international trade within a 'rational' scientific framework and the special problems that arise as a result of the political-economic history of particular countries and of broader systemic changes within the international economy which cannot be handled politically within the existing institutional framework. The issue of neutrality is one example of this tension. As long as it was believed that politics and economics were distinct, then pursuing neutrality, which is a *political* decision, should be perfectly reconcilable with allowing market forces to determine the extent of commercial relations with other countries. There was no reason therefore to include exceptions to GATT rules for neutrality considerations. And the two European countries whose neutrality was still firmly grounded after the Second World War, Sweden and Switzerland, did not confront membership in the GATT with any of the same ambivalence as that experienced with

[35] E. H. Carr, *The Twenty Years Crisis* (London, 1939) 116–17.

regard to UN membership. Although certain issues with important political overtones were unavoidable in the negotiations leading to the GATT, one of them being the exceptions allowed for security considerations, these were neither initiated by the neutral countries nor given much priority by them. These security issues were nevertheless to acquire importance later on. We must now turn, therefore, to a discussion of the goals and principles of the GATT and how the security issues were handled within its framework.

4 Goals, principles, and exceptions of the GATT

The preamble of the GATT presents the goals of the contracting parties:

that their relations in the field of trade and economic endeavour should be conducted with a view to raising standards of living, ensuring full employment and a large and steadily growing volume of real income and effective demand, developing the full use of the resources of the world and expanding the production and exchange of goods, [and]

to contribute to these objectives by entering into reciprocal and mutually advantageous arrangements directed to the substantial reduction of tariffs and other barriers to trade, and to the elimination of discriminatory treatment in international commerce . . .

The aim of prohibiting non-tariff barriers was thus entered into a code governing world trade, the purpose of which was to curtail severely the possibilities of governments interfering with the free flow of private trade. Behind these fundamental principles was the belief that such an Agreement would lead to a peaceful world.

The key principle of the GATT is the 'most-favoured-nation' (MFN) clause. According to Article I, this provision imposes on the contracting parties the obligation that

any advantage, favour, privilege or immunity granted by any contracting party to any product originating in or destined for any other country should be accorded immediately and unconditionally to the like product originating in or destined for the territories of all other contracting parties.

The importance of this clause is to enforce equality of treatment for all contracting parties and prevent in particular a return to the system of preferential arrangements, which were believed to have contributed to the breakdown of liberal trade in the 1930s.

Quantitative restrictions were to be prohibited on industrial goods, thus leaving the customs tariffs as the sole legal protective device. Other important elements included ensuring predictability in trade relations through the binding of tariffs and publication of tariff schedules.

The GATT was primarily to be a forum for countries to negotiate tariff reductions. To this effect, seven rounds of multilateral tariff negotiations were held between 1947 and 1979. Practically all these rounds of negotiations have concentrated on tariff reductions, but broader issues concerning the problems of the developing world and non-tariff barriers have increasingly acquired importance. During the Tokyo Round, for instance, a whole series of codes on non-tariff barriers was concluded in addition to the negotiation of tariff reductions, and the improvement of some elements of the GATT in favour of developing countries. In September 1986 an eighth round of negotiations was launched in Uruguay which will encompass an even broader range of issues including trade in services.

All treaties and agreements dealing with trade allow for recourse to safeguard action. The GATT, in particular, is designated to deal solely with trade problems and therefore attempts to safeguard the sovereign rights of governments to fulfil responsibilities in areas that transcend pure trade. While an agreement containing too many safeguard clauses cannot fulfil its purpose, it is true, nevertheless, that states show a greater willingness to commit themselves to such agreements when some possibilities exist for such recourse.

The GATT contains at least nine different 'safeguard clauses'.[36] Exceptional circumstances, within the GATT frame-work, that call for the use of safeguards include: balance of payments difficulties, security or health considerations, protection of infant industries in the case of developing countries, and the safeguarding of domestic producers suffering or threatened by serious injury from imports.

[36] XI(2c), XII, XVIII(2), XIX, XX, XXI, XXV, XXVI, XXVII, XXVIII.

Thus we see that many of the original arguments for protection that we reviewed in sections 1 and 2 above were adapted to new circumstances and incorporated into the GATT system. However, the one very significant element on which states never reached agreement, except to include it as one of the basic principles, was welfare. It seems evident that the main reason for this exclusion was the association between welfarism and collectivism which was made by many of the original contractors to the Agreement. This was, or so it may reasonably be argued, a potentially dangerous omission. For, on the assumption that the forces that produced the welfare state will not subside and will ultimately spill over into the international arena, the inability to address this concern on the international level may paradoxically lead to self-destruction, forcing states back to national protection despite their commitments to GATT.

The one particular GATT safeguard clause that comes closest to concern with welfare is Article XIX. Because of this ultimate relevance of welfare to both of the themes with which this study is concerned, that is, the general relationship between national security and the international trading order, and the particular problem posed for Sweden and other neutral countries, it will be useful at this stage to consider Article XIX in more detail as well as Article XXI covering security exceptions.

(i) *Article XIX*

Article XIX states that contracting parties have the right to take emergency action in case imports reach 'such increased quantities and under such conditions as to cause or threaten serious injury to domestic producers in that territory of like or directly competitive products'.

However, certain conditions are attached which in more recent times have made use of this Article highly contentious. The Article has been interpreted to authorize 'emergency protection' if, first, the Contracting Party invoking the clause 'give(s) notice in writing to the CONTRACTING PARTIES [i.e. Secretariat] as far in advance as may be practicable before taking action, and give those concerned an opportunity to consult with it in respect of the proposed action'. Only in 'critical circumstances' may action be taken provisionally without prior consultations. Second, in situations where no agreement is reached during consultations and concessions are withdrawn unilaterally, the exporting country(ies) has or have the right to take retaliatory action. Third, the restrictions imposed must be non-discriminatory. If these conditions are satisfied, protection can be applied on a temporary basis either by the imposition of quantitative restrictions on the offending class of imports or by the suspension, withdrawal or modification of a negotiated tariff.

These conditions were meant to deter states from abuse of the clause, but, for a variety of reasons including the absence of clear definitions of such terms as 'serious injury', 'threat', or what constitutes an 'emergency' situation, and the fact that, despite their commitments under the GATT, industrial governments have in practice viewed economic security as embracing their welfare policies, the Article has been subject to general and increasing abuse and evasion.

Although the evasion of Article XIX has been widespread amongst the GATT's contracting parties, it has been greatly exacerbated in recent years by a threat which the industrial countries have perceived as emanating specially from the group of developing countries known as the 'newly industrializing countries' (NICs). These countries have rapidly increased their export capacity and in response the governments of the developed countries maintain that they have no alternative but to apply selective restrictions. Their justification is on the grounds that if Article XIX action is taken on a non-discriminatory basis, and even if compensation can be offered to the exporting country(ies) considered most disruptive, a number of other exporting countries may be adversely affected, each of which may feel entitled to demand or withdraw a concession on a different product. As Tumlir has argued aptly Article XIX 'is too exacting in the sense that the country invoking it risks retaliation for taking emergency action and it is too lenient in allowing emergency protection to become permanent'.[37]

---

[37] Jan Tumlir, 'Emergency Action against Sharp Increases in Imports', in Hugh Corbet and Robert Jackson (edd.), *In Search of a New World Economic Order* (London, 1974), p. 262.

The difficulty of achieving a satisfactory solution to the weaknesses of this Article results in the importing countries seeking different means of protecting their industries other than through the invocation of Article XIX. Increasingly this has been in the form of unilaterally or bilaterally imposed quantitative restrictions.

Such import restraints may take the form of 'orderly marketing arrangements' (OMAs) or 'voluntary export restraints' (VERs), which consist of agreements among governments or industries to restrict imports of a particular product from a particular source in the name of an 'orderly' liberalization of trade. However, these agreements are less than completely 'voluntary' as the name implies; they are rather determined in practice by the respective situations of the negotiating parties, that is, resources, trade structure, negotiating skills, and ability to retaliate.

OMAs and VERs are not considered strictly legal according to GATT rules, and are thus negotiated outside the framework of the GATT. These arrangements are more or less secret and information is generally only available if one of the parties complains to the GATT. Yet it is apparent that there has been a sharp proliferation in the use of such arrangements in the 1970s. It is acknowledged, moreover, that these agreements are a potential disadvantage to third countries as a result of trade diversion and possible chain reactions. Indeed it has been argued that they represent a potential threat to the whole functioning of the GATT.

To deal with the increasing problems associated with Article XIX and restraint agreements, several suggestions were made during the most recent multilateral trade negotiations, the so-called Tokyo Round. These included:

(a) improved criteria for determining serious injury;

(b) the need for international surveillance by some standing body of safeguard measures;

(c) waiving of rights to compensation and retaliation if serious injury is proven and exporting country interests are not prejudiced.

(d) the possibility of discriminatory safeguard action in exceptional circumstances;

(e) specific time limits for safeguards adopted;

(*f*) necessity of bringing existing illegal restrictions into conformity with the revised rules;

(*g*) the question of whether governments should put forward a programme to assist injured industries to adjust eventually out of certain lines of production as a condition for import relief;

(*h*) differential treatment for less developed countries.[38]

The issue of safeguards was, however, never concluded in the Tokyo Round but has remained a contentious issue and will therefore be taken up again in the Uruguay Round. One of the main unresolved issues is whether safeguards under Article XIX should continue to be non-discriminatory, and thereby difficult to invoke, or should be permitted on a selective basis. Yet Article XIX action has been invoked on a selective basis since the end of the Tokyo Round, most notably in the area of textiles and clothing, such as by the United Kingdom in 1980. At this time the United Kingdom imposed quantitative restrictions on synthetic fibres applying to imports from countries other than members of the European Free Trade Association (EFTA), preferential countries, and countries with which the European Community (EEC) maintained bilateral agreements under the Multi-Fibre Arrangement (MFA). Other industrialized countries such as Canada and Norway have also invoked extended and discriminatory Article XIX action against exporters of textiles and clothing.

The inadequacy of Article XIX in not allowing for selectivity was first perceived in the 1960s. The textile sector, moreover, has continued to present a major challenge to the entire GATT framework. As a result, starting in 1961, a series of special Arrangements was negotiated as an attempt to contain the problem and, in effect, modify Article XIX action to allow for selectivity. Since pressure for restraint in textile trade first arose in the industrial countries as a result of falling employment in their own textile industries, these Arrangements—the latest of which, the MFA, is contained in a GATT Protocol—may also be viewed as a temporary, although unwitting, recognition by GATT of the importance

---

[38] A. J. Sarna, 'Safeguards against Market Disruption—The Canadian View', *Journal of World Trade Law*, vol. 10, no. 4 (1976), 389.

of welfare in national policies of economic security. For this reason—and because it is alleged that low-cost imports pose special problems for small, neutral countries like Sweden—the international restraint agreements in the textile sector will be discussed in detail in Part II of this study.

(ii) *Article XXI: security exceptions*

Article XXI states that 'nothing in this Agreement shall be construed . . . to prevent any contracting party from taking any action which it considers necessary for the protection of its essential security interest' relating to 'fissionable materials or the materials from which they are derived'; or relating to 'traffic in arms, ammunitions, or implements of war and to such traffic in other goods and materials as is carried on directly or indirectly for the purpose of supplying a military establishment'; *or* generally, 'taken in time of war or other emergency in international relations'.

The security clause is the most far-reaching and sensitive exception in the GATT, all the more so since it does not contain reporting requirements. Only in the case of a dispute does some information become public. Circumstances in which such information has been disclosed have been rare. Although the implications of the text are ambiguous and have raised controversy, delegates at the preparatory conference of the Havana Charter recognized that 'some latitude must be granted for security as opposed to commercial purposes' and that 'the spirit in which Members of the Organization would interpret these provisions was the only guarantee against abuse'.[39]

Nevertheless it appears clear in the few cases made public that attempts were made to give broad interpretations to the concept of essential security interests. Those parties contesting the validity of the invocation of Article XXI criticized what they termed a misuse of this term. Two such examples will be cited here.[40]

---

[39] UN Document EPCT/A/SR. 33, Art. 3 (1947), quoted in GATT, Analytical Index 113 (2nd rev. 1966).

[40] The following GATT documents have referred to measures, or the possible existence of measures, under the security exception of Article XXI: GATT Documents L/309/Add. 2 Art. 1 (1955); L/1774, Art. 4 (1962); GATT Press Release 519 (1960); GATT Docs. SR. 16/5 Art. 56 (1960); SR. 19/12, Art. 196 (1961).

In 1949 the United States justified an action under Article XXI when it refused to issue export licences for certain coal-mining equipment ordered by Czechoslovakia. It was claimed by the United States that the equipment was actually intended for mining uranium and hence would be used for military purposes. When the Czechoslovak delegation complained in the GATT about the breach of a trade agreement, the GATT tried to resolve the dispute. The final decision avoided any reference to Article XXI being careful not to give an interpretation to the clause beyond the wording in the text. It was stated in the course of discussions that 'every country must have the last resort on questions relating to its own security. On the other hand, the CONTRACTING PARTIES should be cautious not to take any step which might have the effect of undermining the General Agreement.'[41] The charge that the United States had failed to meet its obligations under the Agreement was, in the end, rejected.[42]

A second example of a dispute involving Article XXI is particularly relevant to Sweden's economic security policy. At a GATT Council meeting on 31 October 1975 the representative of Sweden informed the Council of his government's intention to introduce a global import quota system for leather shoes, plastic shoes, and rubber boots due to the constant downward trend of Swedish shoe production and the rising volume of imports. As these developments were seen as a 'threat to the planning of Sweden's economic defence in situations of emergency as an integral part of its security policy', the Swedish government considered that the measure would have to be taken 'in conformity with the spirit of Article XXI'.[43] In the end Article XXI was never invoked, but a large number of countries criticized Sweden for attempting to misuse the clause when they believed that the motive for the global import quota was purely protectionist. There are also other examples of Article XXI being imposed ostensibly for security reasons, but where the measures may

---

[41] GATT Document CP. 3/SR. 22 Art. 7 (1949) in J. N. Jackson, *World Trade and the Law of GATT* (New York, 1969).
[42] GATT Documents CP. 3/33 (1949), CP. 3/SR. 22 Art. 9 (1949), CP. 3/20 Art. 3 (1949). See also Irving Kravis, *Domestic Interests and International Obligations* (Westport, Conn., 1975), 115.
[43] GATT Document C/M/109, 10 Nov. 1975.

actually be protectionist-oriented, such as United States' oil quotas in the early 1980s.

Thus the main problem with this exception consists, on the one hand, in the ambiguous wording of the clause which lends itself to abuse and, on the other, in the fact that it none the less appears to confine the concept of security to matters of a purely military nature, thus seeming to rule out welfare or industrial policy considerations.

5 The case of Sweden

We have now looked at the theoretical foundations on which the themes in this study will be developed. It has become clear that states have benefited greatly from an increasingly interdependent world. However, the resulting pattern of interdependence has also given rise to problems not anticipated by the founders of the GATT.

One industrialized country which perceived its situation to be particularly threatened by the new pattern is Sweden, on which the remainder of the book will focus. In response to increasing economic interdependence and the greater international division of labour, the Swedish authorities began to call for selective protection in those industries declining most rapidly with the aim of maintaining self-sufficiency. Their fear was that the larger the share of imports in total domestic consumption of a product, the greater is their vulnerability to embargoes and external demands. In effect, Sweden, like other industrialized countries, began to question the rationale for further liberalization of trade and thereby revived one of the traditional arguments on the benefits of self-sufficiency in industries essential to war. In the Swedish case, moreover, this response to interdependence was compounded by additional arguments deriving from the country's status as a neutral country.

The choice of Sweden as the country of study has been made for three reasons.

First, it is a neutral country which perceives its needs as differing from those of allied states. One question to raise in this context, therefore, is: what are the particular problems confronted by neutral states as a result of increasing economic interdependence and integration into the international trading order? Moreover, do neutral states in fact have needs that differ in this respect from allied states?

Secondly, Sweden is unique in the way it has developed a policy of 'economic defence'. Although other industrialized states take certain trade measures based on the national security argument, no state has developed this policy to the same extent as Sweden. The 'economic defence' policy originated in the 1930s in a series of contingency plans for wartime. However, since then the Swedish authorities gradually found it necessary to invoke trade restricting measures in peacetime. These measures extended beyond agriculture, traditionally a strongly protected sector, and energy, neither of which has ever been effectively brought within the scope of GATT rules, to include manufactures and semi-manufactures, which originally constituted the central target of the multilateral trade liberalization strategy. They have since justified this protection in the case of textiles and clothing with claims of the necessity for an economic defence or 'minimum viable production' in case of war or serious international crisis.

Thirdly, Sweden is considered to have a special relationship with developing countries, one which is not guided by strategic or even economic motives although there is a convenient symmetry between Swedish neutrality and Third World non-alignment. For this reason and because of the very generous aid programme run by the Swedes, it has gained respect in the Third World. The extension of Sweden's economic defence policies to include protectionist measures, however, may seriously affect the export possibilities of the developing countries and may therefore undermine the special relationship. This tension between Sweden's deliberate courting of the Third World and its new protectionism is central to the book's thesis: it will analyse economic security from a view which diverges from traditional studies on interdependence discussed in the Introduction. In the case of Sweden the paradox is that economic security arguments have not been used to justify the protection of trade with the countries which Sweden is in effect interdependent, but precisely against those countries with which interdependence links are most tenuous: the developing countries. This concentration on restraining trade with the LDCs brings to the fore the contradictory nature of the economic security argument. Let us now look at the evolution of Sweden's policies in respect of its special position as a neutral country and more generally in light of its economic integration with the Western industrial powers.

Part I The Economic Implications of Neutrality

Library of
Davidson College

2 The Concept and Practice of Neutrality

Introduction

As we have seen, the international trading order that was established in the post-Second World War period, made no particular exceptions for neutral countries. It was consistent with, although not explicit in, the philosophy of the founders of the Bretton Woods system and GATT that neutrality was a purely *political* issue which had few, if any, economic implications and therefore would not undermine international economic co-operation. This view was so firmly held by the participants in the post-war international economic order that no mention of neutrality was made in the negotiations for the new institutions, even by the two European countries who managed to retain their neutrality in the two world wars, Sweden and Switzerland. Except in the area of agriculture, almost sacrosanct for neutrals as well as for all other industrialized countries, liberal international trade was seen as perfectly reconcilable with—if anything, even beneficial to—neutral countries. Indeed, in keeping with the liberal tradition, trade was expected to enhance economic strength, which was considered an important prerequisite for neutrality, and to lead to more peaceful economic conditions for all states.

The concept and practice of neutrality was not, however, a product of the liberal age but emerged much earlier during the period of consolidation of state power when circumstances were radically different. At this time the smaller new states found that their security needs could best be met by remaining neutral in the wars of their more powerful neighbours. Power was, however, based on economic tools as much as military superiority while wars were local and limited, thus creating for the neutral countries security requirements very different from those perceived in the period following the Second World War.

One of the aims of this chapter is to look at how the policy of neutrality has been adapted over time to changing perceptions of security needs. Because of the broadening

definition of war as well as the increasing complexities of
international relations, the requirements for maintaining
neutrality, and its concomitant, security, have become
increasingly ambiguous. While the concept of defence formerly
referred merely to military preparations for war, after 1945
it was widened to encompass a series of military, economic,
and social conflicts of different scope and magnitude, both
internal and external. Thus, in addition to an examination
of how the policy of neutrality has evolved in theory and in
practice, this chapter will also address the question of how
neutral countries, Sweden in particular, perceive these new
types of conflicts and in what way, if any, they encroach upon
the pursuit of other policies such as trade promotion.

1 The concept of neutrality

(i) *The role of trade in the history of neutrality*

Neutrality has traditionally referred to the rights and duties
of non-belligerents during the course of a war. As liberal ideas
of free trade gradually replaced the mercantilist system based
on maintaining at all costs a favourable balance of payments
and thus a maximum self-sufficiency, the nature of neutrality
changed accordingly. The development of international trade,
at that time primarily maritime trade, led to growing
difficulties for neutral states in maintaining their rights at
sea. Although the increasing economic interdependence was
hardly noticed in peacetime, maritime trade became a major
cause of—as well as a determining factor in—the outcome
of a conflict. During the course of a war the belligerents
attempted to prevent trade between their enemy and the
neutral states, particularly if this trade consisted of goods of
a 'military' character that could influence the outcome of
the war. Economic resources were therefore an important
element in determining whether a neutral state would be able
to maintain its status. Eventually, a distinction had to be
made between 'military' goods and 'neutral' goods in order
to allow neutral states to maintain normal trading relations.
However, such definitions were very elastic and could include
at the limit almost any product.

The first systematic codification of the rules and of warfare
including the treatment of neutrals was presented in the

Declaration of Paris of 1856. Although it contained certain provisions on neutral trade, it was virtually inapplicable because of the absence of what was considered to be an increasingly decisive factor in the maintenance of neutrality, an acceptable definition of 'contraband' of war. It was the Hague Conventions (1899–1907) that officially defined for the first time the rights and duties of neutrals and incorporated them into international law.

The economic and trade aspects of neutrality were not in the forefront of the rights and duties as laid down in the Hague Conventions. One of the most important duties was that of maintaining territorial integrity which clearly required a strong military defence, but the economic consequences of such a duty was for the state to have at its disposal the necessary war material in preparation for an eventual attack. However, the Article regarding war material does not clarify precisely what this consisted of.[1] An exact definition of contraband was still therefore vague.

As an international legal concept, contraband was first discussed in the Declaration of Paris, 1856, but the definition of contraband was not expressly dealt with until the Conference of London, 1908–9. Before the London conference there had been a number of controversies concerning the issue of which items should be included on contraband lists. Some examples were: foodstuffs, coal and fuel generally, money and precious metals, merchant vessels, and even raw cotton which was declared 'conditional contraband' by the United States in the Civil War because of its use as exchange by the South.[2]

However, the Declaration of London gave a more precise definition of contraband. Articles 22–9 attempted to settle the controversy by listing articles that might 'without notice' be considered 'absolute contraband' and to which further 'articles used for war' could be added by means of a notified declaration from the belligerent powers to other states.[3]

---

[1] Article 7: A neutral power is not bound to prevent the export or transit on behalf of one or the other of the belligerents, of arms, munitions of war, or, in general, of anything which can be of use to any army or fleet.

[2] Julius Stone, *Legal Controls of International Conflict* (New York, 1954), 479.

[3] Robert W. Tucker *The Law of War and Neutrality at Sea*, US Government Printing Office (Washington DC, 1957), 265.

Nevertheless the range of free articles contemplated in the Declaration was practically reduced to nothing as the belligerents increasingly resorted to arbitrary listing. Today war material is considered by many countries as having acquired a much broader definition than was probably intended during the Hague conferences. One author has said, 'Total war, waged with the mobilization of all productive means, has had the effect that there are hardly any goods today that are militarily completely insignificant.'[4] Although these lists in some form are still in existence as is the use of the term contraband, the two world wars completely undermined the progress that had been made in trying to regulate the rules of war trade and the treatment of contraband. 'The belligerent has been confronted with the choice of either permitting goods to enter neutral ports, part of which are certainly destined to find their way into enemy hands, or to impose rigid controls upon such commerce at the risk of interfering on occasion with what is undeniably legitimate neutral trade.'[5]

(ii) *The League of Nations*

The First World War represented a serious blow to the nineteenth-century conception of neutrality and independence of small states. Most were pressured into partiality and those that managed to uphold their neutrality found that the exigencies of the blockade put a severe strain on many of the rights which they had previously enjoyed.

The dilemma that presented itself to the peacemakers at the close of the First World War was how to incorporate into the system more and more small, independent states which had been created by virtue of the principle of self-determination in circumstances where they realized that the concept of neutrality and independence of small states had been at least modified if not destroyed.[6] A compromise was found in the altered conception of international co-operation and security. Thus the Hague Conventions were superceded by the far more comprehensive League of Nations. The League

---

[4] Helmut Kaja, *Neutralität and europäische Integration*, Archiv des Völkerrechts, II Band (1963), 249.

[5] R. Tucker, *The Law of War and Neutrality at Sea* p. 280.

[6] E. H. Carr, *Conditions of Peace* (London, 1942).

represented a continuation of the long history of efforts to regulate war, with one important difference: the Hague Conventions assumed in fact the inevitability of war, while the League sought to prevent it through a system of 'collective security' and peaceful settlement of disputes.

Collective security involved a policy of preventing wars through a system of economic and military sanctions against the aggressor. Any war, according to the Covenant, was 'a matter of concern to the whole League' and any member of the League resorting to war in defiance of its obligations under the Covenant 'shall ipso facto be deemed to have committed an act of war against all other members of the League'. Such a system, in principle and according to the views of President Wilson, made no allowances for neutrality. 'Between members of the League', declared the British government on one occasion, 'there can be no neutral rights, because there can be no neutrals.'[7] Advocates of the League saw little purpose in neutrality since war by its very nature obliged the neutral state either to abandon its rights or fight to maintain them.

Thus the doctrine of neutrality temporarily became obsolete in theory but never in substance. Although the threat of war did not seem imminent in the 1920s, most small or weak states such as Switzerland avoided certain League obligations which they regarded as utopian and which would have implied a renunciation of neutrality. In effect what happened during the interwar period was that a revised conception of neutrality was developed, that of a 'factual' or 'qualified' neutrality. The idea of a statutory neutrality was no longer upheld, the neutral state being allowed in its place to decide in each individual case whether it would stay neutral. In theory this meant that the neutral state would have the right to interpret its rights and obligations in time of peace and war. This new attitude was partly reflected in the recognition of Switzerland's admission to the League.

Faith in the League system declined rapidly in the later 1930s. In particular the Scandinavian states were disappointed

---

[7] 'Memorandum on the Signature of His Majesty's Government in the United Kingdom of the Optional Clause', Cmd. 3452, p. 10, quoted in E. H. Carr, *Conditions of Peace*, p. 51.

by the League's failure to settle the Italo-Ethiopian conflict in 1936. They came to the conclusion that the obligations of Article 16 on sanctions were no longer respected. The outbreak of the Second World War sealed the fate of the whole League system. Austria, Czechoslovakia, Finland, Germany, and Italy left the League and only two countries in Europe succeeded in maintaining their neutrality throughout the war: Switzerland and Sweden. The legal system on which neutrality was based inevitably lost much of its force. As one writer put it,

> The deterioration of semantic accuracy in the use of the term 'neutrality' can be traced back to the efforts of various European small Powers to cloak their frightened reactions to the anarchy of the 1930s in familiar terms. Neutrality traditionally referred to the rights and duties of non-belligerents during the course of a war. Obviously, whatever else it may refer to, the current attraction of policies defined as 'neutral' has nothing to do with legal rights. On the contrary, it reflects political, military, and psychological judgements about the opportunities and dangers of the contemporary political configuration.[8]

(iii) *The United Nations*

The Second World War delivered an even greater shock to the international system and to traditional concepts of war, peace, and neutrality than its predecessor. The scope and intensity of the new kinds of warfare were unprecedented in their horrifying consequences. Even before the war, there had been a sharp intensification of economic warfare which, as we observed in the previous chapter, was widely believed to have contributed to its outbreak. Furthermore, the new international situation was characterized by a growing inequality between strong and weak states which international law was quite unable to rectify. Wars were no longer declared and there was often no clear beginning or end. Perhaps most evident was the increased interdependence among states which was to have considerable consequences on the system in general and on neutral states in particular. 'Absolute neutrality', wrote *Izvestia* in April 1940, 'is a fantasy unless

---

[8] Robert L. Rothstein, 'Alignment, Neutrality, and Small Powers: 1945–1965', *International Organization*, vol. 20, no. 3 (1966).

real power is present capable of sustaining it. Small states lack such power.'[9] In a similar vein, E. H. Carr wrote, 'In modern conditions of warfare a small state cannot defend its independence against a Great Power except by methods which in themselves constitute a surrender of military independence. Interdependence has become an inescapable condition of survival.'[10] At this point it was unclear how, and indeed if, the security of neutral states could be maintained. Experience since 1945 has not provided an unambiguous answer to this question. Although the philosophy of the UN, unlike that of the League, was not inherently opposed to the concept of neutrality, as will be seen, it is not at all obvious that a viable system of economic security is any longer available for small states within the contemporary international division of labour.

Neutrality and other variations on the same theme resurfaced within the UN system by default rather than design. When the UN was founded in 1945 it adopted many of the principles of the League of Nations. Its purpose was to suppress aggression through collective action and work towards the maintenance of peace. However, the collective security system of the UN was not as rigid as in the League. Even more than under the League, the identification of a war situation became increasingly ambiguous.

One important departure from the Covenant was provided by Article 51, which allowed member states to provide for their own defence either singly or collectively. By implication, therefore, it also left them free to pursue a policy of neutrality defined according to the national interest at a particular time and circumstance. There are today in Europe four neutral states in the wide sense of the term: Austria, Finland, Sweden, and Switzerland, although each of these states has its own specific definition or understanding of neutrality. Some other European states, such as Spain and Ireland, have belonged neither to the Atlantic Treaty nor to the Warsaw Pact and so could qualify as non-allies, but whether they could actually be considered as neutrals has been disputed.

---

[9] *Izvestia*, leading article, 11 Apr. 1940, quoted in E. H. Carr, *Conditions of Peace*, p. 54.
[10] Ibid. 54.

(iv) *Non-alignment*

With one or two notable exceptions (Austria, 1955; Laos, 1962), the major change in the concept of neutrality that has taken place since 1945 has involved a shift from the passive to the active voice: states are not now normally neutralized by the great powers but choose to be neutral or, more commonly, non-aligned. There are important differences between the two concepts but also similarities. Although the European neutrals still conceive their policy in terms of physical security whereas the African and Asian non-aligned states emphasize political and economic independence, both groups are equally insistent on the need for a foreign policy independent of any formal political ties.

Non-alignment, sometimes known also as 'neutralism' emerged following the Second World War as a movement of the newly independent Asian and African states to co-operate in strengthening their international position. The concept was based on the idea of avoiding any alignments with either of the great powers, the United States and USSR, and their desire to avoid the political strings which were frequently attached to foreign aid. The developing countries recognized that freedom of action and maximum economic concessions could best be obtained from both blocs by avoiding commitments to either one.[11] Thus non-alignment did not evolve solely out of security considerations as European neutrality had done. Rather, it was the need for autonomy and economic development that was paramount. However, non-aligned states now constitute a very loose grouping and have in fact lost much of their early force and cohesion.

The economic policies of the Third World countries have nevertheless had implications for the industrial world which, amongst other things, have driven a wedge between the non-aligned and some of the older neutral states. The non-aligned movement did not develop out of any specific concern for security *per se* but was rather part of a nationalist movement aimed at development which altered the whole perception of interdependence. While the industrialized countries had promoted interdependence amongst themselves in the name

[11] John W. Burton, *International Relations: A General Theory* (Cambridge, 1965); Leo Mates, *Nonalignment, Theory and Current Research* (New York, 1972).

of peace and prosperity in a context which did not account for the interests of the developing countries, the new reality of interdependence appeared as a particularly alarming 'threat'. Import-substitution policies were gradually replaced by export-oriented development policies and some of the more industrialized of these countries (such as the so-called NICs) became successful at exporting increasing quantities of labour-intensive, semi-manufactured goods. For the industrialized countries this new configuration was one important element which led to a redefinition of the concept of security as well as a re-emergence of the idea that states require 'economic' security or economic defence in addition to military defence. Furthermore it was in this context that a revival of economic nationalism took place among industrialized countries, which involved the use of economic 'weapons' such as quantitative restrictions and other non-tariff barriers to trade. As we shall see, some of the European neutrals have argued that their need to provide for their own economic security in times of economic crisis warrants an even more restrictive response to the Third World 'threat' than that of other industrialized countries.

(v) *Neutrality in the context of changing security perceptions*

It is important to recall that the policy of neutrality was conceived as a system of security primarily for small states. As long as states were relatively independent, as they were in the nineteenth century, this conception of security remained valid. Up until the period between the two world wars, the importance of certain economic aspects of neutrality was acknowledged. In particular, states were aware of the potential danger to their normal trading rights and therefore sought a defence of these rights in international law.

In revealing the complexities of the modern international system the First World War effectively destroyed the basis upon which these rights could be upheld. A new conception of security was sought in establishing the League of Nations which, while acknowledging many of the changes in the international system, failed to make any provision at all for economic security. As became clear from the beggar-thy-neighbour policies of the 1930s, the new economic realities encouraged states to use economic power as a weapon of attack as well as defence.

The shock of the Second World War was even greater than that of any previous wars and had consequences of an unprecedented nature. Because of the Allies', particularly the Americans', belief, that the absence of a liberal international economic order had been among the chief causes of war, post-war policy was aimed at depoliticizing economics and creating a framework based on the principles of classical and neo-classical liberalism. The architects of this framework believed that the security of small states could be guaranteed best by the system of rules in general and the principle of non-discrimination in particular. In contrast to the series of international laws laid down in the nineteenth century which was based on wartime behaviour, this new conception was essentially a peacetime system and made little allowance for war preparation. Given this emphasis, neutral states did not renounce their status but shifted their orientation to one of working for peace. And as we have seen, they were allotted no special rights or exceptions beyond those valid for all states.

In the 1970s, however, new concerns emerged following the actions taken by the OPEC Cartel in acquiring control over prices and supplies of oil. It was now recognized that developing countries were playing an increasingly important role in the world economy, which, amongst other things, resulted in an altered perception of security, or strictly speaking, insecurity among industrialized countries. This new insecurity was based on the realization that inter-dependence could have increasingly negative consequences for states. Although the primary concern of the industrial states was with the vulnerability of their energy supplies, it was progressively widened as certain developing countries established themselves as major, competitive exporters of not only raw materials upon which the industrialized countries had demonstrated dependency, but of semi-manufactured and even manufactured goods already being produced in the West. This new 'threat' from the Third World was ultimately less a function of actual interdependence than it was often portrayed (see Chapters 4 and 5). But security is very largely a matter of perception, and in what was widely viewed as an unpredictable economic environment, the industrial states generally, and the European neutrals in particular, began to broaden their interpretation of war to include 'crises' of an economic nature. This reinterpretation in turn entailed a redefinition of the type of preparation necessary if independence and neutrality were to remain credible policies.

2 Sweden's neutrality

A conscious policy of neutrality was initiated following the outbreak of the First World War under the inspiration of Hjalmar Hammarsköld. Although Sweden managed to maintain its neutrality during this war, in reality its military defence was poor and inefficient. It became clear then that national defence was an indispensable element in maintaining neutrality. It was also in respect of neutrality and military defence that the three Scandinavian states began a new era of Nordic co-operation.

(i) *The Second World War*

Sweden confronted the outbreak of the Second World War with a military defence modernized, but not expanded. It was, in effect, not much better prepared militarily than it had been for the First World War. Again, war had not seriously been expected; defence had not therefore been given the priority that many in Sweden felt it needed in order to resist involvement in a great war. Pacifist sentiments were still strong among the population; the country was still relatively inward-looking, and the standard of living had reached a level high enough to alleviate fears of economic collapse during a war. As one minister stated in 1941, 'It was widely and popularly believed that a policy of neutrality was nothing beyond keeping out of the War'.[12]

The outbreak of hostilities led to rapid mobilization and during the course of the war the maintenance of a strong military defence became a central element of its neutral policy. Moreover the government began to feel the important implications of trade in determining the outcome of the war, and thereby the attitude of the belligerent states. Trade had

[12] W. M. Carlgren, *Svensk Utrikespolitik 1939–45* (Stockholm, 1973).

indeed been a significant factor in the First World War, but it was decisive in the Second World War.

At the beginning of the war the German steel industry was based on annual imports of about 20 million tons of iron ore. Nearly half of this came from Sweden, the rest mainly from France, Spain and North Africa.[13] Steel was a vital material for war production and the Allies applied strong pressure on Sweden to cut off steel supplies to Germany.

For a certain time Sweden successfully negotiated trade agreements with the Western Allies and with Germany by 'balancing off' their respective economic interests. However, economic pressures were used increasingly against Sweden by both sides. Dependent on Germany for coal and on the United Kingdom for metal goods, chemicals, and oil, Sweden was in a precarious position.[14] In these circumstances the government was forced to make concessions which were strictly inconsistent with neutrality, such as allowing the transit of German troops across Swedish territory. The particular trade aspects of Sweden's policies in the Second World War will be examined more closely in the next chapter. Here it is sufficient to note that ultimately it demonstrated that it was more determined to preserve independence and neutrality than to maintain trade regardless of costs.

(ii) *Economic defence*

Although all European countries had a defence policy *per se* as they entered the Second World War, very few had plans geared specifically to economic security. Switzerland had made certain preparations in the Kommission für Kriegswirtschaft (Commission for Wartime Economics) which aimed at maintaining stocks of important raw materials and preparing a system of rationing. Norway also created an organ to deal with problems of economic defence, claiming that the ability to survive economically was the most important aspect of neutrality. From the beginning,

---

[13] Gunnar Hägglöf, 'A Test of Neutrality—Sweden in the Second World War', *International Affairs*, 36 (Apr. 1960), 135–67.

[14] Ibid. 160.

however, Sweden's policies were the most developed in this respect.[15]

In Sweden the First World War had resulted in a serious exhaustion of food and vital stocks caused by poor planning and organization. After the war, therefore, there was a serious debate on the issue of economic defence addressed to the question of how to provide for military and civilian needs during a war, In 1928 a commission was appointed for 'economic defence preparations', Riks-Kommissionen för ekonomisk försvarsberedskap (RKE) whose task was 'devoted to the execution of necessary preparations so that during war, imminent war, or other extraordinary conditions, the armed forces' needs will be satisfied, national food supply secured, and the growth of the economy guaranteed as far as possible' (author's translations). The establishment of this Commission and the discussions on the preparations for war including economic defence matters reflected the increasing priority given to defence and to the acknowledgement of the reality of total war.

All the interested sectors of the economy were represented, including military defence, agriculture, commerce, welfare, and industry. RKE drew up the necessary plans for all industrial activities, including the crisis management of raw materials indispensable in case of crisis or blockade. It also prepared a series of regulations for trade and transport in wartime.

Among other considerations RKE placed great emphasis on the importance of its relations with industry in order to decide which types of industry were important for wartime mobilization and which raw materials should take priority. Machinery, medicines and energy were seen as among the really vital factors in meeting military needs but certain other elements were also considered as having a high priority, for example, transportation and telecommunications. In view of subsequent developments in the economic defence policy (see Part II) it is significant that although RKE concluded that increases in domestic production levels and the international division of labour were positive developments contributing

---

[15] Olle Månsson, *Industriell beredskap om ekonomisk försvarsplanering inför andra världskriget* (Stockholm, 1976), 17–23.

to an improved defence, the Commission also anticipated that the complexity of this increasing specialization in machinery was likely to pose potential problems for future defence capabilities.

(iii) *Contemporary practice of non-alliance*

After the Second World War a new phase began for Swedish neutrality. External conditions changed considerably with the advent of more and more sophisticated technology, including atomic power. It became clear that a state could no longer depend on its armed forces alone for security against external aggression. Moreover the Cold War between the United States and the Soviet Union created a situation of permanent international tension. In the light of these developments, the foreign policy debate in Sweden addressed two principal questions. (1) What priority should be given to defence? (2) What role should neutrality have in these new circumstances? These questions first arose in connection with the problem of membership in the UN. A reduction of defence expenditures had accompanied membership in the League of Nations, but no such action was contemplated with regard to the UN.[16] There were fears that even a strong military defence would not suffice in ensuring the security of the country in a modern war. There were those who argued that in the new international context Sweden would inevitably be dependent on outside help, a fear which raised doubts about the future of Sweden's policy of neutrality. In the final analysis, however, political opinion was united in favour of maintaining a policy of neutrality backed by a strong defence. Only the Communist party's approach appeared to be uncertain, but even it did not openly recommend that Sweden join the Eastern bloc.

In joining the UN, Sweden accepted the obligation to support decisions of the Security Council but regarded the voting system as providing it with a guarantee that military sanctions would in practice never be required of Sweden. It also made clear that it would do its utmost to avoid being drawn into either of the two power blocs, if divisions became

[16] Bo Karre, 'International Organizations in the Economic Field', *Sweden and the United Nations* (New York, 1956).

evident within the UN system. As regards internal policies, defence would remain a priority.

Sweden's involvement in the UN provided the means for a new and more active foreign policy which it called a 'policy of solidarity'. Although, logically speaking, such a policy contradicts neutrality, it reflected the Swedish official view that the credibility of neutral policies would be judged primarily according to how it contributed to the construction of a new system of peaceful international relations. This policy also resulted in a more precise reformulation of Sweden's policy, namely, 'freedom from alliances in peace-time aiming at neutrality in war'.

(iv) *Total defence*

The next development in Swedish security policy took place in the late 1960s. It appeared at that time—the so-called 'era of détente'—that risks of war between East and West in Europe had diminished, if only because both sides had accepted that a total war would also bring about their mutual annihilation. It was in this political and strategic context that it was sometimes argued that economic and social conflicts were taking precedence over military rivalries. Thus despite, or perhaps because of, détente, which had the indirect consequences of exposing the costs as well as the benefits of post-war economic interdependence, tensions arose more often from economic conflicts between the Western industrialized countries themselves and between North and South than between East and West.

The changing external conditions had a number of internal repercussions in Sweden. Although the policies of free trade and specialization were seen to have bolstered the country's economic growth and contributed positively to Sweden's policy of neutrality in providing the resources from which a strong military defence could be built, the increasing internationalization of the economy resulted in a new feeling of dependence and vulnerability. From 1968 these new concerns began to be reflected in publications by the Swedish Committee on Defence.[17] It was also at this time that the

---

[17] See Lennart Pettersson, *Det sårbara samhället* (Stockholm, 1977).

concept of a general 'security policy' became clearly defined and developed. The official definition read as follows:

Sweden's security policy, like that of all other countries, aims at maintaining the country's independence. Our security policy goal should therefore be, that in all circumstances, and in ways that we ourselves choose, to secure a national freedom of action in order, within our boundaries, to maintain and develop our society politically, economically, socially, culturally and every other respect according to our own values, while we, in connection with this, will work externally towards an international relaxation of tensions and a peaceful development.[18] (Author's translation.)

In subsequent statements on defence in 1972 and 1977,[19] the security policy was further expanded to cover what were seen as new requirements for a credible peacetime policy of neutrality. These developments dealt partly with Sweden's position with regard to such issues as disarmament, but more significantly for the present discussion, with Sweden's participation in the international economy.

International economic co-operation had traditionally been regarded as fully compatible with neutrality, but Swedish officials began to make certain reservations in this regard. The new mood was expressed by one of them in 1979: 'We rely upon a close and extensive economic cooperation across borders even for the future. But measures may become necessary to prevent Sweden from becoming too dependent on other states for supplies of important goods and services. An all too heavy dependence could be taken advantage of in order to demand political and economic favours'.[20] In other words, it was becoming increasingly respectable to question the previous free trade thinking.

Economic defence, furthermore, became an increasingly important element in Sweden's total defence policy. It was defined as a 'general term to cover all measures that are needed in order to make our economy and security of supply capable of adjusting to the changed circumstances that war

---

[18] Proposition 1968: 110, Swedish Parliamentary Statement.
[19] Statens Offentliga Utredningar (SOU), 1979: 42.
[20] SOU 1979: 42, p. 108.

and crisis involve' (author's translation). These included:

(1) building up stocks and preparing crisis measures (substitute production, restraining consumption);
(2) greater co-operation among consumer countries in order to share their combined resources;
(3) decreasing import dependence through reliance on alternative raw materials and energy sources;
(4) spreading import dependence among more suppliers.[21]

A new organ was established to handle questions of economic defence called Överstyrelsen för ekonomiskt försvar (ÖEF) replacing the earlier RKE.

Conclusion

The definition of economic defence in the 1979 declaration had a certain similarity to that developed between the two world wars. However, the scope of the policy was broadened considerably. The implications also changed considerably in that other policies were linked to the broader policy of total defence. While the original ideas of economic defence consisted mainly of preparations for wartime mobilization as well as stockpiling of the most essential goods, the new policy covered a great variety of measures concerning raw material and food supplies, industrial production, communication and transportation, labour relations, trade, and aid to developing countries. It also included not only measures in case of military conflict, but preparations for peacetime crises. It identified a range of conflicts and crises. For each situation an analysis was made of the minimum types and quantities of goods for which supply would be needed. Situations were also considered in which Sweden's independence might be indirectly threatened by disruptions in access to supplies considered vital for defence. The contemplation of such contingencies posed difficult political problems, for example, to what extent the country was capable of being self-sufficient, to what degree self-sufficiency was necessary for the credibility of Swedish neutrality, and how far it was economically feasible given the high costs of defence and the uncertain nature of the risk.

[21] SOU 1979: 42, p. 109.

It was evident that the implications of such a far-reaching policy were much wider than in the past. A security policy representing all measures that the state must take in order to preserve its freedom and independence presented a problem in that it was clearly impossible to determine its exact limits. Indeed, the Swedish government recognized that there were potential contradictions in its various goals. National security now involved the need to balance a complex variety of foreign, military, disarmament, trade, and aid policies. Not all of these could be satisfactorily reconciled. For example, the Swedish authorities believed that economic growth through expansion of trade would promote peace and stability but at the same time would also increase dependence and vulnerability. As we shall see in the following chapters this double effect has led to a contradiction between its international trade commitments to lower trade barriers and the recent policy of restricting imports of textiles, clothing, and footwear from developing countries for reasons of economic defence.

3 The Implications of Neutrality for Sweden's Foreign Trade

Introduction

We have seen that the policy of non-alliance was intended purely as a political orientation implying independence from alliances in peacetime in order to maintain neutrality in war. Since neutrality was seen in purely political terms, moreover, there was no reason from Sweden's point of view not to engage in trade liberalization or to become economically interdependent with the rest of the world regardless of political alliances. During most of Sweden's history, the ability to remain neutral and to maintain credibility was believed to depend primarily on military strength and balanced political relations with West and East. Although economic strength was also indirectly important in providing a backbone of military strength, it only recently surfaced as a primary element in neutrality. Even as Sweden's trade relations developed a strong Western bias, this trade dependence was never directly related in theory to the problem of remaining neutral in wartime, nor to the need to maintain the credibility of the policy in peacetime.

The assumption that neutrality was a purely political concept also meant that Sweden was able to co-operate in the post-war effort to depoliticize trade. In practice, however, Sweden like other neutrals, has been confronted with a series of challenges to its trade policy. In this chapter we shall discuss the major conflicts that arose as a result of attempting to pursue a liberal trade policy and a policy of neutrality independently of one another. We shall see that Sweden supported the attempt to reconstruct a system of liberalized world trade after the Second World War so long as the theoretical separation of politics from commercial relations was respected by other states.

Swedish support of the liberal trade order began in the context of post-Second World War reconstruction administered by the OEEC, and continued with the joining of GATT and finally the attempts to establish a Europe-wide free trade area.

Although neutrality was not originally seen as having implications for trade policy, Sweden's support for trade liberalization was further based on the assumption that the derived benefits of economic strength would serve positively the aims of both the country's neutrality and independence, and its system of domestic social welfare.

For a certain period Sweden was able to pursue its various aims independently. The first economic challenge to its neutrality concerned East–West relations. Despite the attempts by the US to persuade Sweden to join the trade embargo against the Soviet Union, on this occasion Sweden managed to maintain its independence up to a certain point.

A second challenge arose when the EEC was created which threatened to discourage Sweden's exports by erecting a common tariff wall. The implicit aims of the Rome Treaty to establish a political union could not be reconciled with Swedish neutrality, but the dilemma for Sweden was resolved, albeit as a second best solution, when the European Free Trade Association (EFTA) was formed.

A third, more diffuse, challenge arose in the 1970s. One might have expected that a neutral country would seek to spread its interdependence, particularly by encouraging trade with the Eastern bloc and/or developing countries, as a means of mitigating potential conflicts. Yet this was never an explicit objective of the Swedish government nor was there a market in these areas to buttress such aims. On the contrary, the undoubted benefits of interdependence were achieved mainly by increasing trade with the 'old' international economic order, that is, primarily with the Western countries without any thought of the potentially negative consequences of such a one-sided dependency. Trade with the East developed very slowly and with the exception of the credit agreement of 1946,[1] trade has been restricted. With the developing countries relations evolved in a very different and more open context but also remained limited. Paradoxically it was this

---

[1] The agreement provided one billion kr. for purchases in Sweden to be repaid over a fifteen-year period at 2⅝ per cent interest. The large credit appeared to be motivated both by commercial and political factors. First, in anticipation of a serious post-war depression in the West, Sweden wanted to secure new export markets in the East. Second, Sweden wished to establish friendly relations with its large neighbour to the East.

trade, however, which posed the new challenge. The reason was that Third World imports of certain goods such as textiles were viewed as a threat to Sweden's neutrality and security policies in so far as these now covered the country's employment and social welfare system. Since the Swedish authorities remain reluctant even now to accept that there is any necessary contradiction between economic liberalism and neutrality, it is to the foundations of Sweden's strong attachment to free trade that we must first turn.

1 The foundations of Swedish trade policy

(i) *The industrialization process and the need for free trade*

Industrialization began in Sweden as a process of exporting increasing quantities of raw materials that could not be absorbed by domestic industries. Swedish resources consisted primarily of forestry products and iron ore. An expanding export surplus then allowed for greater imports of investment goods which led to the development of more sophisticated and specialized manufacturing. Industries which were previously protected gradually developed a dependence on foreign imports and began to recognize that the country would profit from more liberal trade if it lowered its tariff barriers. At the same time, it was expected that an active free trade policy would increase the value of Sweden's own natural resources for export production.

The free trade orientation remained firmly embedded from that point on. Thus, even in the 1920s during the general trend towards protectionism in Europe, Sweden resisted it strongly. One demonstration of this resistance was the Nordic initiative to convene a meeting aimed at lowering tariffs among the Scandinavian countries, Belgium, Luxemburg, the Netherlands, and later Finland. This meeting produced the Oslo Convention of 1930.[2] Even as the general economic and financial crisis was affecting the whole world and economic nationalist currents were growing stronger, Sweden, along with the other small states of the Oslo Convention, the so-called 'Low Tariff Club', struggled to counter the trend

---

[2] Bertil Ohlin, *Utrikeshandel och Handelspolitik* (Stockholm, 1959), 228–9.

towards autarky. Indeed, by degrees Sweden came to be one of the countries with the lowest tariff barriers.

Although the subsequent disastrous effects of this generalized protectionism might be thought to have vindicated Sweden's policy, it is important to recall that Sweden was at this time not faced by the circumstances which led other states to defend their economic position by measures of trade protection. Sweden's industrialization had merely begun, imports were in demand, there was little slack capacity, and unemployment was not yet a problem. In this context, the post-war Minister of Commerce Myrdal stated that

if world trade comes to be dominated by nationalism, imperialism and the formation of political blocs, the countries likely to suffer most are those which, like Sweden, have no desire to belong to any bloc. Our export industry needs free access to all markets if it is to produce the best results. Thus, there are very sound reasons for Sweden's free trade policy.[3]

During the inter-war period, as well as after the Second World War, there was one important exception to the policy of free trade, namely that of Sweden's agricultural policy. As in other industrialized countries where the agricultural interest represents a stable, conservative element in society, protectionism in this area was very much due to the large sector of the population still engaged in agriculture and the strong farm lobbies. In the Swedish case, however, another important argument in official thinking was the need for economic defence preparations. Given the food scarcities faced by the country in the First World War, the policy of self-sufficiency in agriculture became a priority. It also made better economic sense than in other countries given the policy of neutrality.

Apart from this one exception, it is clear that at the outbreak of the Second World War Sweden was already a firm adherent to the principle of comparative advantage, its government holding strongly to the view that global and domestic welfare would be maximized if every country specialized in sectors providing the greatest competitive potential.

[3] Gunnar Myrdal, 'The Reconstruction of World Trade and Swedish Trade Policy', *Svenska Handelsbankens Index* (Dec. 1946) 17.

A number of changes also took place internally to favour the policy of free trade. Following the worldwide depression of the late 1920s and early 1930s, the Swedish population voted a labour party into power, the ideological orientation of which was rooted in nineteenth-century socialism and its critique of capitalism. However, like most of the parties that grew out of the West European socialist movements, the Swedish Social Democrats had accommodated themselves to parliamentary, reformist politics. Their priorities were security of employment, economic stability through expansion of the public sector, growth through specialization and free trade, and a resistance to social and economic inequalities.[4]

Another significant development in the 1930s was the reorganization and strengthening of the trade union movement. Its reaction to what was felt to be an increasing accumulation of property by a small number of persons and the increasing need for the wage earners to defend themselves more efficiently led to the unification of several smaller unions. In contrast with trends in many other European Countries, however, both the trade union movement and the Socialist Party in Sweden were conscious of the importance of free trade to the nation's welfare, including the goal of full employment.

(ii) *Trade policy during the Second World War*

By the time the Second World War broke out, Sweden had already acquired one of the highest standards of living in Europe. The new wealth and industrialization was felt to be a direct result of the rate at which trade was increasing, in particular with the European countries.[5]

At the outbreak of the war a new coalition government was set up, one of whose primary tasks was to provide for security through adequate supplies of armaments and food. The execution of this policy fell to the State Trade Commission

[4] Andrew Martin, 'The Dynamics of Change in a Keynesian Political Economy: The Swedish Case and its Implications' in Colin Crouch (ed.) *State and Economy in Contempory Capitalism*, (London, 1979), 97.

[5] In 1939 the percentage value share of exports directed to nine future EEC countries (Great Britain, Ireland, Germany, Belgium, France, Luxemburg, the Netherlands, Denmark, and Italy) plus Finland came to 74.1 per cent of total. Imports from this area amounted to a slightly lower proportion of the total, with Germany and Great Britain accounting for the major shares, together accounting for one-half of Sweden's imports from Europe.

in co-operation with the Foreign Ministry and the commission in charge of foodstuffs.

Sweden's main pre-occupation during the war was to maintain close to normal exchanges with all belligerents without being manipulated by them or drawn into the war. This proved to be much more difficult than during the First World War because of the greatly increased economic interdependence. Germany, at this stage, was dependent on Sweden for about 50 per cent of imports of its iron ore and ball bearings, which were vital in producing war materials. Sweden simultaneously maintained substantial trading ties with Great Britain. Throughout the war period, Sweden was faced with the difficulty of fostering the credibility of its policy and of demonstrating to the Allies, as well as to Germany, that it was maintaining an impartial attitude. Despite its efforts in this regard, it encountered increasing mistrust from both the United Kingdom and Germany. Even the US, then a non-belligerent, refused to negotiate a trade agreement, at a time when Sweden was under severe economic pressure and faced the danger of a complete depletion of its stocks. Towards the end of the war, the volume of imports had diminished to one half its pre-war level

TABLE 3.1. *Impact of Second World War on per capita product*

Country, type of product, and pre-war base year	1945	1950
United Kingdom National income, 1937		
(a) Total	111	103
(b) Excluding public authority spending	70	98
France National income, 1937	57	108
West Germany Net domestic product, 1936	78	94
Switzerland Net national product, 1938	90	114
Sweden Gross domestic product, 1939	114	150

Source: Simon Kuznets, *Postwar Economic Growth*, Four Lectures (Cambridge, Mass., 1964), p. 91.

and exports had receded to two-thirds their previous level. However, compared to the other European states, Sweden obviously emerged from the Second World War with its infrastructure hardly touched (see Table 3.1).

It is true that Sweden had been much better organized in the Second World War than during the First World War, in particular because it had established considerable stocks in advance. Furthermore, all production that had been geared towards export markets which were closed off was instead added to the stocks. Thus at the end of the war, with its production machinery still intact, Sweden was able to resume production and exports almost immediately. Nevertheless this fact did not undermine the very substantial threat that Sweden was confronted with throughout the war years. It is interesting to note, therefore, that Sweden elected to pursue a strategy after the war aimed at increasing interdependence rather than halting it. The question of post-war economic policies indeed became one of the most heatedly debated issues in the post-war period. In the end the decision in favour of the liberalization strategy as a means to revitalize trade was clearly a result of the experiences of the 1930s: even if the post-war decision-makers were not convinced that free trade would lead to peace, they nevertheless had ample proof of the destructive consequences of autarky.

(iii) *Post-war reconstruction of trade*

Before the war's end discussions were already taking place to determine Sweden's long-term economic policy. The early debate converged on two principal themes, one focusing on the issue of liberal trade vs. self-sufficiency, the other on the problem of full employment vs. price stability. The two documents that discussed these issues were the Myrdal Commission report published by a special government committee, the Commission for Post-war Economic Planning, and the Labour Movement's Post-war Programme, issued jointly by the ruling Social Democratic Party[6] and the Confederation of Trade Unions (LO). Both documents focused

---

[6] Sweden had a Social Democratic government during the entire period 1932–76 except for the summer of 1936 and during the war years when a coalition government was in power.

mainly on ways to maintain aggregate demand in the face of an anticipated post-war depression. According to Lindbeck, this belief was based on the expectation that the post-war world would be more peaceful than it turned out to be and that governments had not yet learned how to generate full employment.[7] Although subsequently falsified by events, these documents were influential in the development of economic policies in Sweden and are, therefore, worthy of some further discussion here.

With regard to the first theme, namely liberal trade and self-sufficiency, the principle of freeing trade was adopted unanimously as a long-term objective.

The emphasis was, on the one hand, on the necessity of removing the direct controls introduced during the wartime blockade but, on the other, on the need for the government to play a much more important role in the economy than it had before the war. This latter goal was to be achieved through expansion of the public sector and a greater influence on investment activities and foreign trade. However, specific policies were unclear and it was agreed elsewhere in the labour programme that 'to the extent that private enterprise succeeds . . . in giving the masses as much of the good in life as is technically possible at full and efficient use of labour and material factors of production, it can in the future be allowed to function in about the same way as was usual before the war'.[8]

Certain groups put forward the argument that self-sufficiency should be pursued in certain vital sectors. There were some economic as well as political reasons behind this line of argument. The economic reasons included

the falling away of German exports, the rising prices abroad, the worldwide shortage of all kinds of goods and, finally, the direct restrictions that may have to be imposed on certain kinds of imports in order to maintain the foreign exchange reserves—all this prolongs and strengthens that tendency towards self-sufficiency to which the blockade during the war gave rise.[9]

The political defence of protectionism and self-sufficiency rested on the belief that this would be the best means of

[7] Assar Lindbeck, *Swedish Economic Policy* (London, 1975).

[8] *Arbetarrörelsens efterkrigsprogram* (Stockholm, 1944), 45.

[9] Myrdal, 'The Reconstruction of World Trade', p. 13.

preparing the country for a future blockade. If vital domestic industries could be almost self-sufficient then the country would run fewer risks of depleting stocks and declining strategic production.

Nevertheless the general view was opposed to self-sufficiency. The counterargument to protectionism held that lower cost measures could be adopted through stockpiling, state-control of vital domestic industries, or cash-subsidies. This was considered a preferable policy to establishing high tariff walls or using price-raising devices such as the compulsory purchase of home-produced materials for the purpose of maintaining domestic production.[10] It was further pointed out that production of essential goods could be made internationally competitive without protectionism and would in fact benefit from this competition in that the quality of these products would be under constant control. Import restrictions were, in fact, imposed in March 1947 and reached a peak in 1949 due to a foreign exchange crisis. From this point on, however, the Swedish authorities began a consistent process of loosening tight controls on imports and freeing trade generally.

The second important theme that was debated in these post-war documents was the problem of how to combine full employment with price stability. Some of the main participants in this debate include Rehn, Meidner, Lundberg, Myrdal, and Ohlin, all of whom were advisers to or members of this government. Ohlin argued for more reliance on general economic policy methods instead of direct controls. However, given that Sweden had a high employment level after the war, he advocated placing less emphasis on employment and more on price stability combined, if necessary, with a more extensive policy for promoting labour mobility. Myrdal and Rehn developed this idea by suggesting restrictive fiscal policies to depress the economy and avoid inflation. At the same time, to compensate for any resulting increase in unemployment they also advocated retraining schemes and subsidies to those in the process of changing jobs. Both the Myrdal Commission and the Labour programme endorsed these policies.[11] A consequence of these dicussions was

---

[10] Ibid.

[11] Ohlin, *Utrikeshandel och Handelspolitik*, pp. 37–9.

the eventual expansion of social welfare policies to include a variety of regional and labour market policies, which will be discussed in detail in Chapter 5. Here one may conclude that the goals of improving social security and the freeing of trade were endorsed by government and labour and were seen as complementary rather than contradictory.

During the early post-war period, however, the desire to develop a multilateral liberal trading system was frustrated by the chaotic economic conditions which most countries experienced. In practice it was impossible to return to pre-war trade immediately. Special payments arrangements were essential, in a situation of balance of payments difficulties due to the inconvertibility of currencies and to the 'dollar gap' of the early post-war years. International capital movements were also interrupted. However, because states obviously wanted to resume a normal exchange of goods as soon as possible, trade regained momentum despite the cumbersome machinery.[12]

In 1945 the US proposals for an International Trade Organization (ITO) met with widespread approval in Sweden.[13] Even though the US never ratified the ITO

---

[12] Like other countries, Sweden was compelled to negotiate a series of bilateral agreements with special payments procedures, so-called 'clearing agreements'. These agreements consisted of lists of commodity goods for which industries would have to obtain licences in order to export. Similarly lists were made up for the most vital imports. The aim was to draw up a mutually acceptable list with the trading partner which would not put too much strain on prices, industries' capacities, consumer needs, etc. A new agreement was made every year. Such a practice of allotting quotas was necessary because of the serious shortage of goods in relation to requirements.

[13] 'It has always been of the greatest importance for Sweden's trade policy to be able to reckon on alternative markets . . . It is the existence of such alternatives that also gives a small country possibilities to assert itself in international organizations. Should they disappear, the economic size and strength of the individual country must be more decisive than normally would be the case . . . In our exposed political trade situation we have every reason to support the international efforts aiming at better co-ordination and in cases where we cannot bind ourselves directly, at least try to establish close co-operation. There is probably no greater risk for our free trade than that of having our exports and imports regarded by other countries as marginal phenomena, while we ourselves try to make business out of such an unstable situation. We should endeavour to have the other countries look upon our exports and imports as a permanent factor, on which they base their plans for the future with confidence—whether we do this by direct commercial relations, with the assistance of trade agreements, or through various forms of international co-operation.' Ingvar Svennilson, *Perspektiv på Västeuropas Utveckling, 1955–75* (Stockholm, 1959).

charter, a part of it, the General Agreement on Tariffs and Trade, was signed on 30 November 1947 by twenty-three countries. Sweden signed the Agreement in 1950.[14] Since the GATT was designed to handle trade based on free market forces with the minimum of government intervention, it was by definition suited to Western-style market economies only. For this reason and because of the context in which the GATT was negotiated, the Eastern trading area declined membership. From the Swedish perspective, however, the goals of the GATT were not seen to conflict with the policy of neutrality. On the contrary, it was believed that trade would lead to greater peaceful co-operation and that even the Eastern countries would eventually benefit from the system as well. It is interesting to note that Switzerland, which has always applied a more strict interpretation to its neutrality policy, did not become a full member of the GATT until 1966.[15] It is believed that this delay was also due to its highly protectionist agricultural policy.

Thus the trend towards greater international co-operation was set in motion. The creation of the GATT was supplemented by a series of attempts after the war to further regional co-operation, particularly in Europe starting with European economic co-operation in the context of the Marshall Plan, the formation of the Coal and Steel Community, and finally the Common Market. Although the general movement towards trade liberalization was expected to provide long-term benefits to Sweden, certain aspects of these particular developments were to challenge Sweden's neutrality.

2 Sweden and Western Europe

(i) *Sweden's role in the reconstruction of Europe*

Sweden's participation in the reconstruction of Europe after the war was an important first element in the development of its trade policy towards this region. Efforts to assist the

---

[14] Karin Kock, *International Trade Policy and the GATT 1947–67* (Stockholm, 1969), 63–5.

[15] *Feuilles fédérales*, Message du Conseil Fédéral sur l'accession de la Suisse au GATT, 1961, et à l'OECE, 1944.

war-torn countries of Europe began as an independent policy of unilaterally granting credits to various governments for purchase in Sweden of urgently needed goods. Sweden's participation in the Marshall Plan was a natural continuation of its own efforts towards European reconstruction.[16] The object of the Marshall Plan was to help tide the participating European countries over the period of diminished productive capacity and the serious disturbances in the international payments situation which were a consequence of the war. The Organization for European Economic Co-operation (OEEC) was to serve as the administrative instrument for the reconstruction of Europe and was expected to deal with all aspects of economic policy. It was to organize the reconstruction of the industrial apparatus, the restoration of industrial production and facilitate the convertibility of currency. Another long-term goal was to effect a liberalization of trade among the Europeans. The Swedish government was in support of the broad economic strategy, yet the evidence suggests that it was also apprehensive that economic co-operation of this magnitude would require certain obligations from the member states, which might be inconsistent with neutrality.

In particular the Swedish authorities had reservations with respect to the fact that none of the East European countries finally participated in the Paris meeting. This was interpreted by many persons as a foreshadowing of a deep rift between East and West. It was suggested that the East declined the invitation on the grounds that the US was aiming to establish a 'Western Capitalist bloc' to divide East from West. If so, the OEEC would obviously have political as well as economic implications.

One Swedish government statement emphasized with relief that although there was a general danger of 'bloc-formation',

---

[16] The US proposal to assist the reconstruction of Europe with massive grants and credits was proposed in a speech by General George Marshall at Harvard University on 5 June 1947. All European countries, including those of Eastern Europe and the Soviet Union, were invited to participate in the programme and to attend the Conference in Paris for its organization. The Conference lasted from July to September 1947. On the same occasion discussions also began on the establishment of the Organization for European Economic Cooperation (OEEC) which was to administer the programme. Eighteen states finally came to the Conference.

such political bloc-building . . . has not taken place . . . This Conference [i.e., the Paris Conference on the Marshall Plan] was not meant to acquire an exclusive character, but rather stood open for all European states. Those discussions that took place in Paris among sixteen states, has signified a gathering around the problem of reconstruction, not a political bloc-building aimed against some outside states[17]

Despite the possibility of additional international obligations which this participation potentially entailed, Sweden did not ultimately fear a surrendering of its traditional autonomy. The evidence suggests that economic co-operation with Europe was considered natural and the policies for achieving this aim were fully compatible with previous policies. In any event there were no apparent misgivings with respect to the country's traditional policy of non-alliance.

Necessity no doubt also played a part in soothing any Swedish fears at this point. Although at the close of the war Sweden was in a good position to offer aid to its neighbours, by the time of the Paris Conference, Sweden too found itself in the situation of having to request outside help in order to balance its dollar payments.

While the US relief programme was primarily planned on a gift basis, it also included the possibility of credit accommodation and the granting of priority in the allotment of scarce raw materials, which could also have a strategic significance. Sweden's assistance from the US was to be in the form of credits which required repayment. In effect, Sweden was a recipient in relation to the US, but a donor in regard to European countries. Thus these countries, thanks to US aid, could pay for imports from Sweden with dollar currency. This system of placing 'drawing rights' through dollar credits at the disposal of certain participants was known as 'conditional aid' from the US. Such conditionality gave the US direct leverage over Sweden, despite the fact that the latter was not a member of the Western Alliance and, as we shall see, this became a significant challenge to Sweden in the context of US policies in the Cold War.

---

[17] Official government statement, 4 Feb. 1948.

(ii) *The embargo policy*

As tensions mounted between the US and the USSR in 1947 the US initiated an embargo on trade towards Eastern Europe and the Soviet Union. Thereafter a series of events led the US to generalize the embargo by making it a condition of Marshall aid. The most important was the Berlin blockade in 1948, which was interpreted by the US as a Soviet thrust westward. In response to this action the US passed two laws in December 1947 and January 1948, the first empowering the Department of Commerce to control fully US exports to Eastern Europe, the second requiring individual licences on all commercial shipments to Europe.[18] In March 1948 a section was added directing the Administrator of Marshall aid to refuse delivery of US commodities to aid-receiving nations 'which go into the production of any commodity for delivery to any non-participating European country which commodity would be refused export licences to those countries by the US in the interest of national security'.[19]

As measures for the embargo were stepped up, a consultation group was established for the co-ordination of trade policies. The Coordinating Committee on Export Controls, COCOM, comprising the NATO countries, began their discussions under the pressure of the US within the OEEC but continued informally and more directly thereafter outside the OEEC framework. The initial association of COCOM with the OEEC Secretariat was most likely a practical decision but created certain potential problems for non-NATO countries.

In the early stages of COCOM discussions both Sweden and Switzerland participated on an informal basis, which was somewhat surprising in that they were both neutral countries. Very little information is available on the reasons for their participation but it can be assumed from subsequent events that they had very little involvement in the substantive discussions. Their participation was probably merely an offshoot of their participation in the European Recovery

[18] George L. Ball, 'New Export Licensing Policies of the Department of Commerce', *Foreign Commerce Weekly*, vol. xxx, no. 10 (6 Mar. 1948) quoted in Gunnar Adler-Karlsson, *Western Economic Warfare* (Stockholm, 1968), 22.

[19] Statement by Under-Secretary Hoover, 'East-West Trade', *Department of State Bulletin* (9 Apr. 1956), 620; *The Economist* (7 Apr. 1956); Adler-Karlsson, *Western Economic Warfare*, p. 44; ibid. 23.

Programme and the fact of holding initial discussions at the OEEC. Once the embargo was actually put into operation, the neutral states proved unwilling to compromise their neutrality by engaging in a policy of economic warfare.

Considerable pressure was exerted on them, however. As industrialized states both Sweden and Switzerland were potential suppliers of strategic goods to the East. Without the participation of these two states any embargo would, therefore, not be considered effective. The two neutrals, on the other hand, could not be forced into compliance with the same 'technique' as was used in the case of the other countries receiving aid. The neutrals were 'loan recipients' and not as dependent on US aid as the 'aid recipients'. Other methods had to be found. Three possibilities were apparently considered by the US: (1) sanctions against the economies of the two countries because of their non-co-operative attitudes; (2) sanctions against private business interests of the two countries; and (3) direct negotiations.[20]

These methods were in fact attempted. The US set up various committees for the allocation of scarce raw materials. Private enterprises were also pressured directly by officials from the American Embassies in the two countries. In effect, the US was trying to coerce Sweden and Switzerland into conformity with the COCOM regulations.

There was considerable resistance to these pressures in the two countries, but certain compromises were inevitably made. For instance, the criticism most often heard concerned transhipment through Sweden. The government, therefore, agreed to issue import licences with a provision stating that the re-export of commodities was prohibited. Switzerland also agreed to promulgate similar regulations. Furthermore it is believed that the Swedish authorities concluded a 'gentleman's agreement' with the US. According to the reports by various diplomats, the Swedish government produced a declaration of intent concerning the rules which they intended to apply for export and transhipment of goods included in the COCOM lists. Due regard was to be given to the COCOM lists in concluding bilateral agreements with

---

[20] Battle Act Report No. 2, pp. 25–6; No. 9, p. 20, quoted in Adler Karlsson, *Western Economic Warfare*, p. 74.

East European countries. Moreover, all imports financed by credits from the Marshall Plan were to be reserved for domestic use. In return, the Swedish authorities were promised a sharp curtailment of the activities and pressures on Sweden coming from American officials.[21] This is a clear example of how pressure could be applied to Sweden's policy of non-alliance as a result of economic dependence on the West.

Sweden's post-war trade with the East has always remained limited to about 4.5 per cent of Sweden's trade, primarily due to the difference in commercial systems. However, certain factions in Sweden's government, notably those led by the Minister of Commerce, Gunnar Myrdal, did try to encourage trade with the East by negotiating a very large credit agreement with the Soviet Union in 1946. There was a considerable amount of controversy in Sweden over the agreement. Although the anticipated increase in trade after the war with the East never materialized, the agreement was viewed with serious concern in the US and provided additional motives to apply pressure on Sweden.

The argument that the agreement was made to promote credibility in the East was never used directly in Sweden. Negotiations for the credit had begun even before the entry into the war of the USSR and hence were before the Cold War. Yet it was clearly an attempt to reconcile neutrality in the broad sense, that is, maintaining good relations with all sides, with Sweden's policy of depoliticized trade. After his term as Minister of Commerce, Myrdal became Chairman of the Economic Commission for Europe, the central aim of which was to increase possibilities for trade between East and West. As far as Sweden was concerned, the initiatives within the UN Regional Commission may also have represented a means of circumventing the consequences of the embargo, but the expansion of ties with the East through trade never materialized to the extent hoped for.

The pressures on Sweden to curtail its exports of certain technologically sophisticated goods have been sustained well into the present day, although the nature of these pressures have changed somewhat, as has the response within Sweden.

---

[21] Battle Act Report No. 2, pp. 25–6; No. 9, p. 20, quoted in Adler Karlsson, *Western Economic Warfare*, pp. 76–7.

Throughout the post-war period Sweden has remained on a US list of countries that are considered highly risky to do business with and whose exports must be monitored most carefully. Every Swedish company which uses American components covered by export controls must abide by US export regulations. These regulations consist of controls on:

—export of goods and technology from the US;
—re-export of American goods from one country to another;
—export and re-export from one country to another of non-American goods containing American components;
—export and re-export of non-American goods which are manufactured with the help of US technology or know-how.[22]

Firms which do not comply with these rules are liable for sanctions, the most serious of which is to be blacklisted, such as in the recent case of the Japanese firm, Toshiba. While such risks for Sweden have always been acknowledged they are today more serious than ever. The most obvious reason for this is Sweden's increasing dependence on US technology and components for its own economy. Sweden's electronics industry, for instance, is almost completely dependent on outside sources, most notably the US. Moreover, the difficulties of stockpiling such goods or maintaining economic defence preparations have further exposed Sweden to its vulnerability as a neutral country. If the NATO countries—or even just the US—suddenly halted exports of electronic components, Sweden's whole economy could be damaged seriously within a few months. As a consequence of this vulnerability, Sweden finally formalized bilaterally its export control agreement with the US in 1986 after lengthy internal discussions in order to ensure a continuous flow of imports from the US. While the majority of Swedish firms deny that such an agreement would conflict with neutrality, it would appear that Sweden's neutrality has indeed been compromised, as has that of the other European neutrals who have signed similar agreements as a result of their trade dependence on the West.

---

[22] Mikael Holmström and Tom von Sivers, *USAs Exportkontroll–Tekniken som vapen* (Stockholm, 1985).

(iii) *Integration efforts in Europe*

The second major challenge to Sweden's neutrality arose as a result of its increasing economic interdependence with the rest of Europe in the context of European integration. Already by the end of the 1940s there were moves towards regional integration in Europe. This tendency manifested itself in efforts to promote greater political unity and more particularly economic integration. Among the elements which drove the Europeans to take concrete steps in this direction were the following: first, the disastrous economic policies of the 1930s based on nationalism and protectionism were believed to have been an important factor leading to the Second World War; second, the European countries emerged after the war very much weakened economically and politically; third, the colonies ruled by the European powers had either become independent already or were expected to do so soon; finally, it was a unanimous conviction that wars among the European countries could no longer be tolerated due to the disastrous consequences at all levels. As a result of all these factors, efforts were geared to bring about political reconciliation and thereby avoid any repetition of hostilities. Furthermore it was thought that the means to achieve this goal was through a functional approach, that is, through economic co-operation and integration.

Negotiations began in 1950 for the creation of the European Coal and Steel Community (ECSC). Its aim was to secure a regular and expanding development for the basic coal and steel industries and thus arrive at a supranational control over the production of armaments, which would in turn lead the way towards the ultimate goal of a unified Europe. In 1952 the Treaty of Paris established the ECSC between Belgium, France, Italy, Luxemburg, the Netherlands, and West Germany.

Further efforts by the same countries to unite Europe economically were begun on a much broader basis in 1955 and resulted in the Rome Treaty of 1957 establishing the European Economic Community (EEC). It was signed by the same six countries as the ECSC.

At the same time the Scandinavian governments began to explore possibilities of instituting a customs union to lower all trade barriers among themselves. Negotiations were initated several times between 1947 and 1959, but the proposed Nordic Customs Union never materialized. It has often been suggested that Sweden's primary concern was to strengthen its own negotiating position, with the help of its Nordic neighbours, in the forthcoming discussions on a Europe-wide free trade area. It was realized in Sweden that the country had the most to gain from free access to markets in Europe in order to continue the process of specialization and the production of competitive goods such as transportation and engineering goods. As a small country it was particularly dependent on international trade, but it lacked by itself the negotiating strength of the larger European countries. No one at this time seriously anticipated that economic interdependence could have negative consequences. The economy was growing rapidly and the standard of living was increasing continuously. There was no need, therefore, to doubt the benefits of trade.

The Treaty of Rome came into force on 1 January 1958, creating the EEC, a customs union which in time would become a full economic union. Although many of the goals bore some similarity to those of the OEEC, the EEC was much more far-reaching both in its methods and its objectives. The EEC aimed at economic expansion, stability, increased standards of living, and employment opportunities, as well as a complete harmonization of economic policies. The measures by which these objectives were to be pursued included: (1) dismantling all customs duties and quantitative restrictions for intra-EEC trade; (2) implementing a common external tariff and a common commercial policy toward third countries; (3) removing barriers to the free movement of labour, capital, and goods among member states; (4) formulating a common agricultural policy; (5) institutionalizing measures to harmonize economic policies; and (6) associating with non-European countries, particularly with newly independent countries in Africa having close ties with the European countries. The executive management of the EEC was vested in a Commission of nine members whose function was to draw up guidelines for action, submit proposals to the Council of Ministers, and put into effect the decision of the Council. The EEC, moreover, contained implicitly ambitious goals of political unification with a supranational basis.

This latter goal was the biggest stumbling-block for countries such as Sweden, since their neutral policy could not tolerate such potential infringement on their independence.

(iv) *Sweden's policy towards the EEC and EFTA*

The eventuality of Sweden's joining the EEC was a hotly debated issue. As we have seen, Sweden had given priority to the general dismantling of trade barriers. This was indeed considered the most advantageous trade policy for Europe, in general, and for Sweden in particular. When plans were drawn up for the six-nation economic union, which threatened the rest of Europe with a relatively high common tariff, Sweden and Great Britain, amongst other European countries reacted by presenting counter-proposals within the OEEC forum. However, their attempt to create a free trade area comprising all seventeen countries in the OEEC failed after long negotiations which lasted through 1957 and 1958.

Sweden's decision not to join the EEC at its inception was almost unanimously supported. Part of the reason could be attributed to Great Britain's absence. Britain was one of Sweden's most important trade partners and influential neighbours. Both countries, furthermore, were adamantly opposed to Europe's establishment of a high tariff wall against the peripheral countries. Secondly, and more importantly for Sweden, membership in a union aiming at common political goals and supranational decision-making was considered incompatible with neutrality.

The alternative for the neutrals and those European countries which had joined the customs union was to form a purely free trade area without any further ambition to move forward to a customs union or political unity. On 3 May 1960, after a year's negotiations, the Stockholm Convention created the EFTA. The following countries became members: Austria, Denmark, Great Britain, Norway, Portugal, Sweden and Switzerland. It was hoped that after dismantling industrial tariffs within the EFTA, an attempt could be made to negotiate an agreement with the EEC which would secure a general liberalization of trade throughout Europe. In fact the EFTA served two useful if more modest purposes. First, a free trade area without supranational goals was a means for the European neutrals to participate in European integration without a renunciation of tariff sovereignty and political principles. Secondly, it allowed the members of EFTA to acquire a stronger negotiating position against the EEC.

The question of joining the EEC as a full member, or in some form of association, was considered twice by the Swedish government between 1961 and 1963 and between 1967 and 1970. On both these occasions the issue arose as a direct result of Britain's announcement to seek membership in the EEC. However, in 1963 France's veto effectively barred the entry of Great Britain into the EEC for the time being. It was also, therefore, less urgent for Sweden to find a suitable arrangement since Great Britain and Sweden already had a free trade agreement with one another. When the British once more sought membership in 1966 and 1967, Sweden again seriously explored the various possibilities. The government submitted a letter to the European Communities leaving open the type of relationship desired. After long negotiations, Sweden signed a bilateral agreement of free trade with the EEC, similar to those agreements also signed by the other EFTA countries which did not join the EEC. Britain, Ireland, and Denmark, on the other hand, became full members of the EEC on 1 January 1973.

There were a number of political and economic factors under consideration when the Swedish government confronted the problem of its relation with the EEC. Many arguments were put forward in favour of full membership. Foremost among these were commercial and trade reasons. Sweden was dependent on free trade for optimal conditions for continued growth and expansion. In 1965 38 per cent of Sweden's imports originated in the EEC (9). This figure increased to 55 per cent in 1980. Swedish industry required a steady and reliable supply of raw materials for its manufacturing industries. Furthermore, large investments for sophisticated and highly specialized production were only possible with access to foreign markets. Trade barriers erected by customs unions might, therefore, hinder the process of growth through an increased division of labour and natural comparative advantages.

But there were also political reasons: Sweden had participated fully in European co-operation since the war and continuation of this co-operation seemed natural and beneficial. Neutrality up until this point had not barred Sweden from co-operation in solely European matters. Moreover, the Swedish government wanted to maintain its general influence in matters affecting the whole of Europe. As an outsider, Sweden could be affected by decisions taken beyond its sphere of influence. Finally, the government had never clearly set parameters for its neutral policy in peacetime, not even after the Second World War when conditions changed drastically. It is interesting to note, moreover, that the issue of pursuing a policy of self-sufficiency never arose in the context of the EEC debate as during the post-Second World War discussions. Although economic security *per se* was discussed briefly as we shall see, it arose in very general terms, the emphasis being on the importance of 'access to certain supplies during crisis periods' without elaborating on the means of such a defence or the nature of a crisis.

(v) *The role of neutrality*

Although there were other reasons which contributed to Sweden's ultimate decision not to become a full EEC member, the most important was the issue of neutrality. No foreign or security policy commitments are spelt out clearly in the Rome Treaty, but it has always been interpreted as an instrument for securing greater political co-operation among member States.

One of the sensitive elements from Sweden's view was the Community's aim, set out in Article 3, to establish a common commercial policy and empower the EEC to conclude commercial agreements with non-member States. Essentially, this implied not only maintaining a common external tariff but also a common agricultural policy and eventually the harmonization of economic legislation over a very wide area, all of which would inevitably entail a significant curtailment of autonomous decision-making.

The EEC goal of harmonizing trade policies also gave rise to specific concerns. One was the obligation to adjust Swedish tariffs to EEC levels. In practice this would have meant raising its low tariffs on such items as mineral oils and their derivatives as well as crude and refined petroleum and certain raw materials which were not subject to duties at all.[23]

---

[23] *Sverige och EEC*, Swedish Ministry of Commerce (Stockholm, 1968), 25–7.

Although membership in trade organizations such as the OECD and GATT had already bound the trade policies of the EEC and of Sweden fairly closely, these obligations did not extend to Eastern Europe, nor, for a long time, would they apply to the developing countries. Given also the suspicion with which the East regarded the EEC, Sweden's membership was put into question even further. With respect to the developing countries, the problem for Sweden was not so much that of compromising its neutrality but of surrendering its freedom of action. Although the EEC had already partially harmonized its policy towards the Third World, through first the Yaoundé and later the Lomé Conventions, the Swedish government had developed a reputation as 'progressive' in its relations with developing countries which it understandably wished to maintain.

A second problem for Sweden resulted from the Communities' aim of negotiating as one party within international fora, which would obviously further preclude the possibility of independent decision-making if Sweden were to join.

A third concern was Sweden's economic-defence policy and the question of access to necessary supplies during crisis periods. The Swedish Ministerial declaration of 1962 included the following statement:

The other reservation based on neutrality concerns the question of how to secure access to certain supplies considered vital in wartime. Already the Rome Treaty contains special decisions concerning war material. In addition to war material, however, there are other goods such as medicine and foodstuffs which must be secured, partly through the maintenance of domestically produced agriculture. I want to emphasize that it is the result, not the method in which this is reached that is of significance and potential cases are few. Even in this question I think that a common investigation of the situation with the Community could give a satisfactory result.

With respect to war material, therefore, it was not envisaged that accession to the Rome Treaty would confront Sweden with a potential conflict of interest with regard to its neutrality or its economic defence as long as this defence consisted solely of stockpiling measures. The problem would arise if stockpiling was not considered sufficient. Article 223 accepted that measures must be taken in certain cases in consideration of a state's security interests but only so long as they had no detrimental effect on normal competitive conditions within the Community with regard to products not destined for directly military ends.[24] This excluded the possibility of maintaining the production in peacetime of non-military products through subsidies or other non-tariff barriers even when stockpiling was considered inadequate or inappropriate. It also excluded the possibility of taking measures during a less serious economic crisis or in the anticipation of a crisis.

Before 1970 the problem of maintaining production for economic defence needs in ways other than by stockpiling was viewed primarily in the context of agricultural policy and in relation to the production of military goods. A Swedish law concerning the self-sufficiency of agricultural production was passed in 1967.[25] Other goods considered important at this time for economic defence included:

—commodities related to the production of war materials such as certain electronic devices, also goods necessary for repairs;
—commodities related to agricultural production such as fertilizer;
—medicines and other health care items.[26]

Had Sweden acceded to the Treaty, it seems likely that any economic-defence measures in these areas other than stockpiling would have conflicted with EEC regulations.

The ambiguity in defining a war or crisis situation was also a potential obstacle to EEC membership. A 1954 law on economic defence in Sweden discussed three types of situations: war, risk of war, and extraordinary crises in

---

[24] Article 223: '1. The provisions of this Treaty shall not detract from the following rules: (a) No Member State shall be obliged to supply information the disclosure of which it considers contrary to the essential interests of its security; (b) Any Member State may take the measures which it considers necessary for the protection of the essential interests of the security, and which are connected with the production of or trade in arms, ammunition and war material; such measures shall not, however, prejudice conditions of competition in the Common Market in respect of products not intended for specifically military purposes. 2. In the course of the first year after the date of the entry into force of this Treaty, the Council acting by means of a unanimous vote, shall determine the list of products to which the provisions of paragraph 1(b) shall apply.'

[25] Proposition 1967: 95, Swedish Parliamentary Statements.

[26] *Sverige och EEC*, pp. 25–7.

which there is a shortage or risk of shortage of goods necessary for economic defence. In the last case it would have been most difficult to justify to the Community the need for independent action, especially if this 'extraordinary crisis' did not in fact lead to war. Article 224 states that consultations should continue during crises for common measures to prevent one state from disturbing the normal operation of the Common Market.[27] Although there were no clear provisions forbidding a country from taking independent measures after prior consultations, the Swedish government foresaw possible conflicts with regard to neutrality. In this context the government made a statement attesting to the need, in case of membership, to be able to terminate the agreement and its obligations with the EEC spontaneously, an eventuality not foreseen in the Rome Treaty.

In the 1970 debate two new Community projects became factors in Sweden's final decision not to become a full member. These were the Werner Plan to establish an economic and monetary union and the Davignon Plan for co-operation on all important questions in foreign policy. Such plans contained in them principles and objectives not considered to be compatible with Sweden's policy of neutrality. The plan for the eventual establishment of an Economic and Monetary Union of which membership was to be obligatory for EEC states elicited the following comments from the Swedish Minister of Commerce:

Sweden intends to pursue a policy also in the future which preserves our possibilities to fulfil obligations which rest upon a neutral state and which give credence to our will and ability to observe neutrality in the event of war. For this intention to be clearly understood and respected, the policy must be pursued with determination and consistency. International ties cannot be accepted which make the possibility of choosing neutrality in time of war illusory. The policy must be supported by a strong military defence—the economic life

---

[27] Article 224: 'Member States shall consult one another for the purpose of enacting in common the necessary provisions to prevent the functioning of the Common Market from being affected by measures which a Member State may be called upon to take in case of serious internal disturbances affecting public order, in case of war or of serious international tension constituting a threat of war or in order to carry out undertakings into which it has entered for the purpose of maintaining peace and international security.'

so organized that the nation can endure a large scale blockade during a fairly long period. We cannot participate in such forms of co-operation on foreign policy, economic, monetary and other matters which in our judgement, would jeopardize our possibilities to pursue a firm policy of neutrality. This means that we cannot participate within a certain group of states in co-operation in matters of foreign policy which is binding—which aims at the working out of common policies. Limits are also set to our possibilities of accepting a transfer of the right of the decision-making from national to international institutions within the framework of an economic and monetary union.[28]

These factors are the ones most directly related to the policy of neutrality. In fact many other Community policies also influenced Sweden's final decision to negotiate the more limited association agreement on free trade in industrial goods, instead of requesting full membership. These included the Community's regional policy, as well as the goal allowing for a free movement of labour and capital. On the one hand, there was a fear that Sweden's far-reaching social welfare policies might in some way be infringed upon; on the other hand, many industrialists feared the anticipated rising of a high tariff wall around the Community with the consequence of lost market shares. Despite some trade diversion in the early years of the EEC, the free trade agreements signed in 1972 between EFTA and EEC countries dissipated these fears very quickly. Although trade expanded most quickly within each area before 1972, trade *between* the EEC and EFTA expanded more rapidly than trade within either area after 1972.[29]

In 1972 Sweden as well as the other EFTA countries signed reciprocal free trade agreements with the EEC thus establishing what was to become a Europe-wide free trade area. This development did not automatically reverse the previous trends that the original EEC tariff wall had imposed on EFTA countries' export patterns. However, as trade barriers were gradually dismantled between the two areas, there was a considerable boost in trade as a whole. Sweden's import shares from the six original EEC countries also increased between 1965 and 1980, but export shares decreased over this period.

[28] *Sverige och EEC*, p. 29.   [29] GATT Annual Reports.

The EEC has, however, changed radically since its formation in ways which again call into question future relations between the EEC and Sweden. Membership has, of course, grown from the original six to twelve countries and it is on course to achieve by 1992 an 'internal market' where all physical, technical and fiscal barriers to the free movement of goods, people, services and capital are removed. The decisions now being made in the Community have potentially significant ramifications for the future of Europe, such as its research programme into high technology, while the EFTA countries must sit on the sidelines. Most importantly, trade between Sweden and the Community is massive. In 1986 the share of the EC(12) in Sweden's imports came to 57.2 per cent while the share of the EC(12) in Sweden's exports amounted to 50.0 per cent.[30] Moreover, this dependence is very one-sided, leading a number of Swedish businessmen to claim that it will be impossible for the country to remain outside. Nevertheless, in a speech by the Swedish Foreign Minister on 10 September 1987, Sweden's attitude with respect to joining the EEC was clearly unchanged for the same reasons as those presented in 1971, that is, neutrality.[31]

3 Sweden and the developing countries

With the exception of the most developed LDCs, Sweden's trade with the Third World evolved in the context of its aid policies, which have been an important arm of its foreign policy. Concern for developing countries emerged in the 1950s as Third World regions became independent and as public awareness grew within the country of Sweden's own underprivileged groups in the context of its social welfare policies. The goal of Sweden's development policy thus came to be based on the idea of solidarity with the poorer people of the world and was seen as a logical extension of its domestic social security programme. Although various changes have been made in the scope and design of Sweden's Third World policy, the basic principles have remained intact.[32]

[30] EFTA Trade 1986.
[31] Sten Andersson's speech to Uppsala Students' Union, quoted in *The Economist*, 21 Nov. 1987.   [32] SOU 1962: 100, 1968: 101, 1977/78: 135.

Assistance policies were initiated in the context of international or non-profit organizations such as the UN. This was consistent with the idea that dependency had been established previously through unilaterally controlled relationships and that the best assurance against a continuation of this pattern was to establish a multilateral form of development assistance. It also stemmed from the Swedish belief that Western relations with developing countries in the post-independence period had too often been merely a function of superpower initiatives.[33]

In the 1960s and 1970s Sweden's Third World policy became more independent with a consequent shift of emphasis to bilateral aid. By 1975 approximately one-third of its development assistance was channelled into international organizations as multilateral aid, while as much as two-thirds went into bilateral programmes. One reason for this change was that the aims of Sweden's foreign aid policy became much more sharply defined in line with the parallel development of Swedish domestic social welfare policies. Since the two policies were based on the same values, the only way of ensuring that Swedish aid was in fact directed to these ends was to take greater direct responsibility for its administration.

An example is the emphasis given to the principles of democracy, equality, and freedom. A famous report written by Alva Myrdal and put out by the Social Democrats and LO entitled 'Equality' stressed that equalization, and its concomitant backbone of the labour movement, solidarity, should extend to all areas of social life in Sweden and abroad. 'The values accepted by social democracy which stimulate our demands for greater equality are universal in the sense that they apply to all people, regardless of nation, race, or colour.'[34]

This extension of domestic policies to developing countries also found expression in the choice of aid recipients. It is evident that Sweden increasingly distributed aid to 'progressive' and socialist regimes which were already engaged in efforts to redistribute social benefits, such as Tanzania, Cuba, and North Vietnam. Aid also went to

---

[33] SOU 1962: 100, 1968: 101, 1977/78: 135.
[34] Alva Myrdal, *Jämlikhet* (Stockholm, 1969), 145.

national liberation movements or movements opposed to racial oppression such as in South Vietnam and in Southern Africa. A speech made in 1965 by the future Prime Minister Palme highlights the ideological elements in Swedish aid.

What we are witnessing is the revolt of a people against privileged groups. What we are hearing are the same demands for liberty and equality for the great mass of the population as kindled the hopes, and stimulated the belief in the future of the emerging workers' movements in the countries of Europe . . . The fundamental moral evaluation of Democratic Socialism . . . makes it our obligation to stand on the side of the oppressed against the oppressors, on the side of the poor and the distressed against their exploiters and masters.[35] (And, furthermore), there is always a core of Democratic Socialism that remains. In short: a loathing of the class society in all its shapes and forms, a striving towards equality and the hope of community, the desire for liberation on the basis of co-operation and solidarity.[36]

Although in the brief period of rule by the Centre and Right Coalition, 1976–82, attempts were made to alter the direction of aid policy, the basic principles rooted in social democratic traditions seem to have remained largely the same. However, against the background of the world recession, pressures have mounted both to cut down aid and to ensure that unless it continues to be granted, it should yield greater two-way benefits. In particular, the ideas that have been presented involve increased access to export markets and, in general, an emphasis on trade rather than just aid. This change in focus was also a response to a parallel change of emphasis in many LDCs, which aim to industrialize through an emphasis on export promotion and by gaining greater access to developed country markets.

Given its small size, Sweden is particularly conscious of its economic interdependence with the rest of the world. In addition to its dependence on export markets, the country is also dependent on a steady flow of imports, particularly of raw materials. For this reason Sweden has a good reason to develop goodwill with certain LDCs. Although the extent

[35] Royal Ministry for Foreign Affairs, *Documents on Swedish Foreign Policy* (1965), 46.
[36] Cit. F. Fleischer. *The New Sweden: The Challenge of a Disciplined Democracy* (New York, 1967), 64.

of Sweden's trade relations with the developing countries is still very limited, it appears that the official view has always been that the aim of ensuring the goodwill of Third World suppliers is satisfied best by maintaining good relations with the LDCs as a bloc.

Finally it is worth noting that two traditional principles of Sweden's foreign policy, the policy of non-alliance and identification with small states, have also had an influence on the development of Sweden's relations with LDCs.

While this identification with non-alliance and small states had originally been seen primarily in political terms, the Third World demands for a New International Economic Order (NIEO) forced the Swedish authorities to think of the neutrality policy much more directly than ever before in economic terms. This was because, on the one hand, the demands emanated from the mostly non-aligned, developing countries with whom, as we have seen, Sweden had tried to develop a special relationship, and, on the other, they were targeted at the industrial countries of which Sweden was one. As a beneficiary of the 'old' economic order Sweden was not in a position, despite its 'progressive' Third World policy, to align itself completely with the NIEO programme. However, Sweden feared the consequences for its neutrality of a potential North–South division in which it would be forced openly into the Western ideological camp. It was in this context that Prime Minister Palme began to modify his 'small state doctrine'. While many of his early speeches in the 1960s had referred to Sweden's identification with 'small states', the emphasis being on the need to protect the sovereign rights of the weak in a world of superpowers, he now emphasized Sweden's ideological solidarity with the broad category of 'democratic socialist' states, including those in the industrialized as well as developing countries, in a deliberate attempt to distance Sweden in both political and economic terms from both the Eastern bloc and the Western 'capitalist' powers.[37] This was clearly a reflection of his conviction that Swedish autonomy could only be preserved if a way could be found of bridging the gap between the industrial West and

---

[37] Anders Mellbourn, 'Neutralitet och Solidaritet', in O. Kleberg *et al.*, *Är Svensk neutralitet möjlig?* (Stockholm, 1977).

the developing countries, and that this required a new formula which would be distinguished from both traditional neutrality and Third World non-alignment. As we shall see in the case of textiles, this effect has not been unambiguously successful.

In addition to pursuing a progressive aid policy towards Third World countries, Sweden has increased its commercial relations with them. In some cases, these commercial ties have been developed deliberately to complement the aid relationship as a means of maintaining a less one-sided dependence. Exports from Sweden to developing countries increased steadily from 8 per cent of world figures in 1965 to 14 per cent in 1980. Corresponding figures for imports were 12 per cent and 17 per cent. In 1985, however, the developing countries have again decreased their share in Sweden's exports and imports.[38]

Sweden's tariff barriers have been lower than those maintained by other industrialized countries and over 90 per cent have been bound. It is, of course, acknowledged that these low tariffs rarely go far enough to benefit the developing countries. For this reason, Sweden, along with several other developed countries, initiated its own 'generalized scheme of preferences' (GSP) in 1972. The purpose of this scheme was to allow duty-free access for developing countries' exports of industrial or semi-industrial goods. In 1974 Sweden's list of GSP goods was expanded to include all industrial goods with the exception of certain textile, shoe and leather, and agricultural goods. Sweden also lowered tariffs on tropical products in 1977. These measures meant that 90 per cent of imports from LDCs and 99 per cent of imports from the group of countries considered the least developed countries now enter the Swedish market duty free. However, Sweden's system of preferences contained an escape clause which gave the government the right to take certain measures in case goods under the preference system were to be imported in such quantities or circumstances that would cause or threaten market disruption.

Three reasons have been given by the government for excluding textiles, clothing, shoes, and leather goods from the system of preferences. They were: (a) the rate of unemployment

---

[38] GATT International Trade Statistics.

in Sweden; (*b*) the need to maintain production capacity for economic defence preparations, and (*c*) the fact that Sweden had already gone further than most countries in giving preferences to LDC products. Although Sweden is certainly not the only country to claim such exceptions to its GSP, the criticism has often been voiced that the GSP does not cover the products in which developing countries have a comparative advantage. Textiles and particularly clothing are precisely the kind of labour-intensive products which LDCs have been successful at producing and which are potentially significant foreign exchange earners. As we shall see, however, LDCs have increased their exports to the industrialized countries including Sweden, at a fast pace, and have begun to constitute what the developed countries consider a major threat.

Conclusions

To summarize: Sweden's entire post-war trade policy was aimed at a general reduction of barriers to trade, an increase in its own ability to specialize and trade, and hence a more specific role in the international division of labour. Although some discussions were held in the early post-war period concerning alternatives to free trade, these ideas were dismissed rapidly in favour of pursuing policies which were believed to contribute to the country's rapid growth and rising standards of living. To this effect Sweden participated in the various institutions created with the intention of furthering these goals. And since the post-war trading order was revived in a context as consciously divorced from politics as possible, Sweden's neutrality never had to be compromised.

The assumption, however, that the policy of neutrality could remain independent from trade inevitably came into question as trade increased in a very one-sided manner. Since the whole post-war international economic order was designed without considering the interests of the former European colonies as in Asia and Africa, and was also unable to handle the concept of state-trading, a distinct bias became evident in trade which set off a series of challenges to Sweden's neutrality. Yet it was never the government officials themselves who questioned the compatibility of liberal trade and neutrality since it would have implied questioning the whole foundation for the post-war international trading order as well as Sweden's wealth in particular. The question of compatibility was only raised in the 1970s as the developing countries emerged as exporters of certain goods in quantities which were viewed as a potential threat to external as well as internal order. In the following chapters, we will look more closely at this particular aspect of Sweden's trade relations with the developing countries in the context of textile and clothing trade, its relation to both Sweden's domestic welfare programmes and its aid policy, and more generally to the requirements of economic security which stem from the policy of neutrality.

Part II A Case Study: The Textile Trade and Swedish Economic Policy

Introduction to Part II

Having examined the general traditions upon which Sweden's policies have been based and the international economic framework in which it was believed that the broad aims of these policies could be fulfilled, we will now turn to a specific case study of the textiles and clothing sector. It is in this sector that Sweden's neutrality and liberal trade policies have converged and manifested their most apparent contradictions.

Textiles is a particularly appropriate industry for such a case study, partly because of the special international regime which had to be created to handle the particular trade problems that arose within it, partly because arguments for protection have been deployed with more sophistication in relation to textile trade than in any other sector, and partly because it is the only sector in which Sweden has a protective trade policy based on economic defence.

Before turning to these considerations in more detail, it will be helpful to sketch very briefly some of the historical background. The textile sector assumed a rapidly growing importance during the early phases of industrialization and indeed the development of a textile industry is often viewed as a prerequisite for economic growth. However, textiles, and particularly clothing, have always been highly sensitive sectors subject to fluctuations and adjustment problems that are arguably unique to it. It is also the first major industry to have experienced a rapid shift in comparative advantages away from the industrial West first to Japan and then to certain Third World countries.

Except in the US the textile sector was engaged in active international trade from the outset because most countries had to import raw fibres and yarns. During the early stages of industrialization Western countries developed their textiles industry rapidly with the aid of infant industry protection. Clothing production, however, remained a predominantly handicraft activity until the First World War. At this time manufacturing developed through mass production of uniforms and standardized city clothing. Clothing, however, was not traded intensively before the Second World War.

The familiar contemporary problems of 'low-cost suppliers' and 'market disruption' were first experienced in the cotton textile sector. Intervention in this sector began in the United Kingdom, then spread to other industrialized countries in the face of competition from Japan, Eastern Europe, and the developing countries.

The competitive situation for developed country industries deteriorated sharply as some of the developing countries acquired a more dominant role in international trade in the 1950s and 1960s. Production units that were affected by unemployment and social disruptions blamed the situation on the surge of low-cost imports and claimed that their lack of competitiveness was linked to the export-promotion policies of developing countries. Trade protection was demanded as unrestricted imports could no longer be tolerated. This unequivocal linking of events was, as we shall see, deceptive but not without logic. Just as the textile industry in the North had served as a catalyst for the industrial revolution it seemed also that many newly industrializing countries in the Third World, with a comparative advantage deriving from cheap and abundant labour, would advance their production of textiles with great speed, at much lower costs, and soon price their Northern competitors out of business.

Textile production was already long established in many developing countries on a small-scale, cottage industry basis, but the change came about as import-substitution was replaced by export-promotion policies. Given the great demand and absorption capacity of many northern markets and the inability of most developing countries to absorb their own production, exports increased at a very rapid rate. In response, manufacturers in the developed countries, particularly in the US, began to apply pressure on their governments to take concerted action against those exporting countries which they considered to be the primary culprits. They applied this pressure despite the fact that textile trade was also increasing within the industrialized areas. Some voluntary export restraints were negotiated but these were regarded as insufficient by the industry, which now called for a multilateral solution.

It was against this background that the Short-Term Arrangement on International Trade in Cotton Textiles (STA) came into force in 1961, to be replaced one year later by the Long Term Arrangement on International Trade in Cotton Textiles (LTA). Although it was meant to be a temporary arrangement to govern international textile trade and balance opposing interests, it broadened in scope and in the number of participants, and was extended several times. Finally the Multi-Fibre Arrangement (MFA) came into force in 1974, covering cotton, wool, and man-made fibres. It spelt out in detail in a number of provisions and clauses the 'economic, technical, social and commercial elements which influence world trade in textiles'. It was extended three times in 1977, 1981, and 1986, the present Protocol expiring in July 1991. The essential feature of this Arrangement was a set of rules governing the negotiation of bilateral agreements which fix quotas for trade in textiles.

The case study will examine some of the major forces which have led to this special Arrangement, as well as the elements guiding its application. At this stage, two particular points should be recalled which were discussed in a different context in Chapter 1. The first is that the textile Arrangement can be viewed as an extended safeguard in the GATT, intended to handle certain welfare aspects of international trade that were not anticipated by the GATT founders. The second concerns the concept of security and the role of small, neutral states in the international trading order. We shall see how the Nordic States, because of their small markets, and Sweden, because of its economic security requirements, were able to plead for special exceptions to the rules for controlled liberalization.

With regard to the first of these points, we have already noted that all international agreements have safeguard clauses (Chapter 1). Since the GATT was designed to deal solely with trade issues, member states deliberately included in the Agreement the legal possibility of safeguarding what they believed were responsibilities that transcended pure trade, such as matters dealing with national security in the event of military attack. Other safeguard clauses adapted some of the traditional arguments for protection, such as infant-industry and balance of payments arguments, to new circumstances. What the GATT founders neglected to consider was a safeguard clause to accommodate a broader conception of national security which would include welfare considerations, and particularly employment policy, as well as the provision of physical defence. Indeed, a major criticism of the neo-classical theory on which the GATT is based has been the lack of any *explicit* recognition of the State's responsibility to provide social and economic as well as military security. The philosophy behind the GATT did not concern itself, however, with this enlarged concept of security since the assumption was that freer international trade would make possible a more efficient use of national resources, generate increased wealth and a higher standard of living for all. Thus welfare was seen in terms of aggregate national income, the benefits of which were automatic and acquired with the minimum of government intervention. Concern for individual or group security, on the other hand, was associated with the realist or mercantilist view of international relations and more generally with collectivism.

Although, apart from a perfunctory reference in the Preamble, the GATT made no special provisions for unemployment, it did provide a safeguard clause for situations in which a particular industry was being disrupted by a surge of imports. One could argue, moreover, that this clause, Article XIX, was GATT's main concession to welfarism in that it was ultimately designed to ease the social and economic tensions accompanying sharp variations in trade. Given that the MFA also legalized the imposition of quotas in order to give importing-country manufacturers breathing space and time to adjust without undue disruptions, this Arrangement may also be perceived as an extended form of Article XIX. What the MFA did, however, was to confer legitimacy on the principle of selective protection against individual suppliers in the case of market disruption in one particular sector. In this way the MFA also entailed a sharp derogation from GATT's main principle of non-discrimination.

We have so far referred to welfare in the sense that the concept is only implicit in the classical liberal theory of trade and in the GATT, that is, that it results from the automatic distribution of wealth brought about by trade. We have also noted the 'liberal' Keynesian revision of this theory according to which some government intervention is required precisely because there is no automatic distributive effect from international trade and that, therefore, the original theory cannot handle social security problems such as unemployment which are the inevitable results of changes in the international division of labour. Keynesianism thus both widens the traditional concept of security and because it is no longer confined to military security, renders it more ambiguous.

The ambiguity of the concept of security comes out also in the discussion of the welfare of developing, or small or neutral countries. What has been said concerning groups within states can apply also to groups of countries within the international system. Disparities in economic and political power were not given attention by the liberals. In a framework that aimed primarily at efficiency these concepts had little meaning, as all states would benefit from greater wealth.

Since in 1947 most developing Asian and African States were still under colonial rule it is not surprising that their interests received little emphasis in the drawing up of the General Agreement. One of GATT's clauses, Article XVIII, was specifically drafted with their interests in mind. Later, when most of Africa and Asia had become independent and through the active participation of Latin America, Part IV was added to take their particular economic development needs into consideration. Despite differing views on the merits and efficiency of these additions, they represented the first public admission by the governments of the industrial powers that the GATT had not been equipped to handle certain important international trade problems.

The second, and related point, relevant to the case study which was raised in Chapter 1 concerns the security problems of small neutral states. Just as particular clauses for developing countries were virtually absent from the General Agreement, small and neutral states were also given no special exception to the rights and obligations. One plausible explanation for this is again to be found in the liberal assumptions underlying the GATT, namely that peaceful international relations were not based on power considerations but on co-operation and that if states respected the non-discrimination or most-favoured-nation principle, the *raison d'être* of the GATT, small states would automatically be protected from the preferential arrangements that were potentially harmful for them and gain positive benefits from engaging in freer international trade. It was for this reason also that small states had no particular security needs beyond those required by all states for a strict interpretation of national security, that is military considerations. In other words, all states, including the small and neutral states, would gain security collectively from becoming economically more interdependent with the rest of the world. Economic interdependence implied greater security.

The consequences of this blurring of the concepts of security and interdependence began to emerge in the 1970s and even earlier with respect to the textile and clothing industries. While the process of structural adjustment was almost automatic during the expansive 1950s and 1960s, this was no longer the case in the 1970s. The LTA and MFA involved recognition of the need for temporary government intervention to facilitate the process of adjustment. In effect it was a means of further legitimizing the 'liberal' Keynesian conception of group welfare at the international level, albeit in principle only for a temporary period.

At the same time the classical notion of security as confined merely to military defence receded into the background as the memory of war faded and concerns turned increasingly to domestic issues of social security and group security. It was in this context that some states began to see imports from the Third World as a potential threat not only to groups suffering unemployment, but also to the state's independence as a whole. Among these states Sweden was one which perceived its needs to be different from those of other industrial states. Consequently as a small neutral state it negotiated into the MFA a clause which would allow it special exceptions to the 'ordered' liberalization rules embodied in the Arrangement.

In the Swedish case, as elsewhere in the industrial world, the demands for protection were in the first instance based on the rising level of unemployment within the textile sector. At the time of the negotiation of the MFA, however, an additional argument was added, namely that a 'minimum viable production' (MVP) was necessary for national security reasons should a case of blockade or more serious international crisis arise.

The inclusion of an MVP clause, providing for an exception to the 6 per cent growth rate, was included in the MFA to meet the interests of the Nordic countries as a whole. It provides for additional restraint (i.e. a growth rate less than 6 per cent) in order to avoid damage to the 'minimum viable production' of countries having 'small markets', an 'exceptionally high level of imports' and a 'correspondingly low level of domestic production'. The concern of the Nordic countries, Finland, Norway, and Sweden, was that the domestic production of textiles had reached a level below which, for political, social and, particularly in the case of Sweden, strategic and security reasons, it could not be allowed to fall. It has been described as 'vital for the basic needs of the population'.

Each of the next three chapters deals with textile trade policy from a different angle. Chapter 4 discusses the general international framework within which the textile trade policies of all the major industrial countries are implemented and analyses some of the reasons for an establishment of a special trade regime in textiles and what elements were emerging in the international economy which the GATT was considered incapable of handling in its existing form. The rights and obligations that such a new Arrangement imposed are also examined. Finally, and still within the context of this special regime, we shall see whether and how the problems of welfare, security, and neutrality were incorporated into the system.

Within this framework, Chapters 5 and 6 will focus more specifically on Sweden's policies, how its textile trade policies have evolved and what relation they have to domestic policies of social welfare and economic defence.

4 The International Framework: The Arrangement Regarding International Trade in Textiles

1 The origins of a special international regime in textiles

(i) *Background to protectionism in textiles and clothing*

Protectionism in textiles and clothing is not a post-war phenomenon that began with the emergence of independent developing countries. There is a long history of intervention in these sectors which dates back to the industrial revolution.

Although the first major textile production[1] appeared in the United Kingdom, a number of other countries had come to the fore in the nineteenth century, mainly as a result of deliberate government action. Starting as a cottage industry, technological breakthroughs during the industrial revolution transformed the industry to one of large-scale manufacturing encouraged by infant-industry protection.

In the period between 1913 and 1929 manufacturing trade increased by 80 per cent while textile trade grew by just over one-half. In addition to the disruption caused by the First World War, one reason for this disparity was the boost given

---

[1] The textiles sector covers a vast area of production starting with raw threads and fibres of silk, cotton, linen, jute, and wool but also including their transformation into yarn, the conversion of yarn into fabrics, and the assembly of finished products including clothing, household furnishing, etc. Technological change has rendered these production processes increasingly more complicated and has blurred the distinction between each phase of processing. These developments in production create problems of definition. In practice we find that the term textiles is defined in three different ways. First, in a general sense it refers to fibres, yarns, and woven goods, including finished products (clothing, carpets, home furnishings). Secondly, in a more specific sense, it refers only to basic textiles not including the finished products. When used in this way, therefore, clothing would be excluded. Finally, the MFA contains its own specific definition of textiles which is contained in Article 12 of the text. According to this definition, textiles is limited to 'tops, yarns, piece-goods, made-up articles, garments and other textile manufactured products of cotton, wool, man-made fibres, or blend thereof'. It does not apply to 'handloom fabrics of the cottage industry, or handmade cottage industry products made of such handloom fabrics, or to traditional folklore handicraft products'. The STA and LTA, however, included only cotton textiles. To avoid confusion, textiles will be referred to here in the MFA sense unless specified otherwise.

to import-substitution programmes by the supply shortages, particularly among raw cotton producers. It was at this time that Japan began to emerge as a major textile exporter as a result of its ability to find outlets for mass-produced, low-cost fabrics. In response the traditional exporters took measures to protect available markets and to restrict Japanese exports which came to be seen as the major source of the industry's problem in the West.

The United Kingdom enacted the scheme for Imperial Preferences which enlarged the scope for the British preferential market. Although the United Kingdom remained a leading exporter during the Depression, the deterioration of its market shares proved to be irreversible. Other countries in Europe and the US followed by imposing restrictive measures primarily against Japanese exports. These restrictions set in motion a series of events that resulted in the establishment of a multilateral arrangement in textile trade. It became apparent that the adjustment problems of the 'older' manufacturing centres would be of longer duration than anticipated and that the 'new' textile manufacturing centres were not limited to Japan but were spread throughout the developing world. Thus, the attitude to competitive new suppliers and the need for structural adjustments were well rooted before the Second World War.

Despite the strategic role which it played historically, production and trade in the textiles sector have confronted numerous economic as well as political and social problems. While production has been largely surpassed by other manufacturing industries, the industry still employs a significant portion of the labour force. In addition, the period between 1913 and 1959 was marked in the industrialized countries by slow growth and decreased demand in the textile and clothing industries. Part of the decrease in textile trade was a result of the development of domestic production of textiles in traditional import markets and the consequent substitution of domestically produced goods for imported goods. A more important reason has been suggested, that textile trade would have fallen under any circumstances because of the low elasticity of demand for textile products.[2]

[2] Alfred Maizels, *Industrial Growth and World Trade* (Cambridge, 1963) 335.

Finally, protectionism among developing countries may have played a small role in the decline.[3] In any event the decrease in trade was perceived to have dramatic effects on countries such as the US and the United Kingdom which until 1959 had enjoyed a large export surplus in the sector.

It is true that in a period of slow growth and declining demand employment may be sensitive to trade factors. It is also true that a shift in comparative advantage was rapidly taking place in favour of certain developing countries. As industrial techniques and 'know-how' spread to countries such as Japan, Hong Kong, and Korea, and the wage rates became increasingly differentiated, their competitive edge in simpler and labour-intensive industries began to surpass that of the industrialized countries. However, one cannot explain protectionism in the developed countries solely on the basis of these economic arguments. The combined value of exports from developing countries was still very small in comparison with that of industrialized countries. In 1955 total textile exports of industrialized countries amounted to $3.78bn. dollars while that of LDCs came to only $0.66bn.[4] But, for reasons connected with their welfare and employment policies which will be discussed in Chapter 5, the industrialized countries saw protectionism as a political and social solution to the decline of their textiles industries.

(ii) *Events leading to the Long Term Arrangement (LTA)*
Most of the major industrial countries emerged from the Second World War with their textile capacity virtually intact. However, with the fall in demand and the world-wide redistribution of capacity, the industry in the industrial countries was characterized by excess capacity in most aspects of textile production, a tendency that was aggravated by import-substitution policies in a number of developing countries.

There remained a wide variety of trade restrictions at the close of the Second World War which were justified by balance of payments and other domestic constraints. By 1955,

---

[3] Donald Keesing and Martin Wolf, *Textile Quotas against Developing Countries*, Thames Essay No. 23 (London, 1980) 10.
[4] Excluding oil exporting countries; including Australia, New Zealand, and South Africa, *GATT Networks of World Trade* (1978).

however, trade liberalization efforts within the GATT and facilitated by the IMF had resulted in the dismantling of the great bulk of discriminatory quantitative restrictions as well as in a trend to reduce tariffs. It is important to note, however, that non-tariff barriers on cotton textiles continued in force in violation of GATT rules, becoming known as 'hard core' residual restrictions. These consisted of import quotas, licensing controls and minimum price agreements.

Although both the US and Great Britain were the first to feel a real threat from industrializing areas, it was the US reaction to increasing imports that was most significant in spurring the events leading to the establishment of an international arrangement. Textile policies were, however, a clear contradiction to previous US trade policies. Not only had the US initiated the post-war global liberalization of trade by encouraging the establishment of the GATT and the OEEC, it had also been a resolute supporter of Japan's membership in the GATT. Nevertheless in the 1950s a conflict began to emerge between domestic sectoral interests and US free trade policies as Japanese imports were increasingly perceived to be flooding the US market.[5] Reacting to mounting pressures from the domestic textiles industry the US Congress granted the executive branch the authority to regulate textile imports unilaterally.[6]

For a short period the US believed it could stem imports by pressuring Japan to impose 'voluntary' export restraints on its textile exports. However, other countries soon began emerging as serious competitors in textiles trade. Hong Kong, for instance, increased its share of imports in the US market from 13.8 per cent in 1958 to 27.5 per cent in 1960. Egypt, India, Portugal, and Spain also increased their market

---

[5] *The History and Current Status of the Multifibre Arrangement*, US International Trade Commission. Publication No. 850 (Washington, DC, Jan. 1978) 1. 'The US Tariff Commission had the authority to conduct investigations to determine whether imports (on which trade agreement concessions had been granted) were entering in such increased quantities as to cause or threaten serious injury to domestic industry producing like or directly competitive articles.' Furthermore, according to the Agricultural Act of 1956, the President was empowered to restrict unilaterally or negotiate agreements limiting exports from other countries or imports of textile products into the US 'whenever he determines such action appropriate'.

[6] Keesing and Wolf, *Textile Quotas* p. 15.

shares.[7] After unsuccessful overtures for VERs were made to Hong Kong, the US government concluded that from their point of view a global solution within existing international organizations would be the most effective answer to the problem of textiles trade. Once in power J. F. Kennedy launched a programme of assistance to the sector, including proposals for 'an early conference of the principal textile exporting and importing countries' which was intended to lead to an international understanding . . . that will avoid undue disruption of established industries'. This initiative resulted in the Short Term Arrangement Regarding International Trade in Cotton Textiles (STA) which subsequently became the Long Term Arrangement (LTA) and finally the MFA.

Meanwhile, in response to pressures felt in Western Europe, a number of cotton textile producers concluded the Noordwijk Agreement in 1958 under which they restricted the re-export within their markets of finished fabric processed from grey cloth imported from Japan, the People's Republic of China, India, Pakistan and Hong Kong. Participants included Austria, the six signatories of the Treaty of Rome, Norway, Sweden, and Switzerland. This agreement combined with other severe restrictions resulted in some trade diversion by exporters to the relatively open US market.

(iii) *Market disruption*

One central issue that came up in the discussions which led to the STA and LTA as well as the MFA was the concept of 'market disruption'. Again it was the US that took the lead in bringing together GATT contracting parties at their fifteenth session with the purpose of reaching an agreement about what constitutes a case of market disruption. Originally the concept was discussed in general terms; in practice, however, it was seen to apply almost solely to the textile sector.

The US delegate drew attention to the fact that sharp increases in imports over a short period of time and in a

---

[7] 'The Employment Effects in the Clothing Industry of Changes in International Trade', International Labour Office, Second Tripartite Meeting for the Clothing Industry, Report III (Geneva, 1980) 18.

narrow range of products could have serious economic, political, and social repercussions in the importing countries. He also requested that an official GATT study be carried out to examine the problems posed by 'the adverse effects of an abrupt invasion (by sharp increases in imports) of established markets'. This study concluded that many countries did in fact maintain restrictions on a discriminatory basis, particularly in the textile sector and notably against Japan. Thus, on 19 November 1960 the Contracting Parties explicitly recognized the term and in the absence of a complete and exact definition decided on procedures for describing it. The Contracting Parties added that 'there were political and psychological elements in the problem' which necessitated special treatment.

They decided that a case of market disruption was evident in, among others, the following circumstances:

(1) a sharp and substantial increase or potential increase in imports of particular products from particular sources;

(2) these products are offered at prices which are substantially below those prevailing for similar goods of comparable quality in the market of the importing country;

(3) there is serious damage to domestic producers, or threat thereof;

(4) the price differentials referred to in paragraph (2) above do not arise from governmental intervention in the fixing or formation of prices or from dumping practices.'[8]

Although the question of the adequacy of Article XIX in textile trade was not formally dealt with, it was understood that importing countries resorted to means outside the framework of the GATT precisely because Article XIX or any other safeguard was believed to be inappropriate. Market disruption has since become the key concept allowing the importer to take restrictive action against exporting countries, in order to permit internal readjustments to take place. It was meant to facilitate a process of restructuring declining

[8] GATT 9th Supplement IBRD (1961); LTA Annex C.

industries at a rate considered politically and socially acceptable. Quantitative restrictions thus became 'legal'.

Controversy in the application of the concept of market disruption has resulted from a number of ambiguities similar to those contained in Article XIX although certain basic differences do exist.

First, from the legal point of view, in the application of the agreed provisions, it was left to the importing country to determine when and in what circumstances a situation of market disruption existed which would allow it to impose restraints (MFA, Article 3, paragraph 1). However, the absence of a tighter definition of market disruption and of an organ with the legal competence to verify the existence of such disruptive circumstances paved the way for potential abuse. In particular, the key concepts, 'sharp and substantial increase', 'substantially below', and 'serious damage', which appear to be central, were not defined. Furthermore, the idea that anticipated disruption was sanctioned left room for all kinds of interpretation.

Secondly, from the economic viewpoint, Bardan states that 'despite the apparent clarity of the definition and the frequent references to the disruptive effect of low-priced imports in the literature and elsewhere, economists . . . have been hard put to it to unearth any detailed data concerning concrete cases of market disruption'.[9] Dam further suggests that the Working Party that was supposed to study the issue of market disruption produced no final report because it became 'increasingly clear that there was but a difference in degree, and not a difference in substance, between the conditions that gave rise to an ordinary increase in international trade and those that gave rise to the economic impact associated with the concept of market disruption'.[10] The concept of market disruption did not refer to the causes of the effectiveness of exporters who penetrated developed country markets and therefore called the whole concept of normal comparative advantage into question. Where was the dividing line between competition and market disruption? A high level

---

[9] Benjamin Bardan, 'The Cotton Textile Arrangement—1962–1972', *Journal of World Trade Law*, vol. 7, no. 1 (1973) 19–25.

[10] Kenneth Dam, *The GATT: Law and International Organization* (Chicago, 1970) 299–3.

of import penetration has at various times been considered beneficial to growth. Although 'low-cost' or 'low-wage' countries are not explicitly referred to in the definition, restrictions that were already in force applied only to LDCs and Japan. There seems therefore to be an implication that these low-cost exporters are unfair and disruptive by their very nature (i.e. by having developed a comparative advantage), and therefore justify restrictive action. However, given that the cost of labour is one of the primary factors determining a country's comparative advantage, the whole principle is nullified once it is claimed that market disruption is caused primarily by low-cost imports. These arguments are important as the concept of market disruption was to lie at the core of the future MFA.

It is important to recall that the purpose of the agreement on market disruption and the ensuing arrangements on trade in textiles was to allow for a temporary breathing period for industrialized countries to implement adjustment policies. Given the state of their often outdated textiles industries and the significant labour force in this sector, the governments of the industrial countries insisted that time was needed to effect changes without the disruption that uncontrolled imports were believed to cause. On the other hand, it was no longer possible within the international organizations to ignore the very real problems of the LDCs. It was held, however, that they would benefit from an international agreement if it guaranteed them a regulated expansion of their trading opportunities through the gradual dismantling of tariffs and quantitative restrictions.

Following the adoption of the market disruption concept, a permanent Committee on the Avoidance of Market Disruption was established in order to promote consultations and find appropriate solutions. The Committee never became active, however. Negotiations were begun shortly thereafter to incorporate the concept into what became the first international agreement for handling this problem in the context of textile trade.

(iv) *The Long Term Arrangement regarding International Trade in Cotton Textiles (LTA)*

The agreement to establish a separate international legal framework to deal with the orderly expansion of trade in textiles was novel in the history of the GATT and a departure from the principles of non-discrimination and comparative advantage. It justified and legalized the extended use of quantitative restrictions and bilateral agreements, despite the fact that one of the basic principles of the GATT is that protection to domestic industries should be given only through tariffs and no other measures. It was also an acknowledgement that the GATT could not cope with all kinds of trade problems.[11]

During its eleven-year lifetime trade in textiles increased significantly. In addition, quantitative restrictions while not dismantled to the extent anticipated, were at least relaxed, and developing countries were successful in expanding their exports of clothing to a considerable extent. In effect the LTA had achieved some 'order'[12] in textiles trade, and hence fulfilled certain of its goals. However, it is impossible to assess with certainty the extent to which the evolution of trade in textiles was due to the existence of the LTA. The reason for this is that no commercial policy can *itself* explain developments in the direction of trade. Although it is assumed that the application of restraint potentially curbs the growth of trade, these restrictions *per se* do not necessarily result in reduced trade levels. Exporters may be able to fill some quotas, but not others for economic or other reasons. Moreover, rapid changes in demand and consumer taste, to which textile production is highly sensitive, may mean that quotas remain underutilized one year and be insufficient the

[11] The LTA was concluded on 2 Feb. 1962 by 19 governments. The LTA succeeded and replaced the STA, but it embodied the same general principles. Although it was intended as a temporary measure to last five years, at the time of expiry on 1 May 1967 a protocol of extension was signed, followed by a second renewal on 15 Jan. 1970. This second protocol extending the LTA for a further three years expired on 30 Dec. 1973 at which time 30 countries had become members.

[12] The principles and aims of the LTA are spelt out in the preamble and represent foremost an attempt to strike a balance between the interests of exporting and importing countries. It states that 'action should be designed to facilitate economic expansion and promote the development of less developed countries'. Paragraph 4 further states, 'Desiring to deal with [problems of market disruption] in such a way as to provide growing opportunities for exports of these products, provided that the development of this trade proceeds in a reasonable and orderly manner so as to avoid disruptive effects in individual markets and on individual lines of production in both importing and exporting countries.'

next. Needless to say, importers believed the agreement was not restrictive enough to prevent adjustments to be carried out without social and economic disruptions, while exporters complained that their exports and general development interests had not been sufficiently safeguarded.

The Multi-Fibre Arrangement

(i) *The need for a new arrangement*

During the lifetime of the LTA, an important evolution took place in world demand for textiles as a result of: the intensified competition from man-made fibres, the development of blends of synthetic fibres with vegetable and animal fibres, and the changed price-parities between natural and man-made fibres. Already by the early 1970s evidence existed of surplus capacity in the synthetic sector practically all over the world. While the key element in competition, even as late as 1965, was quality in clothing, the price factor became increasingly dominant and favoured man-made fibres.[13] Admittedly these changes were also a result of technological advances, fashion trends, and the growth of end-uses for which synthetics were particularly appropriate (e.g. carpeting, home furnishings, and various industrial uses).

While initially the industrialized countries took the lead in the automatization and production of man-made fibres, industrializing countries also began to compete in this area. Thus competition between the industrial countries themselves, and between them and some LDCs, became even more intense. These developments had significant consequences for international commercial policies since man-made fibres were not covered under the LTA.

Although cotton imports continued to increase and, in 1970, held a significant position relative to all imports, the increase of synthetic fibre imports surpassed that of all other fibres and accounted for 48 per cent of all imports to industrialized countries in 1970. Similarly, clothing imports made of synthetic and artificial fibres accelerated in the 1960s

---

[13] M. Salib, 'The GATT Multi-fibre Arrangement and International Trade in Natural Fibre Textile Production', *COMITEXTIL*, Bulletin 1978/1, pp. 12, 13.

and accounted for 51 per cent of all imported clothing into the industrialized countries.

Developing countries increased their exports of man-made fibres, Taiwan, Korea, and Hong Kong accounting for the largest shares. With the exception of these countries, however, LDCs remained net importers and the share of all LDCs in world trade in these sectors increased very little in the 1960s.

As a result of this evolution, many developed-country governments were subjected to new and intensifying pressures to restrict trade in man-made fibres not covered by the LTA. As soon as some countries began taking bilateral or unilateral action, other countries felt justified in doing so as well, fearing that there would be a large diversion of imports into their own markets. The situation called for a new approach to the whole problem.

Norway and Sweden began to take action in the late 1960s to restrict non-cotton imports. In 1971 Canada invoked Article XIX of the GATT to restrict imports of shirts. It was the US, however, that in 1971 and 1972 not only took the most far-reaching steps to restrict imports of man-made fibres from Japan, Hong Kong, Korea, and Taiwan, but also once again took the initiative by calling for a global re-examination of the problem of textile trade.

(ii) *Events leading to the MFA*

As pressures built up in the US, American negotiators conducted a series of discussions with GATT officials and with European governments to rally support for an extended LTA. These discussions were unsuccessful. The Asiatic countries were then asked to agree to 'VER' arrangements. An agreement also came into being in October 1971, called the 'Multilateral Arrangement Concerning Trade in Wool and Man-Made Fibres' which was signed only by the US, Hong Kong, Korea, and Taiwan and which was complemented by separate bilateral agreements.

One of the articles of this five-year Arrangement contained the suggestion that the arrangement be 'replaced' by a multilateral Arrangement in which a greater number of countries would participate. This was the first step towards a new system.

As a result of these US measures the European countries became concerned that products would be diverted to their markets. They therefore began to respond more favourably to the US proposals for broader international participation. It was becoming evident that most countries wanted a new solution to the textiles problem. Not only did the developing countries want greater protection but the LDCs, an increasing force in international negotiations,[14] also wanted to obtain a larger share of the market through a more secure and liberal system.

Among the issues discussed during the negotiations were the type of arrangement appropriate for textiles, the need for a greater balance between the interests of importers and exporters, the working out of a more stringent definition of market disruption, and the establishment of an independent surveillance body to supervise the implementation of the Arrangement. An overview of these issues follows:

1. The question of whether world trade in textiles should be treated as a special case arose particularly because of the increased involvement of the GATT in the negotiations and because of the timing of these textile negotiations. Indeed, at the same time, negotiations were under way in the Multilateral Trade Negotiations (MTN)–Tokyo Round on issues which concerned not only tariff reductions but also quantitative restrictions and other barriers to trade, as well as the general safeguards problem. All developed countries advocated a specific solution for the international textile trade. In their view, textiles posed a unique problem in that it was the one industry which suffered all the problems experienced separately or severally by other industrial sectors. The 'separate solution' was to be negotiated outside the MTNs. The LDCs, as well as Japan, on the other hand, stated their strong preference for an approach within the framework of GATT or the MTNs. India and Brazil in particular insisted that any multilateral arrangement for textiles should be governed by the principles and objectives agreed to in the MTNs. Furthermore, any multilateral solution on textiles should be considered temporary, and made conditional on

---

[14] The first UNCTAD conference had been held in 1964; later that year Part IV was included in the GATT text to handle problems particular to the LDCs.

the result of the MTNs. Such a stand was quite consistent with the LDCs' interpretation of the problem. For them, the proliferation and discriminatory application of restrictions was the root cause of the difficulties in world trade; therefore their elimination in accordance with the principles and provisions of the GATT would obviate the need for a special solution. In the event the textile problem was treated as a separate specific system, but negotiated under the auspices of the GATT. This decision was partly the result of the US decision not to decrease tariffs on textiles in the Tokyo Round.

2. The issue of balance between importers and exporters involved the identification of specific problems encountered in the textile trade by both sides. Developing countries argued for greater market access for their exports in which they enjoyed a comparative advantage. Exports were considered vital for their economic development programmes, to earn foreign exchange for indispensable imports, for the expansion of employment possibilities, for the increase of their GNP, and for the service of their debts. Particular attention was also to be given to the problems faced by cotton exporters and new entrants who were often in the least advantageous position among LDCs.

Importing industrialized countries, on the other hand, were experiencing stagnation in their own textile and clothing sectors, falling demand and increasing unemployment. At the same time, imports not only continued to grow but were perceived as the cause of severe political and social problems.

Both sets of considerations had to be taken into account in the negotiations. It was conceded also by the industrialized countries that the interests of exporting countries had not been given sufficient attention in the LTA and that a certain imbalance in the interests of the two groups of countries had been the consequence.

3. As it had been defined in 1960, market disruption lacked precision and could be more easily interpreted in the interests of the importing than the exporting countries. The developing countries now asked that consideration also be given to the disruption to their industries caused by import restrictions. Furthermore, they argued that it was unfair to leave to the discretion of the sole importer the decision about whether

or not a situation of market disruption existed. This right had often been used arbitrarily and without sufficient proof.

4. The creation of a standing committee to supervise textiles trade multilaterally was advocated by the LDCs. They argued that an independent body with the right to examine all actions and disputes of the Parties so as to conciliate opposing interests and make recommendations could provide a possible solution to arbitrary and unjust measures that the Cotton Textile Committee had been unable to prevent. Such an institution, to be called the Textiles Surveillance Body, TSB, would be unique among international economic organizations.

(iii) *The Multi-Fibre Arrangement*
The MFA came into force on 1 January 1974. The Arrangement was to last for four years. However, three protocols of extension were subsequently negotiated with various amendments, the most recent of which came into force on 1 August 1986.

Forty-three countries, accounting in 1974 for 80 per cent of world trade in textiles, signed the MFA.[15] Certain of these countries were not GATT Contracting Parties but were nevertheless expected to respect the laws of the General Agreement, conform to the specific regulations of the MFA, and accept its discipline. Upon signing the MFA an importing country must agree to accept continuous multilateral surveillance in exchange for the rights to conclude agreements on import restrictions with individual suppliers and to impose unilateral measures in certain instances. Exporting countries must accept restrictions in various circumstances but can gain from the positive elements of the MFA, namely guaranteed growth, minimum levels of exports, various flexibility facilities, freedom from the danger of unilateral actions incompatible with the GATT,

---

[15] Argentina, Australia, Austria, Brazil, Canada, Chile, Colombia, Cuba, Czechoslovakia, Egypt, El Salvador, EEC (as one party), Finland, Greece, Guatemala, Hungary, India, Israel, Jamaica, Japan, South Korea, Malaysia, Mexico, Norway, Pakistan, Poland, Portugal, Romania, Singapore, Spain, Sri Lanka, Sweden, Switzerland, Thailand, Trinidad and Tobago, Turkey, the US, Uruguay, Yugoslavia, and Zaire. Taiwan was not a party to the negotiations having lost its recognition in the UN and being excluded from the GATT from 16 Nov. 1971.

and surveillance to prevent unjustifiable and arbitrary measures.

(iv) *The principles of the MFA*

The MFA recognized the importance of production and trade in cotton and other textiles 'for the economic and social development of developing countries and for the expansion and diversification of their export earnings' (Preamble, paragraph 1). It also took into consideration the natural comparative advantages of LDCs, and the specific needs of new entrants.

Action should be designed to facilitate economic expansion and to promote the development of developing countries possessing the necessary resources, such as materials and technical skills, by providing larger opportunities for such countries, including countries that are, or that may shortly become, new entrants in the field of textile exports to increase their exchange earnings from the sale in world markets of products which they can efficiently produce. (Preamble, paragraph 6).

Furthermore, direct reference was made to the need for consistency with GATT decisions such as the 'reduction of tariffs and to maintenance and improvement of generalized preferences, in accordance with the Tokyo Declaration', with regard to the harmonious development of the textile trade of developing countries (Preamble, paragraph 7 and 8).

Differential treatment in favour of developing countries had been given general recognition in the GATT through the inclusion of Part IV of the basic GATT text and during the Tokyo Round.[16] In the preamble of the MFA and in the various Articles[17] of the Arrangement, there is further

---

[16] Tokyo Declaration, paragraphs 5–6. (See also Diana Tussie, *The Less Developed Countries and the World Trading System* (London, 1987).)

[17] The main operative Articles of the MFA are Articles 2, 3, and 4. *Article 2* obliges the parties, within a fixed period, to phase out all existing restrictions and to modify them according to the MFA. After a certain period only restrictions compatible with the MFA are allowed. It was hoped that the strict nature of this Article would prevent the maintenance of restrictions incompatible with the GATT that prevailed during the LTA. *Articles 3 and 4* constitute the basis for bilateral restrictive measures and in certain cases provide for unilateral actions (Article 3). They impose the rule that no new restrictions may be introduced on imports of textiles unless it is done in accordance with the provisions of the MFA. These include the possibility of restraints in cases of market disruption according to Article 3 or the 'real risk' of disruption in the case of

explicit recognition of the need to differentiate among exporting countries encountering specific types of difficulties, such as new entrants. But whereas Part IV action requires no concessions from developing countries, the MFA is based on an exchange of concessions.

The main operative Articles of the MFA are Articles 2, 3, and 4 (see notes). However, the most relevant Article to the arguments in this study is Article 1, paragraph 2. This paragraph sets out side by side two principal objectives of the MFA: liberalization of world trade and the avoidance of disruptive effects on individual markets and on individual lines of production in both importing and exporting countries. The last sentence of the paragraph refers to what became known as the 'Nordic clause', or the 'MVP' concept (minimum viable production). The same idea is expanded in the last sentence of paragraph 2 of Annex B which provides details on the implementation of the bilateral agreements. The concern of the Nordic countries (Finland, Norway, and Sweden) was that the production of textiles domestically had reached a level below which—for political, social, and, particularly in the case of Sweden, strategic or security reasons—it could not be allowed to fall. It has been described as a level 'vital for the basic needs of the population'. In Chapter 6 the application of this MVP clause will be examined in more depth.

In essence one can say that the two main achievements of the LDCs in the negotiations of the first MFA were the inclusion of stricter and more precise criteria for determining market disruption and the establishment of the TSB to oversee the implementation of the Arrangement. Two important revisions of the definition of market disruption were first that

Such an imminent increase (of imports of particular products from particular sources) shall be a measurable one and shall not be determined to exist on the basis of allegation, conjecture or mere

Article 4. *Article 11* establishes the Textiles Surveillance Body to supervise the implementation of the Arrangement. Membership consists of an independent Chairman elected by the Textiles Committee and eight members representing a balance of 'textile interests'. Participating countries bound themselves in advance to follow, to the best of their ability, the recommendations of the TSB.

possibility arising, for example, from the existence of production capacity in the exporting countries,

and secondly that

In considering questions of 'market disruption' account shall be taken of the interests of the exporting country, especially in regard to its stage of development, the importance of the textile sector to the economy, the employment situation, overall balance of trade in textiles, trade balance with the importing country concerned and overall balance of payments. (Annex A II; III)

(v) *Developments during the MFA period*

Three protocols of extension were agreed upon, in 1977, 1981, and 1986, the last of which will expire in 1991. Each successive protocol led to a more restrictive framework which was less favourable to the interests of the LDCs. It is, however, still too early to assess the most recent protocol as the restrictiveness of the protocols depends on how they are interpreted and put into practice. In any event the MFA, which was originally intended to be a particularly exceptional instrument to allow for the 'adjustment' of the textile industries in the developed countries, has evolved in ways which were not in keeping with the ideas of many of those who negotiated it. Neither the importing countries nor the exporting countries were satisfied with developments and claimed that aims for which they negotiated the Arrangement had not been fulfilled.

In the mid-1970s most countries experienced a general recession. This general downturn in economic activity inevitably affected textiles. Production of clothing and textiles in the industrial countries declined in 1974–5 and, after a slight recovery, stagnated or declined during the second half of the decade. Consumption also decreased in real terms. In the LDCs, on the other hand, production, especially of clothing, continued to increase during this same period.

It is true that overall trade continued to expand in 1974–5 although it was subject to large fluctuations. However, the import surplus in textiles and clothing in developed countries continued to rise. Clothing exports grew particularly fast from developing to developed countries while textile trade grew less quickly. Deficits in Germany, Switzerland, and the US were entirely accounted for by the clothing sector, while in 1978 the United Kingdom, Norway, Sweden, Austria, Canada, and Australia had deficits in both textiles and clothing.[18] However, several South European countries such as Italy witnessed an increasing surplus in both clothing and textiles.

As a result of this period of decline, difficulties increased for both importers and exporters. In the importing countries there were complaints that increased imports accentuated by world recession, currency fluctuations, and surplus capacity in the textile sector were resulting in the closure of mills, increased rates of unemployment, and uncertainty about the future. Furthermore, consumer tastes were shifting towards cheaper items as a result of fashion shifts and emergence of lower-cost, man-made and synthetic materials.[19] This made even more difficult the stimulation of demand through traditional techniques (changes in fashion, technological innovations, and so on). At the same time, prices of cotton and synthetic fibres fluctuated considerably. All these factors together brought about an ever greater sensitivity to import penetration, particularly from so-called low-cost sources, a greater perception of market disruption, and demands for protection from the industry and workers' unions.

In this respect it is worth recalling that Article 1, paragraph 4 of the MFA provides that adjustment assistance measures should be taken to improve the competitive position of the textile industry, but that they should not interrupt the autonomous industrial processes of participating countries. When applied they should encourage businesses to move progressively into more viable lines of production and into other sectors of the economy and provide increased access to their markets for textile products from LDCs. However, in a period of recession, because of the lack of mobility of resources and other factors, most developed countries were faced with industrial rigidity and rising unemployment with

[18] OECD, *Structural Problems and Policies Relating to the OECD Textile and Clothing Industries* (Paris, 1981).

[19] Artificial or man-made fibres are made from cellulose and include rayon and acetate. Synthetic fibres are petroleum-based and comprise polyester, nylon and acrylique.

all the social and political consequences. This issue of structural adjustments in industrial countries, particularly Sweden, will be dealt with in the next chapter.

Market disruption and import penetration of industrial country markets remained the most contentious issues in the negotiations for the extensions of the MFA. For, while import penetration may not by itself justify a government in claiming market disruption, it has nevertheless assumed a major role in the arguments for protectionism. There is an element of political expediency in these arguments which has become increasingly difficult to contain: most economists who have studied the question have confronted methodological difficulties in measuring market penetration precisely.[20] The balance of the argument suggests, however, that import penetration ratios used by developed countries often greatly exaggerate the problem.[21]

Many developing country negotiators, moreover, have drawn attention to the fact that restrictive measures are taken primarily against developing countries. This raised the question in their minds of why the LDCs' share of industrial country markets are disruptive when the industrialized countries' share of the market is not. In 1977 the share of textile imports coming from industrial countries amounted to 56 per cent, while that of clothing imports in intra-developed country trade was 25 per cent. In exports the share of the developed countries steadily declined from 73 per cent in 1973 to 68 per cent in 1977, while that of the LDCs increased from 22 to 27 per cent in this same period. However, a large part of the increase in the value of trade reflected domestic inflation and depreciation of the dollar. The discussions of the future of the MFA began in this economic context.

(vi) *MFA 2*

The 1977 extension of the MFA for a further four years led to an amending Protocol with certain important 'interpretations'

[20] OECD, *Structural Problems*, pp. 57–63. Problems relate to the choice of the right quotient, and in comparing the ratios of market penetration between countries as well as over-time for the same country.

[21] Vincent Cable, *An Evaluation of the Multifibre Arrangement and Negotiating Options*, Commonwealth Economic Papers No. 15, Commonwealth Secretariat (London, 1981).

which departed from the first Arrangement. It noted the 'unsatisfactory' situation in textile trade and renewed the MFA framework subject to the EEC-imposed condition that bilateral agreements 'could include the possibility of jointly agreed *reasonable departures* (author's emphasis) from particular elements in particular cases', on condition that 'any such departures would be temporary and that participants concerned shall return in the shortest possible time to the framework of the Arrangement' (Paragraph 5.3).

It is believed that if the EEC had not pressed for this clause the MFA would have been extended without alterations. The EEC, however, negotiating as one party since 1973, considered that a reformulation was required 'to permit a more restrictive renegotiation of bilateral agreements, recognizing in advance that proof of market disruption required to obtain a new set of agreements acceptable to suppliers, and to the TSB, would be too onerous and time consuming.'[22] Of course, there was considerable controversy over what was meant by 'reasonable' and to what extent a 'departure' could be interpreted. It was also unclear for how long a period such departures would be valid. After the adoption of the Protocol, delegates from several other countries stated that their acceptance of the Protocol was based on the understanding that whatever allowances were accorded to the EEC should be available to them as well.

The 'reasonable departures' clause was certainly a set-back for developing countries and appeared to reflect a general trend towards greater restrictiveness on the part of the industrial states. While the EEC avoided a 6 per cent growth in access to its market through the above-mentioned clause, other countries began resorting to means outside the GATT or to Article XIX of the GATT on a 'global' basis. These 'global' measures actually discriminated against 'low-cost' countries only. Thus, what had, in the MFA, already been a departure from GATT principles of non-discrimination, now became selective discrimination to the disadvantage of LDCs as a bloc under the guise of a global measure.

---

[22] Ibid. 12.

TABLE 4.1. *Area distribution of world trade in textiles, 1955–82 (%)*

	1955	1963	1973	1982
Exports ($bn.)	4.7	7.0	23.4	51.5
World	100	100	100	100
Developed area	79	74	70	60
(EC intra-trade)	(14)	(23)	(27)	(22)
Developing area	15	18	22	30
(Southern Europe)	. .	(2)	(4)	(5)
Eastern trading area	6	8	8	10
Imports				
World	100	100	100	100
Developed area	52	63	68	57
Developing area	43	30	25	34
(Southern Europe)	. .	(2)	(3)	(3)
Eastern trading area	5	7	7	9

TABLE 4.2. *Area distribution of world trade in clothing, 1955–82 (%)*

	1955	1963	1973	1982
Exports ($bn.)	0.8	2.2	12.6	41.0
World	100	100	100	100
Developed area	71	67	51	38
(EC intra-trade)	(16)	(23)	(26)	(19)
Developing area	10	15	35	48
(Southern Europe)	. .	(2)	(5)	(6)
Eastern trading area	19	18	14	14
Imports				
World	100	100	100	100
Developed area	56	66	78	75
Developing area	26	17	10	17
(Southern Europe)	. .	(0.5)	(1)	(0.5)
Eastern trading area	18	17	12	8

Source: *Textiles and Clothing in the World Economy*, GATT (1984).

(vii) *MFA 3*

In contrast to the previous round of negotiations, this time the LDCs were far more united. Their primary concern was to restore discipline to the MFA and to align trade policies of the restrictive importing countries with the objectives of the Arrangement. To this effect, they proposed the discontinuance of the 'reasonable departures' provision, a stricter application of the concept of market disruption, a more effective functioning of the TSB, and demarcation of parameters in the use of MVP.

The EEC, however, maintained an extremely hard negotiating front supported to a large extent by Canada and Sweden and, in the final weeks, by the US. As a result the developed countries obtained considerable further concessions from the developing countries.

A major innovation in the 1981 Protocol of Extension was the 'anti-surge' clause. This referred to the problems that arose when exporters tried to fulfil underutilized quotas of sensitive products in a 'sudden and substantial' manner. These sudden surges were believed to create market disruption (paragraph 10). In effect, after the removal of the 'reasonable departures' clause from the new Protocol this gave the developed countries an alternative means of safeguarding their internal markets from LDC imports. However, the possibility for mutually acceptable adjustment of quotas when the surge problem arose required 'equitable and quantifiable compensation', for example, in increased flexibility, larger quotas for certain products, or additional quotas for outward-processing trade.

A second concession negotiated by the developed countries was the possibility of reducing quotas for dominant suppliers regardless of trade flows. Although they were not explicitly mentioned in the text, presumably the countries referred to were Hong Kong, Korea, perhaps Macao, and a non-member, Taiwan. The Community also stressed the need for a 6 per cent growth waiver given the prevailing economic conditions of high unemployment and, particularly, a declining rate of consumption.

Reference was made by the developed countries to the importance of furthering the 'economic and social development of developing countries'. Although this aspect was mentioned in the basic MFA, it took on a new significance, since developed countries hoped to make access to their markets conditional upon observance of certain labour standards. Such demands have been made in other bodies and in themselves may be valid, but were largely irrelevant in the MFA context, covering as it does only one sector. Although some LDCs might have been in favour in principle of a 'social clause',[23]

---

[23] This argument is treated in Deepak Lal, *Resurrection of the Pauper Labour Argument* (London, 1981).

most of them dismissed the idea in this context as a form of semi-disguised protectionism. Finally, there was a sentence repeating the notion of the objective of social development (Article 1, MFA).

Further refinements were added to the concept of market disruption. In paragraph 4 of the new protocol,

attention was drawn to the fact that decline in the rate of growth of *per capita* consumption in textiles and in clothing is an element which may be relevant to the recurrence or exacerbation of a situation of market disruption.

The inclusion of this extension to the existing definition, at the insistence of the developing countries, was in some way counterbalanced by the factors of technological change and changes in consumer preference contained in the same paragraph at the request of the LDCs. This additional criterion was a means whereby developed countries hoped to 'share the burden' of 'low-cost' imports. Those countries with a slow growth of per capita consumption felt that the MFA had been unfair even though their per capita imports might have been the same as that of other developing countries.

Despite the extensions and further restrictions this Protocol represented a positive step for the LDCs in that it ensured greater discipline in the implementation of key articles. Much more specific interpretations of articles were given in the text to avoid the broad interpretations often made during MFA 2. Of course the real test of success is in the bilateral agreements, which are the true substance of the MFA. And on this question it appears that agreements became even more restrictive than previous ones.

Sweden and Finland on their part insisted on a more favourable MVP clause. The text finally arrived at is the following:

The Committee recognized that countries having small markets, an exceptionally high level of imports and correspondingly low level of domestic production are particularly exposed to the problems arising from imports causing market disruption as defined in Annex A, and that their problems should be resolved in a spirit of equity and flexibility in order to avoid damage to those countries' minimum viable production of textiles. In the case of those countries, the provisions of Article 1, paragraph 2, and Annex B, paragraph 2, should be fully implemented. The exporting participants may, in the case of countries referred to in this paragraph, agree to any mutually acceptable arrangements with regard to paragraph 5 of Annex B; special consideration in this respect would be given to their concerns regarding the avoidance of damage to these countries' minimum viable production of textiles.[24]

Sweden and Finland had hoped for even greater concessions in the form of a possibility to reduce quotas. Nevertheless, they obtained agreement for an extended clause that allowed for lower growth than foreseen in the MFA.

(viii) *MFA 4*

In the summer of 1986 negotiations were completed for yet another protocol of extension due to expire in 1991. Faced with increasing protectionist pressures in the US the developing countries agreed to an arrangement which many regard as more restrictive: silk and all vegetable fibres are now included for the first time; the rules governing false declarations have been tightened up; and there is tighter provision for the extension of restraints for a further twelve-month period. It is reported that the Community could, at the outset, have accepted MFA 3 for a further four years, but the fear that exports shut out of the increasingly protectionist US market would be diverted to the EC led to an increasingly hard line as negotiations proceeded. The EC to some extent tried to play the role of mediator. However, its efforts to obtain special treatment for the least developed countries were viewed with suspicion by other developing countries. The EC also sought greater access to the markets of the exporting countries, especially the NICs, but this attempt was largely unsuccessful.

Positive elements included EC agreement: not to demand cutbacks in the case of dominant suppliers, to liberalize the anti-surge clause and to remove underutilized quotas. Finally MFA 4 underlines the importance of the aims and objectives of the MFA for the developing countries. The importing countries agreed, for example, to improve their bilateral agreements under the MFA as a means of helping

---

[24] Paragraph 4. Norway had opted out of MFA 2 and 3, invoking instead Article XIX. It has now rejoined, however.

exporting countries increase their earnings from textile products, and those countries invoking the MVP clause are required to make 'meaningful improvements' to their new bilateral agreements.[25]

It is worth adding that although MFA 4 was represented by fifty-four countries a GATT report noted that in 1984 trade in textiles and clothing between MFA members amounted to just less than half of total world exports of textiles and clothing. This suggests that MFA quotas, to the degree that they might limit certain categories of imports, have become even less effective in doing so.

Conclusions

The MFA represented the first main departure from the rules of international trade embodied in the GATT which acknowledged and legitimized the need to ease the social and economic tensions that were believed to accompany sharp variations in trade.

On the part of the developed importing countries, the limiting of imports from low-cost sources and the 'orderly development of trade' was expected to allow sufficient breathing space for adjustments to take place without the additional pressure from the 'sharp and substantial increases of imports of particular products from particular sources' and the unemployment problems for which they were believed to be a cause. They claimed and perhaps also believed that the trade problem in the textile and clothing sectors was indeed a unique and temporary one requiring only a short-term departure from the established trade principles. This departure has, however, now lasted for more than twenty-five years.

Sections of the MFA were intended to be at least as much in the interests of the developing exporting countries as of the developed countries. It was clearly spelt out that the economic and social development of these countries, as well as opportunities for developing their natural comparative advantages, should be encouraged through increased market access.

[25] Malcolm Subhan, 'The Fourth Multi-Fibre Arrangement', *Textile Outlook International* (Sept. 1986).

Both developed and developing countries have been critical of the MFA and its application. The former claim that it has not been restrictive enough, and point to the mounting rather than declining economic and social costs as well as the apparent inability of some developing exporters to fill their quotas. Although developing countries claim to want a return to GATT rules, they are aware of the potential costs that this may involve and therefore generally urge, the abandonment of the MFA but a tightening-up of its provisions and greater discipline in its application. They claim, moreover, that each successive Protocol of Extension has become more restrictive in letter and in spirit, incorporating new concepts and further restrictions which have no basis in economic theory. These include market disruption and minimum viable production, as well as 'cumulative market disruption', 'reasonable departures', the 'anti-surge mechanism', etc.

From the point of view of proponents of liberal trade and the GATT system, the MFA has increasingly been interpreted not only as a provisional instrument allowing textile industries to shelter behind its temporary protection, but also as an instrument for protecting industries in developed countries in every possible way for as long as possible.

Critics of the Arrangement further argue that the enduring nature of the MFA perpetuates a problem faced by many industrialized countries of declining competitiveness in certain sectors without giving manufacturers enough inducement to look beyond the short-term solution. Countries hurt by protectionism are not necessarily large producers—such as Hong Kong, Korea, and Taiwan, who are rapidly diversifying into more sophisticated production—but the rest of the LDCs that are relatively new to textiles and clothing production and trade.

Indeed, on this view, such concepts as minimum viable production have no validity and can easily be dismissed by analysts as a further protective ploy. One can certainly provide arguments to reveal the inconsistencies with which they are associated, some of which will be examined in the concluding chapter of the study.

However, given the seeming inability of developed countries to return to the principles and rules of the GATT which they have long claimed as their professed intention, even after more than twenty-five years of a special trade order, then perhaps some more fundamental questions should be raised. For example, would the international trade order work better without an MFA? It is not obvious that this is the case. The pressures in industrialized countries are now such that without some kind of framework governing textile trade, there is a real danger that the alternative would be a proliferation of illegal restraints with perhaps a contagious effect on other sectors. We have seen that many of the arguments for establishing a special regime for textiles have arisen as the result of a preconceived contradiction—whether it is a 'real' contradiction remained a matter of debate between liberal trade principles and the ability of governments to meet their welfare and/or security commitments on both the international and domestic levels. But if in practice the concept of national security has indeed been widened to include the welfare obligations of governments as this suggests, there may be no alternative but to acknowledge that trade can only be free up to the point where it supports the governments' ability to discharge those objectives; thereafter it must necessarily be managed. While it remains an open question whether this is in fact an accurate description of the present situation, the next chapter will discuss the domestic pressures on the Swedish government, which led it, amongst others, to modify its traditional free trade policy, which certainly makes it a pertinent question to ask.

5 The Textile Industry and Swedish Domestic Policy

Introduction

Having examined the origins and the nature of the special international framework for textile trade, this chapter will look at internal pressures that led to the negotiation of the MFA from the angle of one industrialized country, Sweden. The focus, therefore, is on the domestic sources that have influenced Sweden's textile trade policy.

In recent years Sweden has become particularly restrictive in this sector. Swedish governments have justified this departure from the traditional liberal trade policy on the grounds of the rapid penetration of low-cost imports into its market and the consequent social and economic disruptions. As we shall see, however, the problems experienced by Sweden, as by other industrialized countries, do not have purely external origins but have resulted from a host of structural factors, or more precisely from changes in perception with regard to these factors, and perhaps most importantly from the social democratic tradition within which Swedish governments have seen it as their primary duty to provide social welfare and economic defence. It is particularly interesting, therefore, to see how the authorities rationalized the dilemma that faced them, that of reconciling the increasingly problematic commitment to free trade with the requirements of national defence and social welfare.

1 The historical treatment of textiles in Sweden's economic defence policy

(i) *The initial reasons for an economic defence policy*

The development of an economic defence policy in Sweden was a consequence of the difficulties experienced by the armed services and the civilian population during the two world wars. Having chosen to remain neutral at all costs, the country was particularly vulnerable economically as well as militarily. Without allies to rely on for an uninterrupted flow of imports, and thus being totally dependent upon the good-will of other countries, Sweden had to make arrangements in preparation for future war. Most important were measures to ensure an adequate supply of food and other basic needs such as housing and clothing for the population and raw materials for factories.

A policy of economic defence was elaborated in the inter-war period and put into practice for the first time in the Second World War. The general goals of this policy and the measures implemented for the industrial sector as a whole have been described in Chapter 2. Here the emphasis will be on textiles and specifically on how the policy of economic defence evolved in this sector following its inauguration in the Second World War.

(ii) *Importance of textile production
before the Second World War*

Considered one of the basic needs, textiles was among the first manufacturing industries to be established in almost every country. It expanded particularly rapidly in Sweden between 1830 and 1880 due to cheap raw cotton imports from the US. During this period the production of cotton yarn multiplied more than twenty-fold and the production value of cotton fabric and linen fabric rose by about 20 per cent per annum.[1] Production of wool accelerated at a later stage in the industrialization process. Between 1890 and 1910 production increased in value terms from approximately 20 million kr. around 1890 to 70 million around 1910. By the First World War the country was 80 per cent self-sufficient in wool textiles.[2] The ready-to-wear clothing industry also began to expand around 1890.

Employment in the textile and clothing sector was high during the period leading up to, and just following, the Second World War. Despite considerable fluctuations approximately 17 per cent of the work force between 1869 and 1950 was engaged in textile production broadly defined (see Figure 5.1). The importance of employment in this sector coupled with

---

[1] Steven Koblik (ed.), *Sweden's Development from Poverty to Affluence, 1750–1970* (Minneapolis, 1975), 95.
[2] Ibid. 129–30.

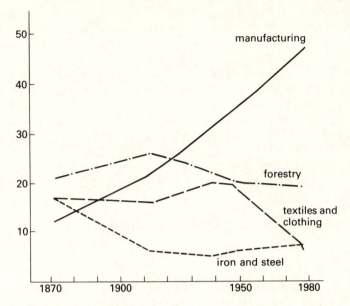

FIG. 5.1. Employment in various sectors, 1870–1979, as a percentage of total employment. From LO Report (1981), 246

low wages therefore provided the incentive for the textile workers to organize unions as early as 1913–14, with the real take-off point being in 1917.[3] Since then, trade union activities have always been a strong element in the textile sector.

The level of textile imports was an important issue for the unions from the very beginning. Table 5.1 shows that the value of textile imports throughout the period leading to the Second World War was high in relation to other products. But it was not until 1930 that the issue was formally brought up at a Union Conference. It was believed that imports were the cause of the considerable fluctuations in employment; and on this occasion, a number of representatives attempted to achieve a consensus regarding the means of preventing purchases from abroad. The motion was defeated, however, due to international solidarity since many of the imports were

[3] Per Petterson, in Beklädnadsarbetarnas förbund—*90 års Jubileumskrift* (Stockholm, 1978) p. 32.

TABLE 5.1. *Value of major imported and exported Swedish products, 1871–1950 (kr. m.)*

Year (annual average)	Agriculture and animal products		Forest products		Paper industry products		Textiles		Minerals and nonmetal products		Metals and metal products	
	Imports	Exports	Imports	Exports	Imports	Exports	Imports	Exports	Imports	Exports	Imports	Exports
1871/75	97	52	2	88	2	4	47	2	21	5	28	48
1891/95	131	83	6	119	6	31	62	9	44	27	40	40
1901/05	197	59	6	159	8	54	58	3	86	54	76	72
1911	238	118	16	180	10	120	82	5	95	98	99	127
1916	333	232	16	334	17	288	100	24	321	170	183	409
1921	430	152	16	194	25	291	132	26	161	128	216	247
1931	363	117	22	174	20	347	225	15	201	138	272	278
1941	281	73	13	213	20	280	267	1	418	228	394	510
1950	1,323	435	88	670	38	1,763	806	101	942	598	1,379	1,505

Source: Historisk statistik. III. p. 58.

made by union workers belonging to the International Textile Workers' Union, of which the Swedish Textile Union (Beklädnadsarbetarnas förbund) was also a member.[4] Nevertheless, import tariffs were maintained at a rate higher than for manufactured imports generally, most likely as a result of pressure from the relatively high rate of imports and the significance of the industry to the home market and employment.

By the outbreak of the Second World War, there were 475 factories employing approximately 29,000 textile workers. Of these, 280 factories and 23,000 workers were engaged solely in clothing production, leaving the country practically self-sufficient in clothing, but highly dependent on imported raw materials.[5]

(iii) *Self-sufficiency and economic defence during the Second World War*

During the 1930s Sweden was approximately 80 per cent self-sufficient in textiles, clothing, and household goods. Between 1936 and 1938 domestic production as a percentage of total domestic consumption was on average 79 per cent for cotton, 91 per cent for wool, 67 per cent for rayon, 84 per cent for silk in the category of woven goods; and in the category of knitted goods: 88 per cent for cotton, 84 per cent for wool, and 81 per cent for rayon.[6]

These supplies, however, were based almost completely on imports of raw materials and foreign goods. Domestic supply of textile raw materials was insignificant, consisting only of small quantities of wool (600–700 tons washed), linen (800 tons) and rayon (900 tons),[7] while imports of raw textile materials amounted to 120,300 tons. Two-thirds of total imports of textile goods consisted of raw materials and one-third of manufactured goods.

Until the outbreak of the war the most important suppliers of wool were Australia, Great Britain, New Zealand, South Africa, and South America, each of which was essential for a special type of wool. Cotton came primarily from the US which accounted for 80 per cent of total imports.

---

[4] Ibid. 33.
[5] *Kläder och skor: Försörjningen i en kristid* H/1972:3, Department of Trade, p. 293.
[6] Ibid. 293.   [7] SOU 1950: 49, p. 562.

This substantial dependence on raw materials began to be looked upon as a serious liability in the 1930s. Thus, when general industrial plans for an economic defence were being drawn up by the RKE, provisions were also made for textiles. An inventory was first conducted to determine the availability of private stocks of raw materials and general supplies. In 1940 an ordinance was passed conferring on the government the right to make purchases and build up stocks in preparation for a blockade and requiring it also to prepare contingency plans for rationing. Large stocks were therefore built up of wool and wool yarn (44,000 tons) estimated to account for at least one year's need of such goods.[8]

In 1939, when war was imminent, a number of authorities were established to centralize control over the supply, production, and rationing of each economic sector. These included a Food and Agriculture Commission, an Industry Commission, and a Trade Commission; all of them were under the Authority of RKE. After the war in 1947 the Industry and Trade Commissions merged, since experience had shown that economic defence questions involving the one inevitably also involved the other.

Imports were maintained at a high level during the first year of the war, even surpassing the previous levels so that more than a year's supply (10,000 tons of wool and 44,000 tons of cotton) existed by the time the so-called Skagerak blockade took effect in April 1940 in connection with the German invasion of Denmark and Norway. The stocks of raw materials were therefore relatively full.

After a one-year interruption trade relations were restored with some countries, particularly with regard to cotton and wool. In addition significant imports of rayon and cellulose were secured through special trade agreements with Germany and Italy that lasted throughout the war. Thus the situation never became too serious and normal trading resumed almost immediately at the end of the war.

Nevertheless, certain measures were taken to secure additional domestic production of raw materials. In 1940 a State Linen and Hemp Authority was created under the State Food and Agriculture Commission to plan for further production

---

[8] *Kläder och skor*, H 1972: 3, p. 294.

and for the preparation and distribution of linen and hemp. State loans and grants as well as minimum price guarantees were provided to subsidize production. By 1943 production had increased to 18,000 tons from 10,000 tons annually before the war, thereby expanding the domestic share of the market. Wool could be obtained in small quantities in Sweden but since few possibilities existed for expanding supplies it was granted low priority.

Government support was concentrated primarily on strengthening cellulose production since the raw material from which it was made, wood, was abundant in Sweden. Thus with state aid Swedish Cellulose AB (Inc.) was set up in 1941 and run co-operatively by the Consumers Union (KF) and the Textile Council. Production increased from 4,000 tons in 1941 to 15,000 in 1944.

Because of the shortage of textiles, controls were invoked to regulate the use of raw materials, to steer production to the most indispensable categories of clothing, and to ensure that clothing was made in the most efficient ways.[9] It is worth mentioning, however, the obvious fact that clothing and textiles are not perishable commodities like foodstuffs. During the war the population undoubtedly made use of old clothes, as well as materials that are available in every individual's home such as curtains, bed linen, and so on to cover emergency needs.

Thus priorities for economic defence planning consisted of maintaining efficient production and stockpiling essential raw materials for producing clothing and other textile products. Economic defence was seen solely in terms of preparing the country for wartime conditions, not as a policy to be maintained on a continual basis in peacetime. Nor did it in any way overlap with employment-creation or other social welfare policies.

(iv) *Consequences of war for production*

By the end of the war, the Swedish textile industry was thriving. Wartime demands had led to an expansion of production capacity and increased demand for labour. All over Europe, a number of small firms had sprung up and continued

---

[9] SOU 1950: 49.

to expand production after the war. Depleted stocks were in need of replenishment and West European firms had to fill the gap left by East European exporters who were now closed off from trade with the West. Sweden participated fully in this general development.

This boom period was of short duration however. Starting with the cotton and wool industries, European textile industries began to decline everywhere in the early 1950s. In Sweden the wool industries were particularly hard hit while in the rest of Europe the cotton industries also began to decline rapidly. Moreover the boom was itself a product of exceptional circumstances: growth in textile industries had already been surpassed by other manufacturing industries before the Second World War. Textiles were therefore already in decline, only temporarily interrupted by the war. Two further wartime developments may indeed have ultimately contributed to the long-term decline of the industry. First, production during the war was geared to increased durability through new combinations of various fabrics, secondly, wartime shortages may have encouraged a shift in fashion from flamboyant to more utilitarian clothing. In any event, since the war evidence has shown constantly falling shares of consumer expenditures on clothing.[10]

To summarize: the production of textiles and clothing had an important place in Sweden's economy up until 1950 but proved particularly sensitive to fashion, changes in demand, and technological change. In the Second World War the economic defence policy was purely a response to wartime conditions and the shortages caused by blockade. At this time the government concentrated its efforts on increasing the supply of textile raw materials, as this was considered the most important element for maintaining sufficient clothing for the population. One major consequence of the war for

---

[10] Hendrik S. Houthakker, 'An International Comparison of Household Expenditure Patterns, Commemorating the Centenary of Engel's Law', *Econometrica* (Oct. 1957), 531–51; Houthakker, 'The Influence of Prices and Income on Household Expenditures'; *Bulletin of the International Institute of Statistics*, no. 2, vol. 36 (1960), 3–16; Hollis B. Chenery and Lance Taylor, 'Development Patterns: Among Countries and Over Time', *The Review of Economics and Statistics* (Nov. 1968), 391–416; D. Keesing and M. Wolf, *Textile Quotas against Developing Countries* (London, 1980), 8.

industry was the rapid technological change and advances in the more capital intensive sectors, which were seen as a positive development. The textile sector did well for a while given the depletion of stocks in Sweden and elsewhere, but was quickly surpassed in importance by other manufacturing sectors.

2 Structural factors and the role of trade in the decline of Sweden's textile sector

The 1960s and 1970s witnessed a continuous rise in protectionist pressures not only in Sweden but also in Western Europe and the US. Because of slow growth in demand and a number of other factors, industrialized countries felt particularly vulnerable to import competition.

The belief that imports from 'low-cost' sources were to blame for the weakening of the textile industries was widespread in developed countries, as was the conviction that textile imports from 'low-cost' sources somehow constituted 'unfair' competition and that protectionist measures would therefore be justified. However, as we shall see, a number of structural and political developments clearly had an impact on these sectors regardless of low-cost imports.

One very important development was the changing perceptions in Sweden and elsewhere concerning the evolving international division of labour. Previously this had been seen as a natural process which promoted structural changes considered positive to growth and in which at any particular time some sectors or sub-sectors would be in decline while others would be expanding. Such shifts in the comparative advantage of industries involved in international trade were not expected to affect the overall level of production, employment or the trade balance. With hindsight it is apparent that this optimistic view was only possible because of the historical experience of an almost uninterrupted period of economic growth. Although there may have been temporary disruptions due to the autonomous process, any slack in employment in one sector was easily taken in by another. It is true that comparative advantages in textiles and clothing were gradually shifting in favour of low-cost producers, but while this no doubt had positive and negative consequences for both parties, some temporary, some longer-term, it was seen as a normal adjustment process according to neo-classical theories of growth. In Sweden such shifts were also perceived by most segments of society as contributing to economic growth without compromising social welfare—and economic defence—policies. However, in the economic climate of the 1970s this ceased to be the case.

(i) *Structure of production*

The 1950s and 1960s in Sweden were marked generally by rapid economic growth accompanied by increased specialization, mechanization, and rationalization. In both industry and agriculture, however, the resulting growth in productivity had certain consequences that were seen to be negative, most notably, a rapid reduction in employment in certain sectors that were increasingly difficult to absorb elsewhere. Textile industries were among those most severely affected, due to rapid transformation in the structure of this industry, domestically and internationally. However, these developments are important to mention as they support the evidence that the decline in employment in this sector was due not so much to imports as to these structural changes.

In terms of production the textile sector in all OECD countries was surpassed by growth in manufacturing generally. This trend which dates from the beginning of the century has continued ever since, albeit with a slowdown after 1973. A number of factors are responsible for the contraction in textile and clothing production, but the three major ones are believed to be changes in demand, technological developments, and the high cost of labour.

With respect to demand, personal consumption remains one of the most important factors in the case of textiles and clothing, since clothing accounts for about one half of final fibre consumption in industrial countries.[11] In Sweden as in most industrial countries the share of clothing in total private consumption measured in prices declined until 1973.[12] The

---

[11] The more industrialized the country, the more significant are household and industrial uses of textiles.
[12] Consumption measured at current as well as constant prices.

low-income elasticity[13] of clothing consumption coincided with decreasing relative prices. Indeed the prices of clothing increased at half the rate of prices overall between 1949 and 1969.[14] However, since 1973 demand has increased relatively quickly compared with total consumer expenditure although the structure of this demand has changed.

Patterns of raw material consumption have also changed in response to price changes. In the 1960s and early 1970s prices of synthetic staples decreased due to advances in chemical technology, the rapid growth of capacity, and supplies of petro-chemical feedstock. Synthetic fibres were found to be much more versatile and less expensive to produce, even for clothing.[15] Furthermore, changes in life-styles and fashion accounted for a preference for lighter and more casual wear which was less costly to produce. Price changes are, however, not the only influential factor in demand. It is possible that the structure and the size of the population as well as the level and distribution of income may have had an even greater effect.

In contrast to the demand factor there is considerable dis-agreement concerning the impact of technological changes on the textile and clothing industries and on trade in particular. It is true that lower production prices have coincided with changing raw material imports and rapidly developing in-dustrial processes by which fibres are transformed into finished products. Technological advances seem to have had their greatest impact on the conversion of fibres into yarn and on the manufacture of fabrics rather than on the 'final' assembly process, which is still relatively labour-intensive. According to some estimates industrialized countries have thus been able to gain a considerable comparative advantage in textile production and gradually shift away from clothing. It is also believed that these developments have had a negative impact on employment.

---

[13] Income elasticity for textiles and clothing was expected to increase considerably according to a prognosis made in 1957, 'Swedish Consumption 1955–1965'. This may have encouraged greater investments in the clothing industry when, in fact, demand was to decline in this sector. Ulf af Trolle, Beklädnadsarbetarnas förbund, p. 37.

[14] SOU 1970: 59, pp. 25–6.   [15] EFTA/CSC/ES 1/83, p. 15.

Technological changes have had a number of consequences for the textile sector. One is that textiles and clothing are moving towards divergent structures, the former evolving towards a more concentrated, capital-intensive system, the latter remaining relatively labour-intensive, but linked to a complex system of distribution chains, wholesale and retail trade, etc. The emergence of synthetic fibres and 'mixes' (mixed fibres natural and synthetic) as well as more efficient means of production have also resulted in lowering costs of the production process.

The changing market and corporate structure has also been important to production and trade. Significant changes took place in the structure of the market throughout the 1960s, particularly in the pattern of retail distribution. Given that most textile production in Sweden was geared to home consumption, these changes had important ramifications and help explain the increasing import dependence. Many small, local, and family shops closed down, unable to compete with the new generation of large department stores. A result of the increased concentration of retail stores was a declining number of persons responsible for wholesale purchasing. Whereas links between producers and wholesalers or retailers in Sweden had traditionally been strong, from the 1960s this ceased to be the case. Buyers began to go abroad in search of lower prices of goods and to take advantage of the strong bargaining position this possibility gave them *vis-à-vis* Swedish producers. In many cases Swedish producers were forced into selling at a loss in order to maintain home market shares.[16] Concentration in marketing is higher in Sweden than in other West European countries with the exception of Great Britain.

In the 1950s the Swedish textile industry had already begun to shrink as the result of the introduction of labour-saving measures. The number of closures of textile companies recorded by the Swedish Textile Workers Union amounted to 120 in the 1950s and 85 in the 1960s. By 1980 635 textile and clothing plants of the 1,332 remaining had closed down.[17] Very few new firms were established during this time.

[16] SOU 1970: 59.   [17] EFTA/CSC/ES 1/83.

Although closures were believed to be largely connected with increasing economies of scale, unit production costs actually decreased minimally in the clothing industry. Because of the stages in assembling that still require manual labour, cost reductions are only significant if the assembly process remains the same for a long period, which is impossible since fashions change so quickly. Furthermore large size can lead to rigidity in terms of production methods and possibly additional labour costs and legislation.[18] As a result of the limited possibilities to decrease production costs in Sweden, textile firms began establishing production units abroad, most notably in the clothing sector. Most of these factories were established in EFTA countries, primarily Finland and Portugal, but also Norway and Switzerland. The prime factor behind this trend was the high cost of labour in Sweden, which, in 1983 was the highest in the world.[19]

The disruptions connected with the decline and the adjustments in the textile and clothing industries have manifested themselves most apparently in the shedding of labour. While productivity in the Swedish textile sector increased at the pace of industry-wide increases, the greater efficiency resulted in a shrinking industry and continuous labour dismissals which became increasingly difficult to absorb elsewhere. Wage and salaried earners in the textile and clothing industries in Sweden declined from 114,000 in 1950 to 27,000 in 1985. In the clothing industry alone, where productivity has been weak, over one-half of the labour force was dismissed between 1970 and 1985 due to declining competitiveness amongst other things.

Despite the significant changes in domestic demand and labour productivity which have been found to be the major cause of declining employment in this sector, much of the disruption has been attributed by the public to the surge of imports of low-cost clothing. What the actual situation is with respect to trade will be discussed in the following section. It is also important to highlight the one important non-structural factor in Sweden that has influenced demand,

---

[18] OECD.
[19] SOU 1970: 59, p. 60; Staffan Hultén, *The Impact of Import Protection and Government Support on the Swedish Textile and Clothing Industry* (Stockholm, 1988).

that is, the high cost of labour. This issue, as will be brought out more fully in later sections, is closely intertwined with Sweden's social welfare policies and is indicative of some major conflicts that have been emerging for Sweden's policy-makers.

(ii) *Structure of textile trade*

(a) *Geographical shifts in textile and clothing trade*

As we have seen, the production of textiles and clothing in the industrial countries has experienced a continual decline. One explanation for this is the shift in comparative advantage from the older to newer industrial centres, mainly to a group of developing countries in Asia, a trend which is not confined only to textiles and clothing, but has been first and most apparent in these sectors. Accompanying this locational shift in production, trade shares have also shifted significantly. In the case of clothing, LDCs increased their share in value terms of world exports from 12 per cent in 1955 to 46 per cent in 1986. The loss of export shares of developed countries was particularly pronounced for Japan and North America. Western Europe's share in total exports declined by much less, however, and was in 1986 at about 42 per cent.[20]

Focusing on world imports of textiles and clothing, the value shares of the developed countries have increased while that of developing countries has decreased. The Western European market accounts for about one half of world imports and is by far the largest market, followed by North America. It is important to note that trade in textiles and clothing within the industrial countries comprises the largest shares of imports even if these shares have decreased over time. Trade in clothing among all industrial countries rose in real terms from one-fifth of world trade in 1955 to two-fifths in 1979 but since 1970 no growth has been evident.[21]

It is true, however, that the share of imports from developing countries has increased markedly, particularly in clothing trade. In Sweden, clothing imports from the industrial countries represented in value terms 80.1 per cent of the total in 1960, 72.3 per cent in 1973, and 68.3 per cent in 1980.

[20] GATT International Trade, various years.
[21] EFTA/CSC/ES 1/83.

TABLE 5.2. *Swedish trade in clothing (ISIC 322) (kr. m.)*

Trade	1960	% share in total	1963	% share in total	1973	% share in total	1980	% share in total
Imports, total	151		238		1,083		3,704	
Developed countries	121	(80.1)	197	(82.8)	783	(72.3)	2,259	(68.3)
Developing countries	18	(11.9)	28	(11.8)	258	(23.8)	977	(26.4)
State-trading countries	12	(8.0)	13	(5.4)	42	(3.9)	198	(5.3)
Exports, total	53		111		402		792	
Developed countries	53	(100.0)	110	(99.1)	397	(98.8)	787	(99.4)
Developing countries	0		0		2	(0.2)	4	(0.5)
State-trading countries	0		1	(0.9)	4	(1.0)	1	(0.1)

Source: EFTA.

The share of imports from the developing countries amounted to 11.9 per cent, 23.8 per cent, and 26.4 per cent respectively in these years, while the state-trading countries accounted for 8.0 per cent, 3.9 per cent, and 5.3 per cent (see Table 5.2). Since 1980 the trend has been reversed to some extent, the LDCs decreasing their share by a few percentage points and the industrialized countries increasing theirs. The share of textile imports from LDCs was much less significant, amounting to only 14.5 per cent in 1980. Imports have clearly increased quickly and it was particularly in the context of the speed of LDC market penetration that the Swedish government began to consider countervailing action. Although exports of textiles and clothing from Sweden have also increased, this is a very recent phenomenon and has not prevented an increasing trade deficit in these sectors.

While imports from the developing countries have clearly increased their shares of Sweden's domestic market, it is difficult to determine an exact causal relationship between imports and domestic production.

Throughout the period of the MFA Sweden's main sources of textile imports have been the EEC (9) (over 50 per cent in 1980), Finland, Portugal, Switzerland, and China. The main sources of clothing imports are the EEC (about 30 per cent in value terms), Finland (20–30 per cent), Hong Kong (12 per cent), Portugal, Korea (5 per cent), and India (2 per cent). The share of the value of imports coming from developed countries has continued to increase steadily. Since 1980 imports have increased substantially from Portugal and Turkey.

(b) *The problem of import penetration*

The industrial countries including Sweden have become increasingly concerned with the problem of rising penetration of the home market by foreign goods. This concept of 'import penetration' is used increasingly as a measure of market disruption and hence as justifying higher levels of protection. Usually understood to mean the ratio of imports to domestic consumption, the assumption in many developed countries is that there exists a certain level of import share that may seriously damage domestic production or threaten to damage it, by causing a substantial reduction in the product price. In the case of Sweden import penetration is said to undermine what is regarded as the minimum viable production for the national economy and is therefore used as the main justifying factor. However, apart from the theoretical and conceptual problems posed by the use of this ratio, there are a host of practical problems in computations of it. Without elaborating on the details of these problems, it is clear that the interpretation of import penetration as an early warning of market disruption is misleading, particularly as it is directed solely against developing countries.[22] It is also for this reason that the concept of minimum viable production, as we shall see, must be looked upon with a certain amount of scepticism.

In Sweden computations have shown that for many categories within the clothing sector, for example, clothing made of knitted cloth, imports make up 80–90 per cent of apparent consumption. For other goods such as wool yarn, home furnishings, suits, jackets, and blazers, the share of imports is much lower, about 60 per cent. A large proportion of these imports of clothing originate in industrialized countries. In the case of knitted wear 81 per cent is imported from industrialized countries, most notably from Denmark and Great Britain. Imports from LDCs of knitted wear decreased from 24 per cent in 1975–7 to 17 per cent in 1979 in value terms, 34 to 25 per cent in quantity. Similar findings have been reported for clothing made of other materials. Finland and Portugal are the two major suppliers, while LDC market

---

[22] Studies have been carried out to determine not only the actual import penetration ratios in various countries, but also the problems associated with their computation and comparability across countries. What is actually meant by import penetration is not always clear because different criteria exist in measuring the impact of imports on domestic industry. For present purposes it is sufficient to discuss these problems in general terms. One problem concerns the definition of the industry and how one differentiates between various products and stages of production. Imports relative to domestic production differ obviously with respect to the product category (e.g. yarn and fabric: sweaters and blouses). Secondly, if imports are calculated in value terms, how does one distinguish the price effect of imports from the price effect of inputs into domestic output? Thirdly, import effects in respect of the tariff differ from those effects in respect of quotas. Other problems of distortion occur if imports are measured in volume terms. See Vincent Cable, 'British Protectionism and LDC imports', *ODI Review*, no. 2 (1977); Emrich, *et al.*, *Imports, Exports and jobs* (American Importers Association, 1978). Keesing and Wolf, op. cit.; Carl Hamilton, *A New Approach to Estimation of the Effects of Non-Tariff Barriers to Trade on Prices, Employment and Imports: An Application to the Swedish Textile and Clothing Industry*, (Stockholm, 1980).

shares shrank from a peak in 1977 of 30 per cent in value or 40 per cent in quantity to 27 and 37 per cent respectively in 1979.[23]

Yet it is the low-cost imports from developing or south European countries that seem to be the main cause for concern in Sweden. In the mid 1960s a number of government and independent agencies were asked to conduct studies examining the implications of increased competition from these countries in particular. The Board of Commerce subsequently recommended in 1968 that bilateral agreements should be negotiated with Yugoslavia and Hong Kong owing to the disruption caused by imports from these countries.[24] This study was then followed by others substantiating the need for further protection from low-cost sources.

However, no studies have been able to prove that imports from low-cost sources have in themselves caused the decline in the textile sector; nor that they have caused balance of payments deficits. There is also no substantiated evidence that they have generated social disruptions due to accelerating unemployment in the sector, or regional disturbances as a result of destabilization of the textile 'belt'. On the contrary, many economists have argued that in industrial countries generally there is a very minor loss of employment due solely to imports from LDCs. For example, one such study on the situation in the United Kingdom attested to the fact that the annual reduction in jobs resulting from LDC exports between 1970 and 1975 came to 0.005 per cent in the production of yarn, 0.8 per cent in cotton textiles, and 1.7 per cent in clothing.[25] Recent research on the Swedish industry supports

---

[23] Tekoindustrierna, SIND PM 1980: 16, p. 25–6.   [24] H 1972: 3.

[25] José de la Torre concludes that with the 'exception of the Netherlands, net import penetration has not been the main direct cause of job losses among the various European industries. While imports rose in some cases both absolutely and relatively, some countries expanded their exports as fast as or faster in the context of a strategy of product specialization. Others reacted by significant improvements in their productivity which had a much more serious impact on employment than had the increased imports. Second, the often prescribed remedy for all declining sectors that they must achieve higher productivity may enhance the industry's international competitiveness, but it will not add to the employment rolls in mature industries characterized by low income elasticity of demand. The solution to the employment problem must lie elsewhere in the economy, or in other branches of industry.' José de la Torre, 'Public Intervention

TABLE 5.3. *Contribution to employment associated with change (man-hrs m.)*

	Import share	Productivity	Apparel demand	Observed employment change
Textiles, wearing apparel and leather	− 19	− 217	97	− 139

Source: J. Bojö and P. Wissén, 'Sysselsättningseffekter av importkonkurrens—några resultat för Sverige', *Ekonomisk Debatt*, no. 5 (Stockholm, 1979).

studies on other countries. Bojö and Wissén, whose research on changes in Swedish manufacturing employment associated with changes in import shares and other factors between 1963 and 1975 was cited in a UNIDO Study on Swedish industry,[26] concluded that even for the textile, wearing apparel and leather industries the loss of employment associated with productivity growth was ten times more important that the loss of employment due to import competition (Table 5.3).

The rapid decline in this sector is nevertheless seen as intolerable by the Swedish government as to varying degrees it is by the governments of other industrialized countries. They claim that they have been forced to take action in order to ease the social and political disruption that is a consequence of massive job losses. The evidence suggests, however, that

Strategies in the European Clothing Industries', *Journal of World Trade Law*, vol. 15, no. 2 (Mar./Apr. 1981), 136.

Donald Keesing studied the problem of import penetration and concluded that: '(1) The developed countries continue to generate the bulk of the World's exports of textiles, all textile products and even clothing; (2) The developing countries' industries are simply too small to threaten the extinction of textiles and clothing industries in developed countries, as is sometimes suggested; (3) Developed countries collectively enjoy a large and sustained surplus in textile trade offset by a larger and growing deficit in clothing; . . . (5) Outside a relatively narrow range of products, import penetration by developing countries is modest. Developing countries' exports of clothing seem to have taken between 8 and 18 per cent of the overall market for clothing in developed countries and much less (directly) for textiles. Moreover, the impact of trade on the size of the industries overall is much less than these figures suggest because of exports, especially of textiles'. Donald Keesing, Martin Wolf, 'Questions on International Trade in Textiles and Clothing', *The World Economy*, vol. 4, no. 1 (Mar. 1981), 99–100.

[26] 'Future structural changes in the Industry of Sweden', UNIDO/IS.191 (1 Dec. 1980), 20–2.

very often measures are taken that have the most visible or tangible short-term effects without consideration of the actual factors involved or the long-term implications of these measures. Government responses to the textile industries' problems in Sweden as well as some of the major internal pressures guiding this policy will be treated in the following section.

3 Structural adjustments and industrial policies

We have now seen how little evidence there is to support the premise behind the MFA that low-cost imports are the cause of market disruption in developed importing countries. The analysis could, of course, be taken further and qualified in a number of ways. Yet it seems clear that a number of other factors have contributed to the decline of the industry besides imports from developing countries. This fact does not, however, alleviate the problems encountered by the labour force and, concomitantly, the government whose post-war policy emphasized the development of a social welfare state.

Sweden has had Social Democratic governments for most of its post-war history. In economic policy the government's priorities always included in simplified terms a commitment to maintain high employment and efficiency as well as income equalization and adequate working conditions. As long as the economy was experiencing rapid growth with low inflation no major conflicts appeared between social welfare policies and free trade. Indeed the progress in the one encourages progress in the other. There was, however, a policy in the 1960s of reaching full employment goals with a minimum of inflationary impact which led to a deliberate productivity-raising structural transformation of Swedish industry. Domestic production was in many cases successfully replaced by imports while new jobs were created in expanding export industries. Moreover this transformation occurred at the expense, as we have seen, of the labour-intensive activities such as textiles, clothing, and footwear industries.

The development of an overall 'industrial policy' was a logical response to the disruptions associated with structural adjustments. The concept of industrial policy is a vague one but is usually understood as a variety of internal and, in some cases, external support measures aimed at either easing the structural adjustment of the industrial sector as a whole on a national or regional level, or assisting specific sectors that have the potential to regain momentum but which, for cyclical or other reasons, require temporary assistance. Ultimately it is believed that it reflects a concern with employment rather than with maintaining an industry *per se*. For this reason too, it should not for example, be confused with the policy of supporting industry, for reasons of national defence. In many countries the armaments industry has been provided with government subsidies but historically this policy has always been considered quite separate from industrial policies to support manufacturing industries generally.

Structural change is viewed as an inevitable accompaniment of the changing international division of labour. More recently the concept of structural adjustment has been defined as 'the transformation of national patterns of production and factor allocation in a *socially optimal* way in order to accommodate shifts in comparative advantage as revealed by unhindered trade flows' (author's emphasis).[27]

But although the shift in emphasis from an autonomous process to, as it were, social engineering is a relatively recent one, it is apparent that policies to assist or regulate structural adjustments have been practised in many countries from the early 1900s and hence do not really constitute a new phenomenon. One important policy instrument in this respect was—and to a certain extent remains—the tariff. However, successive rounds of tariff negotiations deprived governments of this means of promoting domestic production and controlling structural adjustments, thus leaving a vacuum which governments in many cases believed had to be filled by other means. These other means ultimately took the form of non-tariff barriers such as quantitative restrictions. It must be added, however, that the tariff had a different impact from other instruments of industrial policy in that it did not interfere with the basic price mechanism. For this reason it was also the only instrument that was acceptable in the GATT system providing it was applied on a non-discriminatory

---

[27] *Protectionism and structural adjustment*, UNCTAD TD/B/888, 15.1.82.

basis. One important element that distinguishes traditional tariff protection from the 'new protectionism' is that the latter implies discrimination, justified on the grounds that a threat can come from one country or group of countries.

It was the recession of the 1970s that revealed this vacuum. As governments throughout the industrialized world faced conditions of accelerating inflation and rising unemployment, they discovered that they could no longer rely on macro-economic demand management policies; or rather that such policies were no longer sufficient to restore economic stability. Structural adjustments that had earlier been perceived as positive and natural were now considered disruptive and alarming: with sluggish demand and surplus capacity, no new outlets were available for unemployed workers. Sweden was no exception. How, then, the Swedish government responded to this challenge and the background to its approach will be seen below.

(i) *Motives for government intervention*

At the end of the Second World War the Social Democratic party and the labour movement had jointly proposed a stronger role for the state in the economy. The motivation for such a programme was to encourage greater efficiency in industry through structural change and to make it more competitive internationally. They recommended not only government intervention if necessary, but also the introduction of greater democracy through worker participation in industrial decision-making. The programme was not very specific and was finally ignored, partly because it engendered bitter political controversy, but also because evidence accumulated that Swedish industry could perform successfully in international markets without government intervention.

Consequently, policy documents published in the 1950s and 1960s[28] laid stress on the need for competition and structural change but only recommended positive (i.e., market)

---

[28] *Fackföreningsrörelsen och den fulla sysselsättningen; Samordnad Närings-politik* (1961): 'The Swedish industry has to be in the front line in exploiting new technical fields, for methodology, material and ready product, if we shall be able to secure full employment and a continued fast rise in the standard of living. Therefore it is necessary that the structure adjusts continuously to developments'.

adjustment policies.[29] Thus as trade was liberalized, industry was forced automatically to restructure and invest in new activities that would be more profitable. At the same time the government was able to fulfil its far-reaching social goals connected with full employment and wage solidarity by relying on a rapidly growing GNP rather than by controlling production. Political support was maintained by redistributing government resources to those groups which bore the greatest burden of adjustment.

It was not until the mid-1960s that the social costs associated with structural changes began to manifest themselves acutely and that the 'socially optimal' adjustment process acquired political significance. This was partly a result of economic problems that were being encountered throughout the industrial world,[30] but the Swedish authorities also had to react to a number of specific internal pressures.

The trade unions were the first to change their attitude. While they had previously been fully supportive of technical and structural changes, arguing that adjustments should be accelerated in the interest of productivity and prosperity, they increasingly began to question the benefits of a totally free market approach. Indeed, as early as 1961 a working party appointed by the LO called for a 'co-ordinated industrial policy' and the establishment of a new ministry to deal with industry and employment problems.[31]

Such early demands were undoubtedly primarily concerned with employment and location policies, while investment decisions were still expected to be left in private hands. However, whether as a result of this union pressure or independently, government intervention gradually became more extensive. Assistance was begun on a small scale and indiscriminately as between industrial sectors, although it was particularly directed towards the depressed regions of

---

[29] 'Positive adjustments' have been defined by UNCTAD, TD/B/839, 19.1.81. as including intervention to the extent of helping labour and capital to move into more productive areas by way of retraining schemes, relocation allowances, etc.; imports are seen as playing a potentially positive role in stimulating restructuring.

[30] See Martin Wolf, *Adjustment Policies and Problems in Developed Countries*, Staff Working Paper No. 349 (Washington, DC, 1979).

[31] Göran Ohlin, in Raymond Vernon, *Big Business and the State* (London, 1974).

northern Sweden. Gradually the government embarked upon a more extensive programme of aiding industries in various aspects of production, employment, location, and exports, a process which culminated in the establishment of a National Investment Bank in 1967 and a Department of Industry in 1968. The appearance of several other agencies and boards concerned with industrial development followed.

The government's aim was, on the one hand, to reduce the disruptions associated with rapid structural change and, on the other, to promote self-generating industrial expansion as part of a general revitalization of the economy. Moreover, given Sweden's small size, high degree of economic specialization, and dependence on extensive trade for continued growth, the government had a large stake in stimulating Swedish companies to maintain a competitive position internationally. In 1967 the importance of promoting export growth was underlined when the country experienced its first balance of payments deficit since 1949.

The Social Democrats also had a further aim in intervening in the private sector.[32] In the late 1960s the increasing concentration of domestic banks and multinationals meant that they emerged as powerful forces in domestic politics and attracted considerable public attention and criticism as a result. To counteract this trend there were demands that the Social Democrats should exercise more state influence on the management of the most dominant firms.

Thus the emphasis of government shifted from that of fostering efficiency in the industrial structure to that of carefully weighing the cost versus the benefits for society, of structural adjustments and of trying to balance growth with socially acceptable developments.[33] The government's new 'selective' policy as opposed to 'general' fiscal and monetary management of the 1960s seemed to offer new possibilities for responding to local and regional problems while at the

[32] One should note that the Social Democrats are not totally united in their policies, particularly in more recent times. While one wing stresses the dangers of protectionism and too much intervention by government, the other firmly believes in the need to strive for self-sufficiency, hence protectionism, in key sectors.

[33] The Social Democrats made reference to this consideration for the first time at the 1967 Party Congress—UNIDO 1S/191, p. 31.

same time demonstrating a continuing commitment to wage-earner interests.[34]

Two important cornerstones of Social Democratic policy must also be viewed in this context, the 'solidaristic wage policy' and the 'active labour market policy', both of which were developed during the period of rapid growth in the 1950s and 1960s. The 'solidaristic wage policy', which meant equal pay for the same type of work, was an attempt to reduce wage differentials between regions, sectors, and skill groups. One necessary condition for the successful pursuit of this policy was the centralization and strength of the trade union movement as well as continued smooth relations between the unions and government, both of which were achieved in the 1960s. A consequence, however, of this policy was severe pressure from rising labour costs on labour-intensive low-wage branches, namely textiles and clothing.

To counter these negative consequences of income distribution selective policy measures were introduced, primarily through increasing the effectiveness of placement services and of demand-oriented training and retraining services offered by the Swedish labour market administration. During the 1960s, when this 'active labour market policy' went into full operation, the facilitation of labour mobility from the weaker to the stronger regions and sectors of the economy was to a large extent successful.

In the 1970s, however, two things changed. First, the world-wide recession reduced the number of available jobs in the private sector which could not be rectified by simply increasing the efficiency of labour mobility. Second, the labour movement raised its level of aspirations and it became increasingly problematical to move people to where the jobs happened to be, instead of moving jobs to people. At this point the government responded by increasing intervention, first by expanding the active labour market policy from an

---

[34] These policies were undoubtedly inspired by two well-known trade-union economists, Gösta Rehn and Rudolph Meidner. They argued that it would be impossible to tackle unemployment problems in communities suffering from structural contraction by general fiscal and monetary expansion, because it would only result in excess demand in the rest of the economy. General economic policy was to be practised in so far as to contain inflation, while selective measures were proposed to relieve distress in stricken areas. See Göran Ohlin 'Adjustment Assistance in Sweden', *Adjustment for Trade* (Paris, 1975).

instrument of facilitating labour mobility to an instrument providing substitute employment in deficit areas; and second, by embarking upon an endless spiral starting with regional and sector-specific subsidies and then continuing, in the textiles and clothing sectors, with trade restricting measures. Let us look more specifically at the role of trade unions and the solidaristic wage policy in the context of textile and clothing imports into Sweden.

(ii) *Role of trade unions*

The Social Democratic party grew out of the trade union and consumers' movements. Ever since the establishment of the Central Federation of Trade Unions (Landsorganisationen, LO) which represents a large majority of the salaried labour force, there has been continuous support for the government policy of trade liberalization. Originally the advantages of liberal trade were seen in terms of access to cheap imports which, in their contribution to economic growth and rising living standards, would directly or indirectly benefit the workers. More recently liberal trade was regarded as a positive factor in promoting rationalization and specialization in industry, in other words, in adjusting to a changing international division of labour. Even in the midst of the recent recession the Swedish LO on the whole believed that liberal trade, being a prerequisite for economic welfare in aggregate terms, was necessary to finance the social welfare state. The LO's position, with respect to protectionist measures, was that economic dependence could not be reduced in this way. Observation of other government policies has shown that protectionism does not result in more security or less unemployment.[35]

The one exception to this general support by the trade unions for liberalizing trade was as early as 1930 in the textile sector and particularly in the mid-1950s as textile industries began to decline. Although imports of clothing and textiles actually accounted for only a very small percentage of domestic consumption at that time, industry expressed concern at the unfavourable consequences imports might have on prices in Sweden.

---

[35] *Näringspolitik för 80-talet*, Report to the LO Congress (1981).

In the 1960s rapid structural adjustments were taking place as a result of deliberate policies, economic growth, and technological advances. Among the textile unions much of the autonomous adjustment process was believed to be a consequence of increasing pressure from imports. However, the unions agreed not to resist these adjustments despite the social disruption they were thought to provoke. Indeed at the Textile Congress of 1961 a very positive attitude was expressed on behalf of the industrialization and export potential of the developing countries:

Developing countries, which represent the majority of the world's population, constitute an immense future market of utmost importance for Western industrialised nations. Because developing countries have such a great need for capital goods of the kind produced in our country, we have everything to gain from increased trade with these countries, even if this will probably contribute to an additional shrinking of our textile industries. If we do not want to accept an increased exchange of goods with these countries, then all talk about help for them becomes more or less meaningless.[36]

This stance by the union, however, had one important condition, that the government in return establish a more active labour market policy. This was, as we have seen, to include retraining programmes and compensation to labour for moving from one job to another, as well as a wage policy based on the solidarity principle, that is, a levelling out of wages through changes in tax policy. It was thereby hoped that those losing jobs in the textiles sector would be compensated by being retrained for new jobs in other sectors while textiles and clothing would have the chance to become more competitive at a lower but more specialized level of production. Higher wages were expected to follow.

After initial success in effecting an active labour market policy the Textiles and Clothing Workers Union, which was part of LO, became aware of the potential influence of the unions on government policy. When it also became apparent that there would be no let up of pressure on the textile industry the unions gradually intensified pressure for greater government intervention, this time including protection. In

---

[36] *Beklädnadsarbetarnas Förbund—90 års jubileumsskrift* (Stockholm, 1978), 4–5.

the early 1970s one of the union's most vigorous campaigns was centred on a demand for restricting low-cost imports originating primarily in South-East Asia. Strength in this campaign was partly a result of the merging of various textile and clothing workers' unions in 1972 to form one larger union.

The share of domestic consumption accounted for by imports began to increase in the late 1960s. For many years following the Second World War Sweden had been only 20 per cent dependent on imports of clothing. But by 1968 dependency was up to 30 per cent and by 1980 to about 80 per cent. Even though close to 70 per cent of these imports came from other industrialized countries, much of the resulting domestic disruption was blamed on the low-cost South-East Asian countries. The unions reconciled their new assessment with their original position in favour of trade with the Third World by arguing that the unacceptable increase resulted from a distortion of free trade by the multinationals. On this view low-price imports coincided with an expansion of so-called free zones in capitalist developing countries in which multinationals were believed to exploit the local labour force and consequently to export at very low prices while maintaining large profits.

This change in attitude may have numerous explanations. There was in any event a generalized view that economic growth could not be pursued at the expense of other more humanitarian aims such as further social reforms, the environment, and so on. Unions in Sweden as elsewhere became more demanding, a trend which was accentuated as the recession in the 1970s became apparent. This particular feeling of solidarity with the Third World was, as described in Chapter 3, partly as a result of Palme's active involvement with development issues as well as a general emerging antagonism towards capitalism.

Supported by the LO, the Textile and Clothing Workers Union took the position that a regulated trade in textiles was not directly inconsistent with the union's general adherence to liberal trade, but it called for acknowledgement for both advantages and disadvantages. If it was to be supported by the unions, the advantages should be shared equally by society as a whole, not just enjoyed by the multinationals.

Free trade was not to be accepted at any price and was not to be seen as a goal in itself. Furthermore importing from developing countries should not, it was held, be confused with development assistance which aimed to benefit the whole population of the recipient developing country. The Swedish government should demand a social clause requiring better labour conditions and wages, in line with those offered by industrialized countries in return for less restricted imports of clothing. As noted in the previous chapter similar arguments were also advanced during the MFA negotiations, most notably by the EEC, but were never accepted. The debate has, however, been revived more recently in Sweden.

A further exception to the free trade principle raised in the latter half of the 1970s by the unions concerns the protection of textiles in order to maintain an economic defence. The goal of economic independence or self-sufficiency began to be looked upon as a goal in itself, although the unions also held that measures to protect independence must be weighed carefully against international trade obligations and the risk of retaliation.[37]

(iii) *Wage solidarity*

One of the most important Social Democratic campaigns in the 1960s and 1970s was to reduce wage differentials by raising the wages of those in the lowest income brackets. Textile and clothing workers have traditionally been among the least well paid in the whole manufacturing sector. Although it has changed for textile workers, clothing workers in industrial countries generally are low-skilled workers of whom a large proportion are women and drawn from minority groups. This is also the situation in Sweden. Until the late 1960s, however, textile and clothing workers' unions primarily fought for equal wages between men and women. On the whole the unions continued to have faith in the free market mechanism and did not apply pressure on the government for intervention. Firms unable to compete were closed or merged with more successful firms while those employees who lost their jobs were transferred to more profitable sectors with the help of an active labour market

---

[37] *Näringspolitik för 80—talet*, (1981).

policy. Economic policy of the post-war period concentrated on selective job-creating measures to remove tendencies to unemployment in the weakest sectors of the economy rather than on increasing the level of aggregate demand. Thus any tendencies to unemployment were to be confronted directly where the problem arose, instead of maintaining the employment level by an expansive general policy on the demand side.

Up to a certain point this policy was successful. Structural adjustments, however, took place so quickly in the 1960s and textile workers were disadvantaged for several reasons peculiar to that industry. First, it was concentrated primarily in one region of Sweden, Borås, where investment activity was insignificant and alternative jobs difficult to obtain. Second, adjustments took place even more quickly in this sector than in others, due to technical advances resulting in a rapid shedding of labour. Third, the large proportion of women employed in the sector meant that relocating would often entail finding new jobs for two members of the family.[38] Fourth, low wage differentials between jobs and firms hindered the adjustment process: the more productive firms were unable to offer higher wages with the result that there was little incentive for workers to leave stagnating firms which were none the less supported by government subsidies. This fourth reason will be examined below in more depth.

At about the same time as textile industries began to experience difficulties LO, as we have seen, launched a campaign for a solidaristic wage policy that aimed to reduce wage differentials between different sectors of the economy. Given the low wages in the textiles sector and the support provided to the textiles unions by the LO and Social Democratic party, this programme was bound to have implications for textile workers.

Considerable progress was made in effecting this goal already in the 1960s. An important further step was taken in 1971 when the government intervened in private sector wage bargaining for the first time, declaring that low-income

---

[38] The larger percentage of women in the sector had considerable implications in Sweden. Due to the strength of women's pressure groups it became politically difficult to declare them redundant.

TABLE 5.4 *Labour cost in various world textile industries, spring 1980 ($US)*

Developed countries	Average cost per labour-hour	Developing countries	Average cost per labour-hour
Belgium	11.82	Greece, north	2.95
Netherlands	11.68	Portugal	1.68
Germany, FR,		Argentina	3.33
north	10.65	Mexico	3.10
Sweden	10.43	Chile	1.93
Switzerland	9.65	Hong Kong	1.91
Germany, FR,		Uruguay	1.76
south	9.64	Brazil, São Paulo	1.57
Norway	9.62	Iraq	1.57
Denmark	9.12	Brazil, south	1.27
Italy	9.12	China (Taiwan)	1.26
France, north	8.57	Brazil, north	1.14
France, south-		Tunisia	1.13
east	7.25	Syria	0.96
Austria	6.42	Turkey	0.95
United States	6.37	Singapore	0.94
Canada	6.25	Morocco	0.85
United Kingdom	5.75	Korea, Rep.	0.78
Finland	5.62	India	0.60
Ireland	5.13	Honduras	0.42
Spain	4.90	Egypt	0.39
Japan	4.35	Pakistan	0.34
Greece, south	4.03	Thailand	0.33

Note: These data should be taken as indications of relative magnitudes only. They are based on wages (including social charges) of spinning and weaving workers, mainly in the cotton industry. Werner Associates have, however, looked also in general at wages in other sectors of the textile and clothing industries and have come to the conclusion that wage costs in these other sectors are somewhat similarly related between countries as the figures shown in the table.

Source: Werner Associates, Inc., USA.

groups should have the highest percentage increases.[39] Table 5.4 shows that in Sweden's textile sector, which in national terms comprised one such group, labour costs in 1972 were already among the highest in the world. Between 1970 and 1979 salaries and social benefits among Swedish clothing firms in Sweden rose by 92.1 per cent which was

[39] Assar Lindbeck, *Swedish Economic Policy* (London, 1975), 144–5, 156–7.

about double the increases for the manufacturing sector in general.[40]

It is often suggested that these high income levels are largely the cause of the deteriorating competitiveness of Swedish textiles. In fact it is not only hourly labour costs that determine competitiveness of an industry. There are many other factors such as raw material prices, the share of processing in the total manufacturing costs, transportation and storage, and so on. The technical and capital intensity are also primary elements determining levels of competitiveness. However, the combination of factors that are characteristic of the Swedish clothing industries in particular, that is, high labour costs and labour-intensive production do not contribute favourably to Sweden's textile and clothing industries when competing with quality products made at a much lower cost. Thus, while it would be politically impossible and even absurd to attempt to lower Swedish labour costs to the level of Hong Kong's or India's the policy of wage solidarity must indeed have consequences for the competitiveness of the industry, especially if productivity does not rise in step with wages as is the case for clothing. Moreover, because of the large discrepancy of labour costs between Sweden and many developing countries, the government believes it will be impossible for Swedish textiles ever to compete with them. As we shall see in Chapter 6 it is largely for this reason that they have justified the imposition of quantitative restrictions against low-cost suppliers including all developing exporting countries and demanded the inclusion of the minimum viable production clause in the MFA.

(iv) *Sector-specific policies and economic defence*

The new industrial policies were reinforced with respect to the textiles sector in the early 1970s when the government adopted a sectoral approach to industrial policy. In response to pressures from declining industries the government embarked upon a programme of support for textile and clothing manufacturers, that is, beyond what had already been done on a general, industry-wide basis. Once subsidies and other forms of financial support were

---

[40] Textile Revue no. 55, 6.10.80.

initiated, they grew both in scope and scale at a very rapid pace.

Changes in market conditions that provoked the gradual decline in the Swedish textile and clothing industries have already been discussed. It has also been mentioned that the speed with which structural changes were taking place was viewed by the Swedish authorities with particular alarm. According to official statements one of the government's primary concerns was the rapid increase in imports as a proportion of domestic consumption and the projected consequence of this development for the defence of the country in case of crisis. Although policies aimed at economic defence will be examined further in the next chapter it is worth mentioning here that economic defence subsidies were only one out of several types of subsidies which were provided to the textiles and clothing sectors at about the same time. One may therefore ask if legitimate criteria were used to demarcate this type of aid from other types of sectoral assistance. In other words, had the goals and means of maintaining an economic defence ultimately been worked out independently or were they simply a further response to the general decline of the industry and tackled within the general context of industrial policy?

In 1971 a group of experts was set up to study the problem of supply capacity for defence and to recommend various means of maintaining an adequate domestic supply of textiles and clothing. Specific recommendations aimed at the problem of economic defence included subsidies for investment in new machinery and buildings as well as for government procurement. A new law was passed in January 1973 obliging authorities that generally made large purchases of textile or clothing goods to consult with ÖEF (The National Board of Economic Defence) if foreign bids were lower than Swedish offers. It was later decided that ÖEF would be granted decision-making power regarding such purchases. Subsidies were provided to cover costs of the more expensive domestic goods.[41]

These measures were not sufficient to arrest the decline of the industry. In 1975/6 new bills recommended increasing

[41] DSH 1977: 1.

aid for state purchases and stockpiling, subsidies, and other measures to strengthen its competitive position.[42] One important form of assistance for economic defence purposes was a subsidy to maintain stocks of cloth for uniforms or military needs. Such stocks were to cover needs lasting three years.

From this time on it becomes increasingly difficult to distinguish between overall industrial policy and economic defence measures. For example, under the latter heading management education and development programmes were initiated, which provided courses and conferences with the aim of stimulating development in company management and finance, production and marketing, personnel management and co-operation. An export promotion programme was launched to provide initial expenses in market analyses, marketing and product adjustment, with a view to promoting a more efficient industrial structure.

Further government assistance was given in the form of credit support facilities which were particularly relevant in agreements with ÖEF. Companies which maintained agreements with ÖEF[43] and benefited from credit support such as depreciation loans were, as a condition for assistance, expected to increase investments and to maintain a certain level of production and production capacity. These interest-free loans were to be written off during the 10–15 year period during which the company was bound by the agreement. The credit support system was administered by ÖEF. Support was given to a programme of rationalization within the ready-made clothing industry by encouraging new production techniques. Finally, further 'extraordinary' regional and labour market policies were implemented. Such policies were usually carried out in the context of the industrial sector as a whole although some special consideration was given to textiles and clothing industries.

---

[42] Prop. 1975/6: 57, NU 1975/6: 15, rskr 1975/6: 197. Prop. 1975/6: 206, NU 1975/6: 70, rskr 1975/6: 415, 1976/7: 105, NU 1976/7: 41, 1976/7: 305.

[43] To maintain production capacity of cotton yarn, agreements were reached in 1977 between the government and the Swedish cotton industry. Another agreement to maintain production capacity of textile fibres and cord yarn during the period 1976–84 was concluded between ÖEF and a Swedish company.

Despite these measures to stimulate production, the official view was of an acute textile supply problem. The government's solution required more official surveillance and control over the development of the whole sector. In 1977 a special Council was therefore set up for the textile and clothing industry under the Department of Industry. It included government officials, employers and employees. The prime task of the Council was to follow long-term trends in the textile and clothing industries and to analyse potential consequences of these trends. A special Board was established in 1978 to co-ordinate government measures aimed at the textile sector. Among those represented on the Board were ÖEF, the National Industrial Board, the Labour Market Board, and various textile and clothing firms and employees' representatives. As a consultative body the Board advises the government on policy and programmes for restructuring and rationalizing the industry. In 1978 the government also took over three major and a few minor companies which it subsequently merged into one large company.

In reviewing these developments it is impossible to draw a clear line between government-inspired policy and policies that were formulated in response to interest group pressures. In the textiles and clothing sector specifically it is difficult to avoid the conclusion that government intervention was almost purely a consequence of internal pressures. One factor that favours this view is the considerable amount of support and protection afforded to the clothing industry relative to the textile industry particularly in the early stages. Textile firms, which would presumably be the most important to an economic defence policy (clothing can after all be made at home), were the first ones to fall yet it was not until the clothing industry began to decline that the government decided to step in. It is important to add that clothing firms were much more labour-intensive than textile firms, and thus could generate more union support. Furthermore clothing manufacturers were better organized than textile manufacturers.

Despite positive results from such government actions there remains a considerable concern over production and production capacity for economic defence needs. Increasingly attention has turned to this aspect of industrial policy. It is also the Authorities' belief that very little more can be done internally by way of subsidies and other adjustment measures. Thus they are confronted with an increasingly sharp dilemma. At some point the government must ask itself what the most cost-effective means are not only for maintaining a stable sector but also for providing a viable economic defence. To begin with, subsidies are expensive and cannot be maintained indefinitely nor are they meant to be. The original intention was to discontinue support as soon as firms demonstrated an ability to stand on their own feet. However, the burgeoning of subsidies of various kinds has shown that it is not so easy. It is feared that a relationship of dependency will develop as firms begin vying for various forms of assistance. Such a symbiotic relationship between government and business could then create a vicious circle leading to increased protectionism.

Secondly, many reports in Sweden and elsewhere have concluded that government intervention of this sort is damaging to the economy in the long run. One study concluded that support to 'lame-duck' industries in Sweden, such as many of the clothing firms, in an attempt to save jobs was counterproductive to restoring the foreign balance of payments and stabilizing the economy. More specifically it examined the macroeconomic consequences of subsidies and concluded that they may reduce unemployment in the short term, but that effects on the distribution of resources and growth in the long run are likely to be negative. In other words, adjusting to changing comparative advantages would only be postponed by giving subsidies.[44] Thus, according to this argument it seems that while, in principle, adjustment subsidies are meant to phase out dying industries they often seem to have the opposite effect in practice.

Thirdly, as domestic pressures continue to bear on the state resort to trade policy measures has been perceived as necessary. They are easier to administer than subsidies though arguably less efficient. At the same time they seem to be more acceptable from a budgetary point of view as their cost is not immediately perceptible.

[44] Bo Carlsson, Fredrik Bergholm, Thomas Lindberg, *Industristödspolitiken och dess inverkan på Samhällsekonomin*, Industrins Utredningsinstitut (Stockholm, 1981).

The choice is not as clear-cut, however, as this review of the arguments suggests. It is not always possible to make a distinction between subsidies and trade policy measures in terms of effect. As will be seen below even subsidies can have trade distorting effects and can therefore be considered a form of protectionism. Many writers have coined the phrase the 'new protectionism' to cover all forms of non-tariff measures. As Krauss has written 'The new protectionism . . . refers to how the totality of government intervention into the private economy affects international trade. The emphasis on trade is still there—hence the term "protection". But what is new is the realization that virtually all government activity can affect international economic relations'.[45]

4 Adjustment assistance measures and non-tariff barriers

We are now presented with a further problem, that of distinguishing between internal and external measures. The 'new protectionism' is of course not confined to Sweden but the focus will be on its policies in particular.

In the peak period 1981/2 there were about twenty-three forms of subsidies paid to Swedish textile and clothing firms including the economic defence subsidy intended to help maintain security of supply. By 1977 they had increased by at least fifteen times from almost nothing before 1970 (see Table 5.5). During this latter year there was a particularly large upsurge in response to the sharp decline in competitiveness.

Since the mid-1960s there has been growing international concern about the trade distorting effects of a variety of adjustment assistance measures. GATT rules do exist in this area but according to many economists they need to be strengthened. Article III 8 (*b*) of the GATT permits 'the payment of subsidies exclusively to domestic producers'. Article XVI, however, states:

In any case in which it is determined that serious prejudice to the interests of any other contracting party is caused or threatened by

---

[45] Melvyn B. Krauss, *The New Protectionism* (New York, 1978), 36.

TABLE 5.5 *Subsidies paid out to the Swedish textile and clothing industry, fiscal years 1970/71 and 1977/78 (1000 kr.)*

Types of subsidy and loan	1970/71		1977/78	
	Current prices	Share of total subsidies (%)	Current prices	Share of total subsidies (%)
Export promotion	3,535	19.8	17,701	3.5
1. Firm-specific subsidies	2,468	13.9	9,948	2.0
2. Industry subsidy	801	4.5	6,307	1.2
3. Export consultants	192	1.1	1,400	0.3
4. Other	74	0.4	46	0.0
Training and adjustment subsidies	2,182	12.2	70,795	13.9
5. Education	1,018	5.7	2,500	0.5
6. Firm-specific adjustment	0		4,900	1.0
7. Subsidies to make firms merge or co-operate	0		2,000	0.4
8. Industry subsidy	0		3,000	0.6
9. Refunded interest payments and honoured guarantees	0		1,000	0.2
10. Specially refunded interest payments and honoured guarantees	0			
11. Efficiency increasing subsidies	0		35,800	7.0
12. Research and development	1,164	6.5	15,700	3.1
			5,895	1.2

continued

TABLE 5.5 *continued*:

Types of subsidy and loan	1970/71 Current prices	1970/71 Share of total subsidies (%)	1977/78 Current prices	1977/78 Share of total subsidies (%)
Subsidies to maintain preparedness in case of blocked imports	<u>0</u>		<u>116,300</u>	<u>22.9</u>
13. Subsidies conditioned on maintaining a certain level of production	0		76,000	15.1
14. Investment subsidies	0		30,400	6.0
15. Government procurement	0		9,000	1.8
Regional subsidy	<u>12,100</u>	<u>67.9</u>	<u>2,950</u>	<u>0.6</u>
16. Subsidies to firms in depressed areas, including subsidies to encourage firms to move	6,400	35.9	900*	0.2
17. Introduction and education subsidies	4,300	24.1	1,800*	0.4
18. Pure employment subsidy	1,400	7.9	n.a.	
19. Transport subsidy to firms in the north	0		250	0.0

continued

TABLE 5.5 *continued*:

Types of subsidy and loan	1970/71		1977/78	
	Current prices	Share of total subsidies (%)	Current prices	Share of total subsidies (%)
Labour market subsidies				
20. Subsidies to labour over 50 years of age	0		300,670	59.1
21. Subsidy to training when unemployment is the alternative	0		227,300	44.7
	0		60,930[†]	12.0
22. Subsidies to firms threatened by closedown			9,440	1.9
23. Special employment subsidy	0		3,000	0.6
TOTAL	17,817		508,416	
TOTAL in fixed (1974) prices	23,851		377,163	
24. Environmental and energy policy measures (including subsidies to environment improving activities, reduced energy tax, and subsidies to energy-saving activities)	Up to 31.12.77: Approximately 3 m. kr.			

continued

TABLE 5.5 continued:

Types of subsidy and loan	1970/71		1977/78	
	Current prices	Share of total subsidies (%)	Current prices	Share of total subsidies (%)
Loan and credit guarantees				
25. Guarantees for industry loans	3,850		17,270*	
26. Handicraft and industry loans	3,000‡		11,900§	
27. Government banks' loans	0		93,200	
28. Export credit guarantees	1,400		5,600¶	
29. Tariff reduction on imported textile machinery	yes		yes	
TOTAL	8,250		127,970	
TOTAL in fixed (1974) prices	11,044		94,933	

*The period 1.7.77–31.12.77 only.
†The period 1.7.77–31.3.78 only.
‡The calendar year 1972.
§The calendar year 1977, includes the leather and leather goods industry.
¶The fiscal year 1976/1977.

Note: Exchange rates: 1970/71 $US1 = 5.15 kr.; 1977/1978 $US1 = 4.41 kr.
Source: P. G. Nyberg, 'Selektiva näringspolitiska åtgärder för TEKO industrin', mimeo, Statens Industriverk (Stockholm, 1978) from Carl Hamilton (1980).

any such subsidization, the contracting party granting the subsidy shall, upon request, discuss with the other contracting party or parties concerned, or with the CONTRACTING PARTIES, the possibility of limiting the subsidization.[46]

Under Article VI a country can also levy a countervailing duty if it determines that the effect of a domestic subsidy by another country is such as to cause or threaten to cause material injury to one of its industries or an industry in some third country.

Subsidies are accepted now almost as a fact of life although efforts are being made, notably in the OECD, to negotiate restrictions on certain categories, particularly export subsidies. One study was carried out in Sweden by Carl Hamilton to determine the effects of NTBs on import trade and employment with regard to the Swedish textile and clothing industries.[47] Two questions were raised in particular. What would the volume of imports have been in the absence of subsidies? What impact did subsidies have on employment in the textile and clothing industries?

With regard to the first question, the simulation suggested that in the early years of subsidies, between 1971 and 1973, imports would have been 5 per cent higher had there been no subsidies. In 1976 and 1977 the effect on imports was particularly evident, actual imports estimated as having been lower by 8 and 31 per cent respectively than would have been the case in the absence of government subsidies. Subsidies have therefore had considerable trade-distorting effects in the textile and clothing sector.

On the question of employment effects, estimates were made treating textile and clothing industries as one, and assuming subsidies were distributed uniformly across the sector. Results of Hamilton's study showed that between 1973 and 1977 a total of 28,900 man-years were 'saved' of which 34 per cent were in 1977. Subsidies on the whole were found to be more efficient during boom years than during recessionary periods in terms of subsidy costs in relation to jobs 'saved'. Of the five years studied the least efficient years

---

[46] GATT, *Basic Instruments and Selected Documents*, vol. IV (1969).

[47] Carl Hamilton, *A New Approach to Estimation of the Effects of Non-tariff Barriers to Trade on Prices, Employment and Imports: An Application to the Swedish Textile and Clothing Industry* (Stockholm, 1980).

for subsidies were 1973 and 1977, the former only postponing unemployment for one year.

Subsidies reached peak values in 1977 at which time the government not only had to pay subsidies for a particularly high level of potentially unemployed but also an exceptionally high per capita subsidy for these individuals. In other words, Hamilton concluded that subsidies become less effective in proportion to volume and they only managed to postpone the inevitable fall in employment by one to two and a half years.

Further comparisons were made in this study between the cost effectiveness of subsidies and quantitative restrictions. Results showed that the latter were five times more costly to the consumer than the former were to the government budget, US$40,000 and 8,300 respectively.

Domestic subsidies should, in principle, be judged individually without using simple rules to differentiate between 'good' and 'bad' subsidies. Motives for providing subsidies, such as for employment reasons, are just as justifiable in themselves as arguments for efficiency and long-term growth. However, whatever justification is given it is generally agreed that government intervention in many cases contradicts the principles and regulations of the GATT in general and Sweden's international trade policy in particular, in that they interfere with the benefits of trade that result from an efficient allocation of resources. This observation applies then to intervention in favour of welfare promoting measures as well as for reasons of national security. In effect, according to many economists, the inherent contradiction of the state with a strong welfare or defence policy is that it requires a high level of productivity to sustain it, whereas interventionist policies take the emphasis away from efficiency and rising national incomes. Increased intervention will as a consequence result in a more rigid economy which becomes increasingly unable to adjust to the changing environment.[48]

5 MFA and structural adjustments

Sweden's policy towards the textile sector has not consisted solely of subsidies. Tariffs on textiles and clothing follow

[48] See Melvyn Krauss, *The New Protectionism* and W. M. Corden, *Trade Policy and Economic Welfare* (Oxford, 1974).

a classic pattern of escalation (e.g. raw cotton duty-free, cotton yarn 7 per cent, cotton fabrics 13 per cent after MTN reductions, clothing generally 15–17 per cent), but although they are lower than the tariff rates of most OECD countries for textiles and clothing they are higher than the average tariff rate in Sweden for manufactured goods. The authorities in Sweden have also found that subsidies and tariffs are not sufficient in meeting the numerous problems faced by these industries. They have, therefore, increasingly made use of the options at their disposal within the framework of the Multi-Fibre Arrangement.

During the first half of the period in which the LTA was in effect, Sweden made little use of its possibilities for negotiating bilateral agreements to restrict imports from the exporting countries. Intervention of any form was at this time still discouraged. Gradually, however, import restrictions were imposed on those countries which were thought to be penetrating the Swedish market most rapidly. When negotiations began in 1972 for the MFA the situation in Sweden's textile and clothing industries was such that the authorities found it necessary to negotiate a special clause taking the country's particular problems into consideration. Thus the MFA entered into force encompassing a special 'Nordic clause' which recognized the importance of avoiding damage to the minimum viable production of 'Countries having small markets, an exceptionally high level of imports and a correspondingly low level of domestic production'. From this point on, as we shall see in Chapter 6, Sweden's bilateral agreements with exporting countries have escalated in quantity and scope, alongside the intensification of adjustment assistance measures.

The LTA and MFA were established on the principle of market disruption in industrialized countries due to the rapid influx of imports from low-cost developing countries. However, the MFA states specifically that 'Actions taken under this Arrangement shall not interrupt or discourage the autonomous industrial adjustment processes of participating countries.' Furthermore, it goes on to emphasize that actions taken under the Arrangement 'should be accompanied by the pursuit of appropriate economic and social policies, in a manner consistent with national laws and systems, required by changes in the pattern of trade in textiles and in the comparative advantage of participating countries'. The intention was to use such policies to encourage businesses which were 'less competitive internationally to move progressively into more viable lines of production or into other sectors of the economy', thus allowing for increased access to their markets for textile products from developing countries.

As a result of the dissatisfaction on the part of developing countries with the insufficiency of the adjustment measures taken by the importing countries, on the grounds that they were not allowing them (as was intended) a greater access to the developed countries' markets, a major study was prepared for 1980. The results[49] showed that firms had indeed taken advantage of technological innovations and had improved their competitiveness, but that 'it was not possible to establish a direct link between changes in production and trade figures and adjustment processes or measures that have taken place or are being undertaken'. It proved to be even more difficult 'to relate the information available on adjustment processes and measures to the provision of increased access'. In other words, how much evidence of adjustment is necessary to warrant increased access? It was pointed out that governments concerned have found that there are inherent problems in evolving a suitable methodology which would establish this relationship.

With regard to Sweden it is apparent—from the information supplied by the government to the Textiles Committee—that measures have been taken to encourage business to improve the viability of current lines of production, and to move progressively into more viable lines of production. Labour and regional policies also encourage business to move out of the textile sector into other sectors of industry. No assessment of the effect of these measures has been made however.

Concerning access to the Swedish market, the response was that production had already decreased substantially in the last decade. It was, therefore, 'doubtful if adjustment in forms which would imply a further decrease in the production and productive capacity of the industries concerned would be

---

[49] See COM.TEX/15, GATT/AIR/1611, GATT/AIR/1612. COM.TEX/16.

consistent with the objective of avoiding damage to the 'minimum viable production', as well as of securing the supply of essential textile and clothing products'.[50] It was further reported that imports of clothing in 1979 accounted for almost 80 per cent of the total supply in volume terms, 33 per cent in value terms. In this context it was noted that Sweden is the world's largest importer per capita of textiles and clothing from developing countries.[51]

It is clear that Sweden is confronted with a dilemma. On the one hand, it is argued that Sweden's wealth and extensive social welfare policies have been made possible through accordance with GATT principles. On the other hand, the government is faced with the possibility that at a certain point free trade is likely to be incompatible with its security and welfare policies.

The argument for national security reappears frequently in Swedish official statements. It is, moreover, often mentioned in connection with developing country imports. If it is indeed the case that LDC imports are the cause of Sweden's declining 'security', then there seems to be no possibility of meeting its obligations in the MFA, nor towards the LDCs. However, even in this case, the 'security' achieved from protection seems tenuous. Major weaknesses are already appearing in this argument. The subject of the next chapter will be to examine whether there is, indeed, a clear link between security and Sweden's protective MFA policy. If protectionism and industrial policy complement each other and if both are necessary to uphold security objectives, it seems that Sweden must inevitably lock itself into a vicious circle for it is hard to see how, according to its own official view, more vigorous growth can be recaptured with large subsidies and the multiplication of trade restrictions.

---

[50] COM.TEX/16, part C. Adjustment measures and policies relevant to Article 1: 4.

[51] COM.TEX/W/53.

6 Swedish Economic Defence and the Multi-Fibre Arrangement

Introduction

The structure of Sweden's economy has continued to change at a very rapid rate as a consequence of technological advances as well as of liberal trade policies and the changing international division of labour. This transformation has had many positive effects on Sweden. However, it has also altered the Swedish government's perceptions with respect to its national security and the plans necessary for an effective economic defence.

Developments in the basic needs sectors, such as textiles and clothing, have been a primary focus of economic defence plans under such changing conditions. To address the concerns of these sectors the authorities conducted various studies during the post-war period to determine the current situation and future trends and to propose various means of safeguarding needs in case of war or international crisis. While a traditional economic defence has consisted of stockpiling and contingency plans for reorganizing production during a war, the continued decline in production of certain goods has led the authorities to take alternative measures for maintaining an economic defence, namely to provide support to the industry in peacetime to prevent a decline below what is considered a minimum viable production.

The various types of support measures granted to the textile and clothing sectors specifically or on a more general level were discussed in the previous chapter in the context of Sweden's social welfare policies. As we have seen, the subsidies that comprise the various industrial, labour, economic-defence, and other policies have multiplied since 1970. However, while ÖEF administers the subsidies for economic-defence purposes, the government has increasingly promoted quantitative restrictions and other trade policy measures as a complement to subsidies for economic defence. Although it has always been emphasized in Sweden that trade protection is harmful to an efficient allocation of resources, trade policy measures were increasingly justified by Sweden's need as a neutral country to maintain what it considered a minimum viable production (MVP). However, this trade policy, justified on the basis of economic defence, is administered independently of ÖEF and has never been endorsed by it. Moreover ÖEF supports the textile sector primarily for economic defence reasons, while the government protects primarily the clothing sector with its MVP clause. This clause was incorporated into the original MFA signed in 1973. Since that time the clause has also become the subject of considerable controversy in international circles. It has been invoked with increasing frequency and charges that it is being abused have multiplied.

This chapter will examine the rationale behind the inclusion of trade restrictions as part of an overall economic defence. Before 1973 trade policy measures were in peacetime never specifically linked to economic defence. For most sectors only in general terms did Sweden and other countries pursue liberal trade policies with the broader implicit aim of maintaining more peaceful international conditions, hence greater security. Thereafter, so far as textiles were concerned—as we shall see—Sweden's policy demonstrated an apparent belief in an opposing philosophy, that of maintaining security through protectionism.

1 Textiles and clothing in Swedish economic defence policy

(i) *Changing conceptions of economic defence planning*

The policy of economic defence in Sweden was first formulated in the 1930s. During the First World War the supply shortages and the lack of any plan to reorganize the economy for wartime conditions were considered to have had intolerable consequences. Thus the drawing up of a programme for wartime preparation beyond that concerned with the armed services became fundamental. Plans were initiated for stockpiling essential raw materials sufficient to cover a six-month period and for the mobilization of productive resources in case of war.

The aim of economic defence plans has always been to prepare the domestic production apparatus for adaptation to a situation of war, to provide for the country's needs, and to compensate for diminishing imports. However, the conceptions concerning the nature of the war or crisis to which plans must be geared and priorities given have continuously been changing. In 1948 the emphasis in stockpiling was on food and clothing. After the Korean war stockpiling was increased to include a wider scope of raw materials and fuels to last two years. In the 1960s the policy was based on the supposition that imports might be interrupted for an indefinite period and that large sections of the population might have to be evacuated from one area to another.

When plans for the textiles and clothing sectors were first elaborated in 1968 calculations were based on needs for a one-year period during a total blockade in which large-scale evacuations might be necessary. Plans were to cover three categories: (1) clothing supplies for evacuees; (2) supplementary supplies and replacements of worn clothing primarily for children and those being evacuated during the first six months; (3) replacement of worn clothing during the following six months.

The concept of 'total defence' was first implemented in the late 1960s. At this time, instead of planning for a total blockade, plans concentrated on various types of wars or crises that could affect different sectors of the economy. The state was becoming increasingly concerned that the process of specialization had proceeded so far that certain industries risked extinction altogether. Furthermore it was believed that a certain self-sufficiency would guarantee a greater freedom of action during an extended crisis and improve conditions for, and hence credibility in, remaining neutral.

In this new context the question of supply of textiles and clothing was again studied by a specially formed group of experts, Försörjningsberedskapsutredningen (FBU).[1] These studies were primarily based on analyses of supply durability, or the period during which existing supplies were expected to last, as well as minimum standards thought to be viable during a war.[2] It was later realized, however, that goals

---

[1] FBU (Committee on Supply Preparations), set up by the Swedish Riksdag in 1971.

[2] DSH 1972: 3.

established to maintain an adequate defence covering all sectors of the economy would be impossible to fulfil. Present planning is therefore somewhat less ambitious. As a result of the changing concept of defence planning, clothing needs were no longer to be determined by the possibility of a large-scale evacuation[3] but by the eventuality of a blockade lasting from one to three years or even longer.

The study put out by FBU in 1972 was subsequently taken up by the National Board for Economic Defence, ÖEF, for comment and further elaboration. Its final report on the textiles and clothing sectors, published in 1973, produced the estimate that an import level of 10–20 per cent of normal levels could be anticipated. Production plans were to be based on the need to survive a three-year partial blockade, and stockpiling plans on a two-year partial blockade, the time difference stemming from the greater flexibility with which stocks can be manipulated.

(ii) *Supply durability and standards*

In the 1977 government report on 'total defence',[4] the question of supply durability was again addressed. Goals were established with regard to two types of crises, one of short duration and one of longer duration. For a shorter crisis period, such as of one year's duration, no major adaptation of the productive apparatus was expected to be necessary. In such circumstances, however, the authorities were to aim at maintaining large stocks of manufactured and other necessary goods not normally produced at home. For a crisis of long duration the emphasis of planning would be to maintain production capacity or to adapt the production apparatus.

The various types of crises that have been studied include a crisis which involves war among the superpowers in Europe resulting in a partial or total interruption of trade; an attack in which political demands or a military invasion is directed towards Sweden; and a peacetime crisis in which production, employment, exports, and consumption cannot be maintained due to a drop in imports of vital goods as a result of inter-national tension.[5]

---

[3] Prop. 1972: 75, FöU 1972: 17, rskr 1972: 231.
[4] Prop. 1976/7: 74, SOU 1977: 1, FöU 1976/7: 13, rskr 1976/7: 305.
[5] DSH 1977: 1.

The crises on which ÖEF plans have focused include primarily blockades resulting from war between the super-powers in which Sweden is attacked. Some calculations will be shown below representing the anticipated effect of such a blockade, 'D1', which lasts one year approximately. Calculations are based on various hypothetical situations divided into four periods in which imports amount, on average, to 90, 70, 15, and 0 per cent of normal levels. To this calculation is added a fifth period after the crisis lasting two years in which imports would amount on average to 40 per cent of normal levels.

The standards that are aimed at in a crisis, expressed in relative terms, represent a certain percentage of normal consumption but take into consideration the differences in productive capacity of each good. Furthermore, surveys were taken in 1970 and 1976 to estimate the average amount of clothing already existing in homes.[6] These surveys included questions such as the length of time individuals expected their clothing to last. Evaluations were subsequently made by two groups, FBU and the Committee on Textiles and Clothing.[7] Although they came to somewhat different conclusions concerning needs, both groups set their standards for crisis periods at about one-half of the amount of clothing normally maintained, older persons requiring somewhat less than average and growing children somewhat more.[8] Moreover some products were estimated to wear out faster than others, such as socks, underwear, blouses, and shirts. Calculations were adjusted to domestic production capacity and could be used as a basis for a wartime system of rationing. On the whole, however, the results of the surveys show that most people in Sweden believe they have sufficient clothing in most categories to last at least two years on average. It must be pointed out, however, that most people currently buy new clothing when the fashions change or when they tire of something, rather than when clothes are actually worn out beyond repair. Such questionnaires therefore probably

[6] DSH 1972: 3, DSH 1977: 1.

[7] DSH 1977: 1. Much of this information is extracted from the above-mentioned Committee's report as it summarizes previous findings.

[8] The tables were taken from calculations made by the second of these groups, the Committee on Textiles and Clothing (Beklädnadsutredningen).

understate the actual period during which civilians' clothing would last.

Calculations have been made to estimate the amount of production that would be necessary to keep the population clothed during a two- or three-year crisis at various levels of trade.[9] Supplies could be maintained either through

---

[9] The present production capacity, according to estimates, is sufficient with respect to clothing, particularly outer wear, tops and bottoms, and shirts and blouses during both a two- or three-year blockade. However, considering the continuous decline in the sector, it was recommended that developments be closely monitored.

(a) *Knitted-wear sector*
The production capacity is sufficient for tights and thick socks, but would be insufficient for thick socks, ankle- and knee-socks in the event of a three-year crisis with 18 per cent of normal imports. Production of mittens and hats would also be insufficient, but supplies could always be supplemented by hand-knitting at home.

(b) *Woven textiles*
Woven textiles here include categories of actual woven textiles as well as knitted textiles which are made by knitting or crocheting in a knitting machine. Hospital textiles and home furnishings are also included in this category. There are about one hundred weaving firms in the country, many of which are small. Although production capacity is deemed sufficient, a greater concern for the ÖEF is the strong concentration within the industry. It is estimated that 25 per cent of normal imports are necessary to maintain sufficient supplies during a three-year crisis. The machinery used for producing woven textiles is very flexible and can therefore be used for various sub-categories. This is not as true for knitted textiles but this latter category is produced in surplus. However, Sweden is almost completely dependent on imports of yarn for producing textiles.

(c) *Spinning*
Yarns can be spun mainly from natural fibres such as cotton and wool or shorter synthetic (petroleum based) or man-made (based on artificial or cellulose) fibres. Depending on imports, it is estimated that yarn must be produced in the amounts 33,000–69,000 tons during a three-year crisis. The maximum that can be produced in the country is 65,000 tons average per year. Thus a certain capacity exists for spinning but it is limited and only exists with regard to coarse yarns. Stocks are therefore necessary for finer yarns and extra shifts would be necessary for the production during crisis periods. Machinery for the production of yarns cannot be adapted to different types of yarn production. However, possibilities exist in Sweden for producing sisal- jute-, linen-, propane-, and glass-yarns. Moreover, yarns produced domestically could be used in combination with yarns existing in stocks.

(d) *Fibres*
Cellulose or artificial fibres are produced by only one firm in Sweden. At full capacity this firm is capable of producing 30,000 tons per year of which 90 per cent is exported. 35,000 and 70,000 tons of fibres are necessary to produce respectively 33,000 and 65,000 tons of yarn. As mentioned above, 33,000–69,000 tons of yarn are estimated necessary to cover needs during a three-year crisis; thus the production of fibres is at a minimum. In the event of war, these rayon

continuous production using additional shifts, or by maintaining stocks, or a combination of the above. It is interesting to note here that while ÖEF is requested by the government to make estimates for a three-year supply capacity of clothing, this is not the case for other sectors. There is, for instance, currently only a one-year supply for oil.

(iii) *Economic defence in textiles and clothing*

The two prevalent methods of maintaining an economic defence in textiles and clothing consist of stockpiling and maintaining continuous production or a combination of the two. A policy of stockpiling cotton and wool existed as early as the 1930s. Production capacity, on the other hand, was considered sufficient in the various stages of textile and clothing production until the early 1960s. The scope of stockpiling has continued to grow while support measures for production were begun in the early 1970s.

(a) *Production*

It was shown in the last chapter how much production had decreased overall in the past two decades. Domestic production of yarns, fibres, and clothing as a percentage of total supply is particularly low. The country is relatively self-sufficient only in knitted wear and cloth woven from continuous synthetic and man-made fibres. Thus the authorities launched a programme in the early 1970s of artificially maintaining production in certain sectors which were considered incapable of surviving international competition. The various methods of maintaining continuous production when it is not normally profitable consist of trade measures; government assistance measures at the various investment, production or consumption levels; and obtaining agreements from firms that they will use domestic inputs in production. General measures such as manipulating taxes or exchange rates can also be used.

fibres could, however, also be mixed with cotton or wool as in the Second World War. Stocks of cotton and wool fibres are also minimal, however, respectively 5,600 and 2,000 tons, and fibres made from cellulose cannot be used for all purposes. This sector is therefore considered the most vulnerable in case of crisis, yet it is the most vital, being the 'raw material' for all domestic production of made-up articles.

TABLE 6.1. *Civilian needs for certain important clothes ('000)*

Goods	Three-year crisis			Total	Two-year crisis Total
	Year 1	Year 2	Year 3		
Outer wear (incl. jackets)					
Men	830	1,390	1,200	3,420	2,220
Women	555	1,290	1,340	3,185	1,845
Children	1,000	1,500	1,500	4,000	2,500
Tops					
Men (sweaters and jackets)	1,860	2,690	2,860	7,410	4,500
Women (sweaters and suits)	2,650	3,080	3,390	9,120	5,730
Children	2,000	4,000	4,000	10,000	6,000
Bottoms					
Men (slacks)	3,240	2,990	5,200	11,430	6,230
Women (slacks, skirts, suits, dresses)	1,980	2,360	4,970	9,300	4,330
Children	2,000	4,000	4,000	10,000	6,000
Protective clothing, overalls					
Men	2,000	2,000	2,000	6,000	4,000
Women	1,500	1,500	1,500	4,500	3,000
Shirts, blouses					
Men	2,000	2,500	2,000	9,500	4,500
Women	1,500	2,000	3,000	6,500	3,500
Children	1,000	2,000	2,000	5,000	3,000
Underwear					
Men	7,500	9,300	9,300	26,000	16,800
Women	6,800	11,300	11,300	29,400	18,100
Children	3,700	4,400	4,400	12,500	8,100
Socks and tights					
Men	13,200	18,000	18,000	49,200	31,200
Women	31,200	34,000	34,000	99,200	65,200
Children	7,600	7,600	7,600	22,800	15,200

Source: Beklädnadsutredning, Ds H 1977: 1.

Maintaining production for purposes of economic defence, however, carries a high cost burden and has a number of other disadvantages. If the competitiveness of these industries continues to decline despite subsidies and other forms of assistance, the costs of increasing assistance will obviously increase and surpass the benefits which may, in any event, be somewhat tenuous. ÖEF has therefore considered the

TABLE 6.2. *Production needs for clothing during a three- or two-year crisis (items m.)**

	Three-year crisis Production needs when imports:				Lowered standard	Possible production	Two-year crisis				Possible production
	125%D1 48%	100%D1 38%	75%D1 28%	50%D1 18%	100%D1 38%		125%D1 48%	100%D1 38%	75%D1 28%	50%D1 18%	
Outer wear											
Tops	20.6	21.5	23.5	28.6	(12.3)	40.0	11.8	12.8	13.5	16.1	23.0
Bottoms	17.8	19.9	23.7	23.4	(12.7)	46.0	9.9	10.0	11.2	14.2	26.0
Protective clothing and overalls	10.2	10.2	10.2	10.2	(7.6)	29.9	6.7	6.7	6.7	6.7	12.0
Shirts, blouses	7.5	7.6	9.6	14.0	(5.6)	20.0	4.6	4.7	4.7	6.2	12.0
Underwear	46.9	53.2	60.6	71.9	(38.2)	82.0	28.5	31.4	37.8	44.8	46.0
Hats, mittens, etc.	18.7	19.5	20.9	22.1	(13.6)	15.0	12.9	13.8	14.6	15.3	9.0
Thick socks, ankle and knee socks	72.4	77.1	82.8	88.5	(51.6)	97.0	44.1	47.7	50.5	55.1	51.0
Tights	75.2	75.2	75.2	75.2	(55.3)	97.0	115.0	48.7	48.7	48.7	77.0
(Million m2)											
Woven textiles	89	109	144	192	(73)	158	45	61	78	106	88
Knitted textiles	51	55	63	75	(52)	325	31	32	37	45	185
(Tons)											
Corded yarns	18,000	19,600	24,300	31,600	(11,800)	33,600	10,700	11,800	12,900	17,400	18,700
Combed yarns	150	300	850	1,800	(50)	3,200	—	100	250	700	1,800
Cotton yarn	14,800	19,200	25,600	35,600	(9,800)	28,700	8,700	10,400	13,400	20,100	16,300
Continuous fibres: synthetic	12,100	13,500	15,300	17,500	(8,700)	—	7,900	8,600	9,500	10,900	—
man-made	—	—	—	200	—	—	—	—	—	—	—

*With varying assumptions with regard to imports expressed as percentages of imports in situation D1 (38% of normal) and of peacetime normal imports
Source: Beklädnadsutredning, Ds H 1977: 1.

possibility of subsidizing passive capacity (*malpåse*), that is, allowing for a certain decline in production but subsidizing firms to maintain their machinery so that they may be put to use in the event of a crisis or other disturbance affecting imports. However, the risks associated with this possibility are, according to the government, first, that the machinery quickly becomes outdated and, secondly, that it would be difficult during a crisis period to assemble manpower having sufficient skills to start up production. This would be particularly true for production of yarns and fibres and for repairs of the machinery. Furthermore, some machinery for the basic textile industries must be used continuously for technical reasons. However, these risks seem rather minor if there were actual wars or crises when compared with similar circumstances in other sectors such as electronics. With regard to production of clothing, on the other hand, there is less of a need for highly skilled personnel. Moreover it is estimated that one out of every two households has an electric sewing machine which could easily and effectively be used to repair old clothing or even to make new clothing.

Nevertheless, according to the authorities, an effective economic defence must involve continuous production with only limited reliance on passive capacity. Alternatively a way must be found to have access to trained personnel during crisis periods.

(b) *Stockpiling*

The more traditional means of maintaining an economic defence and an alternative to artificially sustaining production consists of stockpiling. While the production of textiles had previously been considered sufficient not to warrant stockpiling, from the beginning of the 1960s there was a considerable reduction in certain industries. At this time, the spinning industry was increasingly surpassed by more modern techniques in the knitting industry, which resulted in fewer fine yarns being produced in Sweden. Thus basic stocks of raw materials were supplemented with fine yarns. From the late 1960s stocks of woven goods increased; but this was for the purposes of the labour market rather than of economic defence. Finally, buffer stocks of hospital textiles were increased in 1976.

The costs involved in stockpiling are very high. In addition to state purchases, the high costs accrue as a result of investments, transportation, handling, administration, rents, interest, and replacement of old goods. Because of the considerable expenses, the authorities maintain stocks only if the goods cannot be produced domestically. Primarily, this includes cotton and cotton yarns, wool, synthetic yarns, and fibres. The present goal is to maintain stocks of two-thirds the calculated needs and to supplement this only if international tensions increase noticeably.

The new aspect of economic defence that was recognized during the 1960s and the 1970s was that certain sectors of the economy were declining rapidly and that stockpiling alone was no longer a viable means of economic defence. Production subsidies were thus initiated in the early 1970s in order to assist firms to adjust to new conditions and to become competitive. These subsidies reached their peak in 1980/1 when a total of 490 m. kr. were paid although they are gradually being decreased as the industry restructures and becomes more competitive. However, the government could also have raised the possibility of an increased role for the private sector in maintaining stocks such as is the policy of Switzerland and Finland. The actual defence motivations in Sweden became even more questionable when 47 per cent of the ÖEF programme budget (1984) was devoted to the textile sector.

Trade policy measures such as the use of quotas were first thought of as an alternative to subsidies to be used only as a last resort in connection with economic defence. There were two obvious reasons for this reluctance to engage in trade policy measures: first, the Swedes risked retaliation by other countries and, second, such measures could undermine the country's obligations with respect to the GATT. Nevertheless, such latitude as was available to Sweden within the GATT, specifically in the context of the MFA, began to be employed to the fullest advantage and, or so the government's critics maintained both internally and externally, they increasingly adopted a protectionist stance which went well beyond the letter and spirit of the Agreement. How Sweden has utilized the provisions of the MFA in pursuing its textile trade policy will be the subject of the next section. It must, however, be emphasized from the start that the policy of applying trade restrictions based on the government's official economic-defence objectives has never been endorsed by the Director of the ÖEF. In an interview with the author (summer 1984) he stated clearly that he did not believe that a trade policy for economic defence purposes could ever fulfil Sweden's desired security goals. If anything, they were counter-productive, especially when applied in the clothing sector which, he believed, should not be covered at all under the policy of economic defence.

2 Swedish policy within the MFA framework

(i) *The evolution, a co-ordinated textile trade policy*

The period of rapid growth in the 1950s and 1960s is often associated with the liberalization of trade within a multilateral framework. Post-war developments, such as the creation of the EEC, and EFTA and the multilateral negotiations within GATT for large-scale tariff reductions, were fully in line with this general tendency. But even in the middle of this period of unprecedented growth, certain forces opposed to liberal trade were already emerging, notably in textile trade. As with agriculture, no-one in the 1940s or 1950s could have predicted the problems that these sectors would encounter during the later post-war period. Yet the coming into force of the LTA in 1962 in fact legalized, within a multilateral framework, the use of unilateral and bilateral trade restrictions under certain specified conditions. However, given that the LTA was meant to be temporary and similar in many respects to the Article XIX clause, it seems unlikely that potential conflicts were anticipated by those who conceived and negotiated it.

When the LTA was negotiated Sweden's role and stake in it were minor. Although from the 1950s the decline of the textiles sector had been a concern in Sweden, it was not yet seen by the state as a problem for economic security originating in developing countries, nor as one to be remedied through trade measures. Nevertheless some trade restrictions had been initiated in the 1950s outside the scope of any international trade agreement. In 1958 some of the European countries, including Sweden, concluded an agreement known

as the Noordwijk Agreement which aimed at restricting the
re-export to each others' domestic markets of fabric processed
from grey cloth coming from certain Asian countries. Bilateral
agreements had also been established as standard practice in
the commercial relations between Sweden and the centrally
planned economies. These agreements—which were
periodically renegotiated and covered many, though not all,
products—consisted of quotas generally established for
textiles of all fibres. Agreements which among other things
specifically covered trade in textiles were reached for an
indefinite period with China in 1957, and for five-year periods
with the USSR in 1970, Poland and Bulgaria in 1972, and in
1973 with Czechoslovakia, the German Democratic
Republic, and Romania. Licences were required for imports
from most Eastern bloc countries and specific ceilings were
fixed when necessary. Also, at the commencement of the LTA
Sweden maintained a quota, agreed upon 1 April 1959, on
imports of practically all textile items from Japan. For imports
from Taiwan, a non-member, Sweden applied restraints on
socks, knitted under-garments and outer-garments, and woven
under- and outer-garments, by value quotas established under
import licensing provisions.

Thus, as imports from low-cost sources were increasing, the
Swedish government foresaw certain potential benefits from
participating in the LTA. However, during the course of the
LTA the composition and geographical distribution of the
textile trade underwent numerous and rapid changes which led
the participants to seek solutions to textile trade problems outside the LTA. Increasingly Sweden and other LTA participants
resorted to voluntary export restraints[10] and import licensing.

Even with the LTA in force Sweden continued to negotiate
restraint agreements outside the scope of the Arrangement
with respect to certain wool and man-made fibre apparel
products which were covered by the LTA.[11] Such trade

---

[10] VERs are usually stated in volume terms for each CCC category (Customs
Cooperation Council Nomenclature, formerly Brussels Nomenclature (BTN)) as
number of shirts, tons of towels, etc. Later, volume and value quotas were used.

[11] Article 9 of the LTA states, 'For purposes of this Arrangement the
expression "cotton textiles" includes yarns, piece-goods, made-up articles,
garments and other textile manufactured products in which cotton represents
more than 50 per cent (by weight) of the fibre content, with the exception of
hand-loom fabrics of the cottage industry.'

restrictions were imposed on Hong Kong (1968), Korea (1967), Macao (1970), Singapore (1972), and Taiwan (1968). The only two countries with which LTA restrictions were maintained were Japan[12] and Hong Kong.[13] Although the government was increasingly resorting to trade policy measures in general to deal with its declining textile industry, the problems were clearly less in the cotton sector than in wool and man-made fibre apparel sectors. Finally, after eleven years of the Arrangement regarding cotton textiles, participants agreed that a new arrangement was necessary to incorporate non-cotton products and newcomers to trade in this sector.

(ii) *The inclusion of a national security element*

When negotiations for the MFA were initiated in 1972, Sweden had begun to see its situation with regard to the textile and clothing sectors as increasingly serious. Some internal measures had been taken as part of the labour market and regional policies, and in the early 1970s adjustment assistance—and export-stimulating—measures were added to stimulate the development of more competitive industries. Yet the need was increasingly seen for a further safeguard clause in the event that internal measures were not sufficient to prevent these sectors from further decline. The MFA negotiations were therefore an opportunity for the Swedish authorities to include a special clause that could be tailor-made to suit the specific situation in which they perceived themselves to be.

The policy statement submitted by Sweden in connection with the preparation for the Study leading to the negotiation of the MFA included the following remarks:

By participating in the work of GATT, EFTA and other organizations, Sweden assumed a number of obligations in the field of trade policies. Sweden has, however, found it necessary in a number of cases to make certain exceptions from its basic free trade policy. These deviations are intended as temporary and they have been implemented over the last few years in situations of sudden and serious market disturbances, usually in connection with rapid increases in imports of certain textiles from new producer countries in South and East Europe and Asia.

---

[12] COT/M/5.   ·   [13] COT/M/9, COT/M/10, COT/100 and Add. 1.

Such developments have seriously complicated the gradual adjustment of domestic enterprises to a new competitive situation and have *jeopardized the continued existence even of the viable parts of the business of vital importance for the country and the national security* . . .

As to the economic and social reasons and objectives of the restrictive trade measures mentioned earlier, the reader is referred to what has already been said concerning Swedish trade policies in the field of textiles. In addition it should be noted that the *sizeable increases in imports and the reduction in the degree of self-sufficiency have given rise to fears that Sweden would not be able to maintain a satisfactory supply of textiles and clothing in case of a blockade.*[14] (Author's emphases.)

Swedish negotiators were successful in their aim to include in the MFA a 'minimal viable production' clause. This clause was agreed to as follows: 'In the case of those countries having *small markets*, an exceptionally *high level of imports* and a correspondingly *low level of domestic production*, account should be taken of the avoidance of damage to those countries "minimum viable production" of textiles.' (Author's emphases.)

Serious disputes concerning the 'MVP' clause did not appear until after 1977, yet the question may legitimately be asked why other parties agreed to such a clause which was later to become a source of such contention. The most likely answer lies in the acknowledgement that Sweden has always been among the more liberal countries in the GATT and the question of possible abuse of any GATT clauses never occurred to the other negotiating parties. Moreover, by the time the MFA negotiations began, Sweden already had the highest per capita imports of clothing of any West European country, and was able to present its case in such a way that convinced other member governments that it was really in a special situation (along with Norway and Finland)[15] and merited certain exceptions to the rules. Developing countries may have accepted the clause for similar reasons; that a safeguard clause was justifiable given the rapid speed with

---

[14] L/3797, 1973.
[15] Sweden, Norway, and Finland negotiated the 'MVP' clause as a bloc. For this reason, the MVP clause is also known as the 'Nordic clause'.

which the sector was declining in Sweden, the special problems of adjustment, and the consistently good relations with the Third World countries. Beyond this, the validity of the 'national security' argument seems not to have been questioned and further proof was not demanded.

Perceptions were certainly changing within Sweden concerning the vulnerability of the country. Many believed that the policy of liberal trade was leading the country into a precariously dependent position and that conditions had to be altered in order to render more credible the policy of neutrality. Until the late 1960s all discussion about changing international conditions and the increasing economic vulnerability of society was met with scepticism if not disbelief.[16] But by 1971 such ideas had begun to be taken seriously. For example, a group of experts was called upon by the Swedish Parliament, the Riksdag, to study the state of security of supply with regard to textiles and shoes. The study was finished in January 1972 in time to have an impact on the Swedish demands in the MFA negotiations.

(iii) Sweden's performance during MFA 1

The new textiles Arrangement entered into force 1 January 1974, covering a greater number of products and adding several significant new elements to the system of internationally agreed rules for the conduct of trade in textiles. One of these was the institution of continuous international surveillance in the form of the Textiles Surveillance Body (TSB). Participants to the Arrangement were required to disclose to the TSB all information about agreements concluded bilaterally or measures taken unilaterally in order to allow it to make a continuous review and evaluation of them. The TSB in turn was required to submit annual reports to the Textiles Committee on the operation of the Arrangement, as well as a more complete report for the major review of the Arrangement in the third year. The first major report appeared in 1976 and covered among other things the relative frequency of recourse to the main operative Articles of the Arrangement. Articles 3 and 4, and the extent to which restrictions had increased or diminished since the signing of the MFA.

---

[16] Nils Andrén, FOA.

During these first years of the MFA Sweden's actions were generally in conformity with its principles and regulations. There was even evidence of Sweden's increasing access to its market.

Sweden concluded bilateral agreements under Article 3 with Hong Kong, India, Korea, and Macao covering specific products. They were later renegotiated as Article 4 agreements which are supposed to be more liberal in overall terms including particularly growth and flexibility. Malaysia and Singapore were then also included on this list.

Although the product coverage of most Swedish agreements in this period remained selective, restraints were introduced on some new products and liberalized on others.[17] However, by adopting the system of annual agreements Sweden managed to avoid providing for an annual growth of exports. Each new agreement instead necessitated negotiations on quota levels for which there were no established minima. Sometimes they were raised substantially, sometimes hardly at all. In some cases there were apparent cutbacks on past restraint levels (India and Malaysia).

Conflicts in Sweden's agreements came up only once during this initial four-year period. In June 1975, after failing to reach agreement under Article 3 with Mexico, Sweden decided to ask the TSB to make an examination and recommendation—Mexico's imports were claimed to be the cause of market disruption—but the TSB, while agreeing that a real risk of market disruption might exist, concluded that the Swedish claim could not be sustained. The TSB finally recommended that the two parties consult again with a view to finding means of eliminating these risks and ensuring an orderly development of trade. Shortly afterwards, however,

---

[17] In the case of Hong Kong, two items were liberalized and three, including socks, added to the list of restrictions. Two out of three items were liberalized for India; for Macao, knitted undergarments were placed under restrictions. In the agreement with Singapore one item was liberalized but product coverage was extended to shirts, knitted underwear and sweaters, woven trousers and blouses. Restrictions with Japan were gradually phased out except for one new item. For Korea new restraints were introduced on sweaters, overcoats, and jackets and trousers. Finally two new restrictions were concluded under Article 3 with Pakistan and a non-participant, Malta, covering knitted under-garments, bed linen and towels of cotton, and trousers. COM.TEX/W/SB/186 and COM.TEX/W/SB/196.

imports from Mexico declined and Sweden no longer considered it necessary to continue with negotiations.

It was in 1977 that protectionist pressures began to mount and Sweden's bilateral negotiations and attitude in the MFA began to take an increasingly contentious character. While Sweden's restraint agreements were really no more comprehensive than, for example, the EEC's, the shift in trade policy both in substance and in style took a number of countries by surprise. There was a feeling among other participating countries that the MVP clause was being unduly extended.

When the MVP clause had been negotiated the intention was to allow Sweden the possibility of lower growth rates regarding LDC imports than the MFA requirement of 6 per cent annual growth. It appeared, however, that Sweden was beginning to interpret this clause in an increasingly loose and open-ended way.

The MVP clause was not understood to cover the flexibility provisions such as the provisions of Annex B, paragraph 5, relating to 'swing'. Flexibility according to swing provisions implied that the restraint level for any one product might be exceeded, normally by 7 per cent, provided that the aggregate level for all products within the overall quota was not exceeded. Swing was also to be permitted both between groups of products and between individual products. However, in three of Sweden's agreements negotiated during 1977 with Macao, Malaysia, and Thailand the TSB noted that no provision had been made for swing. It was assumed by the TSB that the parties had agreed to waive this right, but no written explanation was notified to the TSB, nor was any further comment provided.

Some of the most frequent disputes in the application of the MFA arose from unilateral measures taken under Article 3:5 which normally resulted from failure to conclude a bilateral agreement. In 1976, Sweden found itself in this situation with regard to imports from India of bed-linen and women's blouses. Following unilateral action by Sweden under Article 3: 5, India presented a complaint to the TSB. Complaint was in this case considered justified since Sweden had neglected to follow the prescribed procedures for the application of unilateral measures which called primarily for notification to the TSB. The two countries were unable to come to agreement by the time the first MFA expired. The dispute with India resulted in considerable ill feeling. As mentioned previously, India is one of Sweden's most important aid recipients. A number of developing countries denounced Sweden's actions of providing aid to India in favour of industrialization on the one hand and then, in effect, on the other denying the country the possibility to industrialize by preventing it from developing in areas in which it has a comparative advantage.

An agreement was finally reached with India concerning bed-linen, but restraints were maintained on women's blouses and extended to woven cotton shirts. Moreover the TSB held that Sweden had presented insufficient information on imports demonstrating evidence of market disruption.

Discussions with Pakistan concerning growth provisions remained at a standstill throughout 1975, 1976, and 1977. No agreement on growth was reported to the TSB by either party until 1978 when a new Article 4 agreement had been decided upon.

Sweden did, however, take unilateral action under Article 3: 5 on imports of cotton blouses from Pakistan and, as in the case of India's exports, no agreement was reached by the time MFA 2 was negotiated. Explicit reference was made here to the provisions of Annex A and Sweden's need to protect its minimum viable production, a claim which Pakistan disputed. The TSB intervened to recommend further consultations and, in the meantime, to replace the unilateral restrictions by voluntary export arrangements.

An Article 4 agreement was concluded with Singapore on its exports of shirts and blouses, sweaters, pullovers, trousers, and some knitted under-garments. There were no swing provisions in the agreement.

Certain relevant actions were also taken outside the scope of the MFA which reflected the increasingly protectionist trends in Sweden. An 'import licensing' system[18] was

[18] The effect of this kind of 'supervision' on exporting countries is discussed in J. N. Bhagwati and T. N. Srinivasan, 'Optimal Trade Policy and Compensation under Endogenous Uncertainty: The Phenomenon of Market Disruption', *Journal of International Economics*, 6 (1976), 317–36.

established from 1 January 1976 requiring licences for all imports of textiles and clothing except those from the EEC and EFTA but including Portugal. It was indicated that such a system would improve supervision of imports and thereby upgrade economic defence preparations in case further restrictions became necessary.[19]

Restrictive measures taken *vis-à-vis* non-MFA-members included two bilateral agreements with Malta and one with Portugal. The latter was particularly controversial given the free trade arrangement, EFTA, of which both Sweden and Portugal were members. Very little publicity was given to this agreement; in fact, it was only by mistake that it became publicized. Furthermore, Portugal was one of Sweden's traditional aid recipients. Gradually this aid relationship was to be replaced by one based on greater 'equality' but the new restrictions seemed to reflect an unusual precedent.[20]

Although there is seemingly a contradiction here between trade policy and Sweden's other economic agreements with Portugal, the restrictive textile agreements were accepted by the Portuguese. Some LDC trade representatives have confirmed that the contradictions exist but that Sweden circumvents them by using the argument that aid policies have indeed been progressive and exceptions should therefore be allowed.

Thus, during this first phase Sweden had made significant deviations from its MFA obligations, even when the economic situation had not yet deteriorated very much.

(iv) *The MFA Protocol of Extension—an attempt to tighten up Sweden's policy*

By the time the first 'major review' was completed in 1976, negotiations were scheduled to begin, 'in order to consider

---

[19] *Aktuellt i Handelspolitiken* 9/1975, a periodical published by the Department of Trade, containing speeches, statistics, etc.

[20] In this context, a declaration was signed, 11 Mar. 1975, between Portugal and Sweden with the aim of increasing economic co-operation. 'The Parties agreed to increase cooperation with the aim of furthering economic and social development in Portugal. Conditions for such cooperation were considered particularly favourable in the following areas: industrial development, construction of housing, education, transportation and telecommunications'. Included in the declaration were plans to investigate possibilities to establish a multilateral fund for industry and development in order to further industrial development in Portugal. *Aktuellt i Handelspolitiken* 3/1975.

whether the Arrangement should be extended, modified, or discontinued'.[21] The MFA already covered a much more extensive range of products than the LTA and its provisions had been elaborated to contain detailed rules governing the level and growth of quotas and flexibility provisions between products and over time. Yet trading conditions were constantly changing. Consequently the dual purpose of the MFA to provide for liberalization of restrictions within a legal framework and for the orderly development of trade began to rest on an increasingly fragile balance.

Negotiations to determine the future of the MFA were initiated in the context of a recession and a particularly acute pressure on the textile and clothing industries in the OECD countries. None the less, there were significant differences in the evolution of trade among participating countries. Among the developed, importing countries, import demand was the strongest in the EEC but the overall situation was seen by many observers to be deteriorating the most rapidly. Sweden's import surplus in textiles and clothing increased from $585 million in 1973 to $870 million in 1975, the period covered by the major review. Imports per capita from LDCs were $42 and from all other sources $118.[22]

Most importing countries expressed their desire in principle to renew the Arrangement. The EEC and the Nordic countries, however, aimed at a more restrictive MFA. The Community sought drastic solutions to curb imports. After three years of recession, they insisted on the need to 'stabilize the market'. In effect they sought a freeze in the growth of imports from all sources. Their rationale for protecting their market included additional factors such as the rate of import penetration, evolution of domestic consumption, cumulative effects of imports, and the price factor taken in isolation in interpreting market disruption. However, the Community was not alone in its preoccupations. The situation in the Nordic countries had deteriorated considerably in the textiles and clothing sectors. Norway and Sweden in particular wanted a strengthening of the minimum viable production clause. Considering the rapid decline in production and employment in Sweden, the government clearly intended to

---

[21] Article 10, paragraph 5. [22] COM.TEX/SB/196, p. 47.

pursue a more offensive policy. From the previous chapter it is evident that a number of internal political and economic factors had resulted in pressure on the government to negotiate more stringent bilateral agreements and an MFA more favourable to Swedish interests.[23]

The outcome of the negotiations was, however, not purely a result of domestic pressures independent of the position of other MFA members. Specifically the firm stand taken by the EEC, negotiating as one party, was undoubtedly influential in Sweden's moves to tighten up its policy. Very early on in the negotiations for a new MFA, it became clear that the Arrangement hinged on the position taken by the EEC as the most dominant importing party. The EEC not only managed to negotiate a very vaguely worded 'reasonable departures' clause,[24] but also made the successful conclusion of bilateral agreements a condition for signing the extension.

The Swedish negotiators increasingly seemed to acquire the attitude that the MFA was an instrument that should be used in its favour and that Sweden should begin to 'take advantage' of its possibilities to restrict textile imports, at least to the same extent as the EEC. Sweden therefore decided to use the MFA to the limit and to start 'playing the game'[25] by following, and indeed going further, than the actions of larger importing countries. Reference was therefore made to the trade problems of the small importing countries with high levels of imports and low domestic production. These were

[23] During the year of negotiations in 1977 a special Council was established under the Ministry of Industry for the textile and clothing industries which included representatives from the government employees and employers. This was a further indication of the importance given to the sector by the government and the increasing control it felt obliged to exercise. The creation of the Council was followed by the formation in 1978 of a special Board to co-ordinate government measures. This latter Board had a significant scope for domestic pressure on trade policy. One may add that nationalizing firms also facilitated access to government.

[24] Paragraph 5.3: 'The Committee agreed that . . . negotiations should be conducted in a spirit of equity and flexibility with a view to reaching a mutually acceptable solution under Article 4 . . . or Article 3 . . . which does include the possibility of jointly agreed reasonable departures from particular elements in particular cases'. 5.4: 'It was agreed that any such departures as mentioned . . . would be temporary and that participants concerned shall return in the shortest possible time to the framework of the Arrangement'.

[25] Words of a government official interviewed in Stockholm.

to be resolved in a spirit of 'equity and flexibility' and their minimum viable production was to be fully maintained.

When the Swedish negotiators pressed for an improved application of the Nordic clause, no one seriously challenged that particular clause. Again this was somewhat surprising considering the apparent lack of real solid evidence to back up the MVP claim. While employment was certainly a verifiable factor, the official justification for MVP was the need for economic defence and no explicit treatment of the security problem had ever been presented in such fora as the Textiles Committee. The blurring of the various Swedish problems seemed to be ignored.

It is true that Sweden still has, in general, a liberal reputation in GATT, and other importers could hardly complain about Sweden when in effect they were also pressing for more restrictive measures in textiles and clothing. Exporting countries were probably also more concerned about curbing the demands of the leading importers, such as the EEC and the US, than about Swedish requests. Sweden's market was far from the most significant.

The Protocol extending the Arrangement was concluded on 14 December 1977. The Swedish government announced that although it welcomed the conclusion of a Protocol it was not yet in a position to sign. Following the EEC, both Norway and Sweden made the satisfactory conclusion of bilateral agreements a condition for signing the Protocol. Norway failed to reach a satisfactory conclusion to its bilateral negotiations with Hong Kong and henceforth declined to renew its membership in the MFA. It instead invoked and maintained Article XIX action, which, in contrast to the MFA, does not contain obligatory growth provisions. Sweden, on the other hand, concluded new bilateral agreements and signed the Protocol in April 1979.

Negotiations ended successfully for Sweden. The Conservative minister of Trade in 1977, Burenstam-Linder, stated that provided the Multi-Fibre Arrangement could be prolonged according to the conditions agreed in the summer of 1977, it should imply improved possibilities for Sweden to curtail disturbing low-price imports given that bilateral agreements could be concluded: 'We have also been assured of an improved application of the Nordic clause.'[26]

In the new Protocol, Sweden successfully negotiated the inclusion of a paragraph reaffirming the importance of its minimum viable production needs. Paragraph 6 of the Protocol reads,

> The Committee recognised that countries having small markets, an exceptionally high level of imports and a correspondingly low level of domestic production are particularly exposed to the trade problems mentioned in the preceding paragraphs, and that their problems should be resolved in a spirit of equity and flexibility. In the case of those countries, the provisions of Article 1, paragraph 2 (MVP of MFA) should be fully implemented.

(v) *Intensified use and abuse of the MVP clause*

Sweden notified the TSB of a large number of bilateral agreements following the renewal of the MFA. Although some MFA countries did ease up some of their restrictions, the majority of importing countries increased both the number of agreements and the range of products covered. New countries had joined the rank of suppliers upon whom restraint agreements were immediately imposed. Forty-one countries participated in the second phase. Growth rates were also often fixed at a lower rate than the norm set by the MFA. In effect there was a loosening up of the framework with less rigid interpretation of and respect for the rules. The new set of agreements was frequently modified and was so complex that it became more and more difficult to analyse. Although the alternative to such an arrangement presented potentially much less favourable possibilities for exporters, the network of agreements under MFA 2 was on the whole more restrictive than under MFA 1 without providing greater transparency in trade relations. The situation resulted in a great deal of concern as to the implications for the future of textile trade, as well as for trade in other sectors and indeed for the whole GATT system itself.

Much of the frustration involved in the relaxation of the system was borne by the TSB which had the increasingly delicate task of supervising the Arrangement. Its difficulties

---

[26] Prop. 1977/8: 82, p. 66.

were aggravated by the need to reach a consensus each time it was notified of a complaint. In some cases parties renounced the procedures of the TSB altogether and worked out their conflicts bilaterally.

Among the major obstructing factors to a smooth functioning of the system were the increasingly liberal interpretations of the MVP clause and the introduction of the 'reasonable departures' clause. Although the latter was negotiated by the EEC, no particular country was referred to specifically in the paragraph. Other importing countries therefore felt that the clause could apply to them as well so that they too could refer to it in their new agreements. On this occasion, Sweden also asserted this right, although referral to the MVP clause was much more frequent.

During the 1970s the decline in production and employment was critical in Sweden. In this context the government gave 'more and more attention . . . to the problems connected with securing the supply of essential textile and clothing products in case Sweden would be cut off from its present source of supply'.[27]

During the course of the renewed Arrangement Sweden's methods of interpreting and applying MFA regulations deviated significantly from its obligations under the Arrangement and have been perhaps the greatest source of contention in the MFA evoking harsh criticism from exporting countries. Even in Sweden some officials admit to 'unorthodox' and 'arrogant' behaviour. A very liberal interpretation of the MVP clause has extended to provisions not only on growth rates but also on all the flexibility provisions including 'swing', 'carry-over', and 'carry-forward'. When the MVP clause was originally drawn up it was indeed vague, but the stipulation was clear that it should apply only to growth provisions and that it should not extend to flexibility. In other words, restraint levels could be fixed at less than the 6 per cent growth rate set out in the MFA if there was evidence of risk or market disruption. However, ignoring, as Sweden increasingly did, the right to flexibility provisions implied a more rigid system for the exporting countries than the one originally agreed,

[27] COM.TEX/S/65, 11.1979.

preventing them from the possibility of filling their quotas by any other means.

In the second 'major review' carried out during 1980, the third year of the MFA, large sections were devoted to Sweden's bilateral agreements as well as the TSB's comments on them.[28]

Of the eleven agreements in the previous phase, ten were renewed. Only the arrangement with Japan was allowed to lapse and two new agreements were negotiated. By the end of the period the restrained exporting countries included Hong Kong, India, Korea, Macao, Malaysia, Malta, Mauritius, Pakistan, Philippines, Singapore, Sri Lanka, Thailand, and Yugoslavia.

During this second phase of the MFA there was a trend in most importing countries towards an intensification and proliferation of restrictions. Japan and Switzerland were the only two industrialized countries which imposed no restrictions on LDCs. The general tightening up of restrictions was applied only against imports from LDCs and state-trading countries despite the sharp increase in US exports to many of the other industrialized, importing countries, sometimes at very low prices. Restrictions against the only developed country, Japan, were progressively dismantled.

The concept of 'reasonable departures' was an EC creation intended for use against dominant suppliers. In fact, all importing countries resorted to departures from the MFA elements and Sweden most extensively. The existence of an MVP clause allowed for a reduction of growth to lower positive rates but never to negative rates. In practice the growth rate was often reduced to zero, cutbacks were frequent, and flexibility provisions were rarely in evidence. Departures were applied not only to dominant suppliers but equally to small suppliers and new entrants who were supposed to be given additional protection under the Arrangement. Quotas were in some instances placed on countries having next to no exports.

---

[28] See Annexe, pp. 204–11.

(vi) *MFA 3*

In late 1981 agreement was finally reached on a new Protocol extending the Arrangement until July 1986. The major conflicts arising during the negotiations boiled down to an accommodation of the Community's minimum requirements of extending restrictions in a period of recession and the LDCs' aim to restore discipline to the MFA. With respect to the Nordic countries, it was agreed that the exporting LDCs would enlarge the scope of concessions available in the MFA for those countries required to maintain a minimum viable production. Sweden and Finland had sought not only to extend their rights for waiving flexibility provisions, but also to modify restraint levels for products where the domestic industry's share sank to less than 40 per cent of the market. Although they were unsuccessful in taking the MVP interpretation to this extreme, they managed to include a vaguely worded paragraph ultimately allowing for a waiver of flexibility provisions subject to mutual acceptance; paragraph 11 read as follows:

The Committee recognized that countries having small markets, an exceptionally high level of imports and a correspondingly low level of domestic production are particularly exposed to the problems arising from imports causing market disruption as defined in Annex A, and that their problems should be resolved in a spirit of equity and flexibility in order to avoid damage to those countries' minimum viable production of textiles. In the case of those countries, the provisions of Article 1, paragraph 2, and Annex B, paragraph 2, should be fully implemented. *The exporting participants may, in the case of countries referred to in this paragraph, agree to any mutually acceptable arrangements with regard to paragraph 5 of Annex B; special consideration in this respect would be given to their concerns regarding the avoidance of damage to these countries' minimum viable production of textiles.* (Author's emphasis.)

They thus legalized past performance in the MFA.

Furthermore, other paragraphs in the Protocol were equally ambiguous and could also be invoked by Sweden in various circumstances.[29] Clearly the position of the Swedish

---

[29] Paragraph 6 of the MFA Protocol was negotiated by the EEC in particular but could potentially be used by other importing countries. It referred to the 'role' and 'goodwill' of predominant suppliers 'in finding and contributing to

government on textile trade had hardened significantly. Although the domestic goal of maintaining at least 30 per cent self-sufficiency was already becoming impossible—indeed, it had already sunk to 20 per cent—the government nevertheless chose to hold to this objective as a guideline. Both the textiles and clothing sectors had continued to decline during the MFA 3 period.

The Community had also insisted that an 'anti-surge' clause would be a condition for signing the renewed MFA. This new element meant that the performance in under-utilized quotas for highly sensitive products would be regulated, with certain thresholds, in such a manner as to prevent sharp and substantial increases in trade. Just as the 'reasonable departures' clause of the second period was invoked by Sweden, so too could this procedure.

Sweden negotiated sixteen bilateral agreements and imposed unilateral restrictions on textile imports from seven East European states including the USSR, plus Albania, China, North Korea, Vietnam, and Mongolia. These agreements were no less restrictive than previous agreements and in many cases much more restrictive. They showed that the Swedish restrictions continued to be directed towards the imports of made-up articles and clothing from developing countries only and were of a comprehensive nature with specific restraints on some groups with the remainder placed in a basket with a limit. Sweden also seems to have invoked the new Protocol in denying totally the flexibility provisions to Pakistan and Sri Lanka. In the agreement with Singapore, limited use of carryover/carry forward was allowed but no swing.

At the time of writing, MFA countries are a year into MFA 4. Sweden has again signed agreements with sixteen countries so far. There are, however, some indications that Sweden is relaxing its restrictive stance. The MVP clause was tightened up for MFA 4 with promises of improved growth rates and better flexibility provisions. Sweden has also decided to limit the number of product groups under quota restrictions. Although the restrictions have been marginally

---

mutually acceptable solutions to particular problems'. This refers to cut-backs for Hong Kong, Korea, Macao, and highly sensitive products in the EEC.

successful in limiting Third World imports, they have not protected Swedish production. Imports have instead increased from other European countries, especially Portugal since it joined the EEC, Italy, Finland, and, most recently, Turkey. At the same time subsidies to the textile and clothing industries are being reduced gradually as the industries show some evidence of improved competitiveness. Finally it appears that the economic defence argument for protecting textiles and clothing is losing credibility even in Sweden, while the employment argument and the social clause continue to have a strong following. ÖEF has changed its name to ÖCB (Överstyrelsen för civil beredskap) which replaces the concept of economic defence with civil preparedness. Textiles and clothing will no longer have the priority in this policy relative to other sectors and there is general discussion of giving greater responsibilities to the private sector.

Conclusion

The minimum viable production clause was included in the original MFA at the instigation of the Nordic countries— Finland, Norway, and Sweden. Given the alleged existence of a special case for 'countries having small markets, an exceptionally high level of imports and a correspondingly low level of domestic production, account should be taken of the avoidance of damage to those countries' minimum viable production (MVP) of textiles'. The clause was drawn up with the understanding that a lower growth rate than the 6 per cent minimum provided in Annex B could be allowed after 'consultations' between the parties concerned. However, the MVP clause has been used in an increasingly abusive fashion to justify departures not only from the growth rate, but also from the established flexibility provisions.

In most industrial countries demands for protection were, of course, in the first instance based on the rising level of unemployment within the textiles sector. However, during the negotiations for the first MFA, the Nordic clause was added and justified by the necessity to maintain a minimum viable production. The concern of Sweden in particular was that the domestic production of textiles and clothing had reached a level below which for political, social, and perceived strategic or security reasons, it should not be allowed to fall. The aim was to prevent the extinction of an industry that was described by Swedish officials as 'vital for the basic needs of the population' and for which an economic defence policy had been specifically designed.

Thus, we have seen that the economic defence policy in textiles and clothing has shifted from being a traditional one consisting of stockpiling and contingency plans for reorganizing production during a war to the more recent measures involving production subsidies and trade restrictions in peacetime.

While subsidies are administered by ÖEF, which is the official authority for handling questions concerning economic defence policy, it is the government itself which dictates trade policy. Furthermore, ÖEF (now ÖCB) insists on providing subsidies to the textiles and knitwear sectors only, whereas trade policy measures are aimed at clothing and made-up goods. According to the Director of ÖEF (1984), the country's economic security does not benefit from trade restrictions, especially when they are directed at developing countries only; nor can clothing be considered a priority sector for economic defence. Nevertheless, the government continues to impose restrictions on imports from developing countries despite the increasing evidence to suggest that such restrictions cannot benefit the country's employment or security. Sweden has become one of the most restrictive of all developed countries in this sector and has only recently shown some evidence of altering its course.

Annexe: Extracts from the 1980 Review

(a) General comments

General TSB comments on the interpretation of the MVP clause were repeated several times in connection with bilateral restraint notifications made by Sweden. 'In the course of its examination of several Swedish agreements during which it had had full regard to the concept of minimum viable production, as set out in Article 1:2 of the Arrangement, the TSB nevertheless found occasion to make an observation of general application in this respect. The TSB held that while fully recognizing Sweden's right to protect its minimum viable production, paragraph 6 of the understanding reached by the Textiles Committee on 14 December 1977, could not be invoked as a general waiver of particular obligations under the Arrangement. It further recommended that, if the agreements to which this comment was attached were to be extended, modified or renewed then both parties thereto should adhere to this principle.' This observation was made in the context of the TSB's review of Swedish agreements with Hong Kong, India, Korea, Pakistan, Philippines, Singapore, Sri Lanka, and Thailand.

(b) Growth rates

One of the most important differences between MFA action and Article XIX action under the GATT is that the former guarantees annual growth in access by exporting countries to importing country markets. In the LTA the growth rate was set at 5 per cent and was later raised to 6 per cent in the MFA although in recent years this rule has hardly been operational. As we have seen, the Nordic Countries had the right to waive this obligation in their bilateral agreements by invoking the MVP clause. In most cases the exporting country agreed to this provision, but during the course of MFA 2 disputes became more frequent. The normal procedure for Sweden's agreements was either to freeze imports from a country at the same level as the preceding twelve-month period or to allow for a 0–1 per cent annual growth rate. These rates were normally stated in volume terms rather than in value, although in some cases since 1976 some countries have been allowed their own mix of export commodities in volume and value terms. However, Article 5 of the MFA states that 'The participating importing country should take full account of such factors as established tariff classifications and quantitative units based on normal commercial practices in export and import transactions'. This refers to the denomination of quotas and restraint levels in volume terms in order to avoid *inter alia* any trade distortion that might arise from variations in exchange rates, inflation, etc. Thus Sweden's actions also in this way derogated from MFA rules and principles.

A further problem in evaluating Sweden's agreements was related to the frequent use of one-year periods. For this reason it was not always possible to differentiate between increases in base levels and growth within the life of agreements. Although the MFA provided specific rules with respect to growth rates, provisions on base level increases between agreements were not as strict and could therefore provide a means of circumventing growth provisions. Swedish agreements were further complicated by the use of non-yearly periods (16, 18, 14 or in one case 11 months) in which growth cannot be calculated easily. Sweden maintained a system of annual agreements in the early part of this phase, continuing a practice that was begun in the first phase. Longer term agreements, however, increasingly became the trend during the course of the second period.

With respect to new agreements notified to the TSB in 1978 it was noted that the Article 4 agreements between Sweden on the one hand and India, Macao, Singapore, Sri Lanka, and Thailand respectively, on the other hand, 'provided for a considerably lower rate of growth than the growth of not less than 6 per cent prescribed in the MFA'. Indeed, Sweden resorted to cutbacks in quota levels in agreements with Korea, Macao, Malaysia, Philippines, Singapore, Thailand, and Yugoslavia. In a further statement, however, it 'recognized that the lower growth rate reflected the parties' understanding that implementation of the 6 per cent growth provisions of the Arrangement could contribute to the then existing threat to Sweden's minimum viable production as foreseen in paragraph 2 of Annexe 3'.

The bilateral negotiations with Hong Kong, Korea, and Macao provoked long discussions in the TSB. All three agreements concluded in 1978/9 involved a cutback or reduction in access and therefore a departure from the MFA provisions. In the Korean case, statements were made in the TSB by the Swedish and Korean members. Although it was agreed that a 6 per cent growth rate could contribute to a threat to MVP, the new agreements consisted of not only lower growth rates in comparison with the preceding agreements, but even considerable reductions. The TSB was also informed subsequently that 'the previous all-fibre agreement had also contained a quota of 900 tons which had been established for a group of products for which the export performance of Korea to Sweden was very small'. Placing high quota levels on products for which the country in question does not have a strong export potential gives an illusion of growth in access when in fact there is none. Concerning Swedish agreements with India, Mauritius (a non-participant), Sri Lanka, and Yugoslavia, the TSB noted the provision of nominal rates of growth usually amounting to less than 1 per cent, and recommended that future agreements should contain further growth. In some cases Sweden took liberties to the extreme in according countries positive growth rates, such as in increasing quotas by one pair of trousers, etc.

(c) Swing

Annexe B, paragraph 5 of the MFA refers to the so-called swing provisions. 'Where restraint is exercised for more than one product the participating countries agree that, provided that the total exports subject to restraint do not exceed the aggregate level for all products so restrained the agreed level for any one product may be exceeded by 7 per cent save in exceptionally and sparingly used circumstances where a lower percentage may be justified in which case that lower percentage shall not be less than 5 per cent.' In a large number of agreements, the TSB remarked that swing possibilities provided do not accord with the above-mentioned provisions, that either, '(i) swing was totally absent; (ii) that swing was lower than the minimum figure provided for in Annex B, paragraph 5; (iii) that the right to swing as between agreements, when several agreements were in existence, had not been granted; or (iv) that swing had occasionally been incorporated in the specific limits of an agreement'.

The absence of swing, an essential element of the MFA for exporting countries, became an increasing concern for the TSB, particularly in the case of Sweden. While it was assumed in agreements lacking swing that exporting countries had waived their rights to this provision the TSB made a statement that if it was 'in return for certain other considerations in the agreement, or as a reflection of a mutual recognition of the minimum viable production principle, the notifying country should note this in a short reasoned statement'. Nevertheless, the absence of swing seemed to lack justification in most cases.

Most of Sweden's agreements made no swing provisions. These included respectively: Sweden's agreements with

Yugoslavia, Pakistan, Singapore, Macao, Korea, India, the Philippines, Sri Lanka, Malaysia, and Thailand. In the agreement with Hong Kong and the first one with Korea the agreed rates of swing amounted to 1 per cent, i.e. lower than the minimum 5 per cent. The reasons presented to the TSB for the absence of swing in all these cases referred to a 'reflection of the mutual recognition of the minimum viable production principle'.

After the major review considerable time was spent discussing a new agreement between Sweden and Brazil. There were no provisions for swing. In reviewing the agreement, the 'TSB took into consideration that the parties to the agreement had specifically cited, as a basis for the agreement, Articles 1: 2 (MVP) and 4 of the MFA, and the Protocol of Extension'. In fact the acceptable term of 'mutual recognition' had not been used because Brazil had not officially recognized MVP as a reason for no swing, nor had the Brazilian member on the TSB asked his government for a formal position on this. It had been a tacit agreement in which Brazil assumed the absence of swing had been agreed to under the Protocol of Extension. Only after a careful review did the TSB find the agreement acceptable and after finding that other elements compensated for this departure. In this light only did the TSB find the agreement to be in conformity 'in overall terms'.

(d) Flexibility provisions: carry-over, carry-forward

Requirements for carry-over and carry-forward are laid down in Article 4: 3 and Annex B, paragraph 5: 'Such (flexibility) provisions should encompass areas of base levels, growth, recognition of the increasing interchangeability of natural, artificial and synthetic fibres, carry forward, carryover, transfers from one product grouping to another and such other arrangements as may be mutually satisfactory to the parties to such bilateral agreements.

'Where restraint is exercised for more than one product the participating countries agree that provided that the total exports subject to restraint do not exceed the aggregate level for all products so restrained (on the basis of a common unit to be determined by the participating countries concerned), the agreed level for any one product may be exceeded by 7 per cent save in exceptionally and sparingly used circumstances where a lower percentage may be justified in which case the lower percentage shall be not less than 5 per cent. Where restraints are established for more years than one, the extent to which the total of the restraint level for one product or product group may, after consultation between the parties concerned, be exceeded in either year of any two subsequent years by carry-forward and/or carryover is 10 per cent of which carry-forward shall not represent more than 5 per cent.'

Many of the observations made by the TSB with respect to the application of these flexibility provisions were similar to those made concerning swing. General remarks concerning flexibility provisions in relation to MVP consisted of the following: 'the TSB had full regard to the concept of the minimum viable production as set out in Article 1: 2 of the Arrangement. While fully recognizing Sweden's right to protect its minimum viable production, the TSB held that paragraph 6 of the Understanding reached by the Textiles Committee on 14 December 1977, could not be invoked as a general waiver of particular obligations under the Arrangement, and recommended that, if the agreement was to be extended, modified or renewed, both parties thereto should adhere to this principle.'

A total absence of carryover and carry-forward was noted in several of Sweden's agreements. They included agreements notified in 1978-9 with India, Singapore, Sri Lanka, and Thailand. However, in new agreements with India, Malaysia, the Philippines, Singapore, Sri Lanka, Thailand, and Yugoslavia respectively it was noted that TSB recommendations had been heeded and the agreements were relaxed. Sweden notified an agreement with Macao to the TSB that provided for carryover from the first agreement period to the second one, but no allowances were made for carry-forward. The negotiations for agreement with Macao was one of the most heated and controversial debates in the history of the TSB, involving attempts by Sweden to cut back on its previous cutbacks. It was finally withdrawn and replaced with only a slightly more liberal agreement. New agreements with Hong Kong, 1/4/79–31/3/81, and Korea, 1/3/79–28/2/81, provided for less flexibility in terms of carryover and carry-forward than the preceding agreements and amounted to only 2.5 per cent.

(e) Notifications

The MFA requires participating countries to communicate details of all agreements within thirty days of their entry into force. In numerous instances, however, the TSB noted that there had been considerable delays in the notification. It must be pointed out, however, that Sweden's record with regard to punctual notifications was perhaps not much worse than that of other importing countries. Despite the TSB's oft-repeated recommendations to comply with the regulations, there were considerable delays, particularly in Sweden's agreements with India and Sri Lanka. Notifications had once been given at the time of expiry and, not infrequently, several months late. Furthermore, information was provided in an especially reserved manner concerning East European countries. The attitude of the Swedish authorities seemed to be that Sweden was a special case in all respects and not obliged to furnish details to the same extent as other countries.

(f) Product coverage

In the period from 1978 onwards Sweden adopted a more comprehensive approach to bilateral agreements with developing exporting countries particularly in the MFA. Clothing and made-up products covered by such agreements were classified into twenty main groups. The scope of specific restraints was extended significantly, and clothing groups not covered by specific restraints were usually included in a 'Rest Group' with a ceiling defined generally in tonnage or, in some cases, in Swedish crowns. Quotas were placed on the whole gamut of made-ups and clothing products from various tops, blouses, pullovers, etc. to underwear, bedlinen, and towels. In some cases Swedish agreements included textile products not covered by the MFA. It was hoped, furthermore, that Swedish representatives would be able to negotiate into MFA 3 the inclusion of hides among the products covered (NU 1980/1: 47), but this was not accepted by the other participating countries. It must be added that product coverage in Swedish agreements included only finished goods, no basic textiles.

(g) Quotas maintained under GATT

All Nordic countries, Norway, Finland, and Sweden, have maintained quota restrictions under the GATT Protocol of

Accession. The advantage with this type of arrangement was that the importing countries would be waived from the MFA requirement of a 6 per cent growth rate. Sweden still maintains such agreements against Hungary, Poland, and Romania. The three Nordic countries had indicated to the TSB that in future negotiations concerning these agreements they would be willing to consider transforming relevant textile quotas into agreements under the MFA, but only Finland has complied so far. Norway, on the other hand, was unable to reach agreements with certain exporting countries and therefore never signed MFA 2. Instead it has taken extended Article XIX action under the GATT against countries such as Hong Kong.

(h) *Agreements with non-MFA participants*

Actions taken against non-participants should be notified to the TSB. In this context Sweden has notified agreements with Malta and Mauritius that are similar to MFA type agreements. Agreements also exist with several centrally planned economies in the form of global quotas, bilateral quotas or import licensing. Such agreements are maintained with Hungary, Poland, Romania, Czechoslovakia, the German Democratic Republic, the People's Republic of China, and Taiwan.

7 Conclusion

Throughout this study we have been confronted with the recurring tension between, on the one hand, the commitment by the industrial Western states to promote the liberalization of trade and live up to their international obligations in the GATT and, on the other hand, the increasing demands on these states to provide economic security not only for traditional defensive purposes but also for the social welfare of the nation as a whole. Although the conflict between these policy goals has earlier origins, it only became apparent in the 1970s as a result of a series of shocks to the system, including the widespread recessionary periods of that decade. It is in this context that governments have begun to perceive the phenomenon of interdependence as a potential threat to their sovereignty and to the security of the state, rather than as a purely positive consequence of trade. Interdependence has in fact exposed the changing nature of security and welfare.

The study has argued that despite the apparently changing nature of security and the adjustment by states to new responsibilities, there has been no attempt to accommodate the enlarged role of the state in providing security for its citizens within the international trade order, either conceptually or by structural change. As we have seen in Chapter 5 the main attempt at reconciling the liberal trade order with the new welfare and industrial policies, namely, the negotiation of a special temporary instrument to regulate textile trade, has resulted in a series of self-defeating measures.

But if the problem is a general one, for countries such as Sweden—on which the study has focused—the new pattern is perceived as particularly threatening. In response to increasing economic interdependence and the greater international division of labour, the Swedish authorities began to call for selective protection in those industries declining most rapidly with the aim of maintaining self-sufficiency. Their argument, as we have seen, was that the larger the share of imports in total domestic consumption of a product, the greater is their vulnerability to embargoes and external demands. In effect, like other industrialized countries, Sweden began to question the rationale for further liberalization of trade. But Sweden went further than most other countries. In raising the question the government effectively revived one of the traditional arguments about the benefits of self-sufficiency in industries essential to war. The trouble with this attempt was that this argument, which had made sense in a world in which states had to be prepared to fight protracted but limited wars and when both international specialization and trade competition were relatively under-developed, could no longer be applied in the new military and economic circumstances. In the Swedish case, moreover, the response to interdependence was complicated by arguments deriving from the country's status as a neutral country, and for two additional reasons.

First, Sweden is unique in the way it has developed a policy of 'economic defence'. Although other industrialized states take certain trade and industrial measures based on the national security argument, no state has developed this policy to the same extent as Sweden. The 'economic defence' policy originated in the 1930s in a series of contingency plans for wartime (Chapter 3). However, since then the Swedish authorities gradually extended the policy to include trade-restricting measures in peacetime. These measures extended beyond agriculture—traditionally a strongly protected sector—and energy, neither of which has ever been effectively brought within the scope of the liberal trade order, and therefore of GATT rules, to include manufactures and semi-manufactures, which originally constituted the central target of the multilateral trade liberalization strategy. They have since justified this protection in the case of textiles and clothing with claims of the necessity for an economic defence or 'minimum viable production' in case of war or serious international crisis.

Second, Sweden is considered to have a special relationship with developing countries. This relationship is not dictated by strategic or even economic motives although there is a convenient symmetry between Swedish neutrality and Third World non-alignment. Both economic and, in a broad sense, strategic benefits may therefore accrue from it. For this reason and because of the generous aid and development programmes run by the Swedes, it has gained respect in the Third World. The extension of Sweden's economic defence policies to include protectionist measures, however, may seriously affect the export possibilities of the developing countries and, therefore, undermine the special relationship. This tension between Sweden's deliberate courting of the Third World, and an economic defence policy in which Third World countries are the major target of Swedish protection, is central to the study. The contradictory nature of the economic security argument has been brought to the fore as it became evident that economic security arguments have been used precisely against those countries with which interdependence is most tenuous rather than against those with which interdependence is in fact a problem. An analysis of Swedish textile policy leads inescapably to this conclusion; yet, as we have seen, it is one that the Swedish authorities have consistently failed to draw.

This final chapter begins with an analysis of how and why the industrial countries in general, and Sweden in particular, were able to conclude that there was no fundamental conflict between a liberal trade policy and economic security. Consideration is then given to how the attempt to combine neo-classical principles with a nationally based economic security policy leads the government into adopting conflicting and self-defeating measures. This examination includes an assessment of the plausibility and weaknesses of the Swedish attempt to devise a policy of national economic security within an international liberal trading system. Finally, given that there is no unambiguously 'right' solution to the conflicting and current demands of economic security and economic liberalism, some questions are raised as to the implications of the new state/society balance for the international trading order.

1 Economic liberalism and security

With respect to the first of these issues, one could argue that the belief in the reconcilability of economic liberalism and economic security has its origins in the theoretical underpinnings of the present international trading order. The classical system of economics with its emphasis on the positive gains from trade was developed largely in reaction to mercantilist theories and to their underlying assumption of zero-sum exchanges and the continued commercial warfare to which it had led. The policy of restricting imports in order to maintain a favourable balance of payments at all costs to the disadvantage of all other states was, in effect, a system of belligerency and was based on the belief in war as inevitable. The objectives of increasing profits and power at the expense of rival states were seen as one and the same interest. But, although power rather than security was the dominating concern of mercantilist governments, several small states were able to develop a policy of security based on neutrality as a way of protecting their trading rights during a period of virtually permanent economic warfare. However, as we have seen in Chapter 1, one consequence of liberal thought was to separate the market from the state, and welfare considerations from those of security, and hence to undermine the economic case for neutrality with regard to 'normal' economic relationships. As a consequence, as the new liberal doctrine gained ascendancy, attention was deflected away from the special trade problems of small neutral states.

The response of the classical liberals was to substitute the focus of international relations founded on power and economic warfare with one aimed at increasing and facilitating international exchanges and promoting economic welfare gains. Broadly speaking, they believed that this system would lead to greater welfare for all and to a more peaceful international system.

Many of the ideas from classical and neo-classical thought were vindicated by the destructive economic nationalism of the 1930s and thus came to form the basis of the 'new' international economic order of the 1940s. At this time, efficiency became the determining criterion of an order which was to be ensured by allowing a free rein to market forces and a strict separation of politics from international commerce. Consequently it was believed that the most efficient way to carry out trade was to encourage an international division of labour based on the theory of comparative advantage.

Despite the very strong classical legacy in the 'new' order there were some important differences as well as similarities. While the old system was based on automatic domestic adjustment to changes in the international division of labour, the new system also aimed at internal stability. Indeed it was positively required if the system was to work. The shock of the Depression and the serious unemployment which was believed to have contributed to the political instability of the 1930s and the rise of fascism combined to necessitate a broader role for the state. The question was: how could this be accomplished without major departures from liberal principles in the direction of collectivism? An answer was made possible to a large extent through the theoretical advances associated with Keynes who prescribed active demand management. But the important point to make here is that the policy significantly reduced in principle the need for trade protection. As one author has pointed out with reference to the GATT,

the stability of this order, therefore, rested on the capability of the contracting parties to manage these crises (which periodically had plagued capitalism and provoked the onset of the major protectionist episodes) without recourse to protection; that is, through the use of domestic macroeconomic policy. Perhaps the best reflection of this reality was the commitment of the principal contracting parties to exercise fiscal responsibility and maintain fixed exchange rates, placing the burden of both internal and external management on domestic policy tools.[1]

The full implications of this change in the operational assumption of the reconstructed liberal economic order were not explicitly recognized in the GATT rules. In some ways indeed the 'new' order was still based on a conception of an older world. The main problem with the post-war order was that no means were envisaged in the GATT to reflect the new role delegated to the state except for a peremptory reference in the preamble to the general desire for full employment, and a further passing reference in Article XII, the balance of payments safeguard clause, which envisaged that temporary protection might be necessary as a result of

---

[1] Douglas R. Nelson, 'The Political Structure of the New Protectionism', World Bank, Staff Working Paper No. 471 (July 1981), 8.

a state's employment policies leading to a sudden surge of imports.[2] Although certain other safeguards were included, the most important of which were Article XXI for security considerations, Article XVIII for infant-industry protection and Article XIX for emergency protection in the event of injury to an industry, these were also all designed for temporary periods only in order to ease the disruptions due to short-term market disturbances. They could not, therefore, deal with longer-term structural problems, nor with problems of unequal distribution, nor with the problems of small or neutral states. They could not do so primarily because, in a liberal order, trade itself is viewed as a form of security and no distinction is made between internal and external security.

Article XXI which permits protection for security considerations provides the best example of this discrepancy between the old order and the new one. According to the classical doctrine the role of the state encompassed only the specific duties of maintaining law and order, a sound currency, and defence. Any other interventions were thought to interfere with free market forces and an autonomous process of structural adjustment. In this way Article XXI was designed to reconcile a traditional liberal conception of security in allowing states to withdraw concessions unilaterally for reasons of national security. But given that it could not be used for problems associated with the broader notion of security as it has been perceived, in fact, throughout the post-war period, it has hardly been used at all.

So long as tariff protection remained at a relatively high level the conflict between the old and new conception of state security was masked. The series of tariff-reducing negotiations carried out under GATT auspices has virtually

---

[2] For an alternative view, see John Gerard Ruggie, 'International Régimes, Transactions, and Change: Embedded Liberalism in the Post-war Economic Order', *International Organization* 36, 2 (spring 1982). Ruggie argues that the reference to employment in the balance of payments safeguard clause indicates that the drafters of the General Agreement took deliberate account of the enlarged role of the liberal state. The fact, however, that Article XII like all the other safeguards envisaged only temporary derogations from the rules—so that, for example, after the return to convertibility in 1958 states found it increasingly difficult to invoke Article XII and had increasing recourse to unilateral action outside the GATT—strongly suggests that the full structural implications of the change were not anticipated.

eliminated barriers among industrialized countries with the exception of textiles and agriculture. In this way, moreover, one could view the root of GATT's problem as lying in its success. As soon as tariffs were largely eliminated a vacuum was left which was inevitably to be filled by other kinds of protection. This protection took the form of various kinds of industrial policy primarily based on subsidies. Within GATT an attempt was made to draw a distinction between production subsidies, which were permitted, and export subsidies which were proscribed. To the extent that this distinction could be sustained therefore (and liberal economists have increasingly questioned the possibility) there was no need to question the scope and adequacy of Article XXI to cover the new and broader interpretation of national security.

To a large extent the 'new' responsibilites of the liberal state did not encroach on international negotiations. Within the trade sphere where they did encroach there was no need to consider the Article because, apart from the disruptions occurring in the trade in raw materials which did not enter into GATT's domain, the most acute problems arose in one sector primarily, that of textiles, and special rules were allowed in this area from an early date. Although the LTA and MFA were temporary instruments in principle, in effect they deflected attention away from the inability of the GATT to handle the negative consequences of interdependence such as unemployment and the special trade problems of the Third World in general. Sweden also managed its particular problem by negotiating the special MVP clause which allowed it greater protection than that accorded to other industrialized countries (Part II). Given that an instrument already existed for textile trade, there was no reason to invoke Article XXI for problems in this sector. On this view the LTA and MFA were ultimately compatible with the liberal design. In both cases the intention was to minimize the social costs of domestic adjustment, which were believed to be temporary, without freezing the international division of labour. And by providing a 6 per cent growth rate the MFA has allowed for a regular expansion of exports without totally limiting structural change.

So long as the system functioned well, for Sweden as for the other industrial states, there was no need to question the foundations of the liberal trading order nor its domestic counterpart. Growth and prosperity vindicated the theoretical division between politics and commerce. For Sweden in particular the success of the system also contributed to the official belief, on the one hand, that the political stance of neutrality was not in conflict with the commercial system and, on the other hand, that security was not an issue of relevance to trade.

A further explanation for neglecting the problems of security was that the major rift in international economic relations in the post-Second World War period was no longer in the market order as it had been in the inter-war period, but across the East–West ideological divide, which among other things separated states according to their adherence to collectivist or market principles. Under these circumstances the security of most industrial states—although not, of course, the neutrals—was provided by the Western Alliance under American leadership. Consequently the theoretically universal market was dominated by a less than universal security system. The strongest European members of NATO were also members of the EEC which was committed to economic harmonization within the Community and to devising common policies *vis-à-vis* third countries. Thus general economic prosperity masked the contradiction between principles of the universal market and those of what was in effect a preferential system of Western security and European integration.

Despite the fact that GATT was dominated by Western capitalist states, the commercial world was never expected to have permanent ideological divisions. Nor was it to be divided according to levels of development. Thus, on the assumption of a separation between politics and commerce, no conflict was envisaged between neutrality, aid to developing countries, and liberal trade obligations. Indeed, a policy of liberal trade was positively required in order to maintain the economic prosperity and strength necessary for upholding a credible policy of non-alliance as well as for maintaining a generous aid policy.

The argument so far has attempted to explain why Sweden and the industrial states generally were able to reconcile economic security and liberal trade as it were 'by default'.

But it does not explain why they increasingly believed the threat to their economic security came from the Third World. In a way of course this belief was from the start an illusion. Protectionism is just as rampant and in some respects more damaging in relations amongst industrial states than in North–South relations, but where power is more evenly distributed, bilateral trade disputes—for example, the US/EEC steel dispute in 1982 and the US/Japan semi-conductor trade dispute in 1987—tend to be settled by an unofficial exchange of concessions. To the extent that the Third World is a prime target for discrimination, however, the answer is partly a matter of economic theory and partly of political history. At the level of theory it is, of course, precisely because they enjoy a real comparative advantage that Third World producers of textiles are regarded as such a threat to Western industry and employment.

The textile sector is the paradigmatic example of how the emergence of the Third World has shaken the system, hence the emphasis given to it in this study (Chapters 4 and 6). It is an industry which developed first on a very small scale, initially as small units, then in larger labour-intensive units. Indeed, in the West, the Industrial Revolution of the nineteenth century began with the mechanization of textile production, and for about a century the development of these now highly industrialized countries owed a great deal to the vigorous expansion of their textile industries and their access to world markets including those of what is now described as the developing countries. As the economies of the Western countries became increasingly more capital- and skill-intensive it was natural that they would diversify their production and trade and leave such activities to other countries lower down on the scale of industrialization which were still relatively labour-intensive. Or rather this was what was regarded as 'natural' under liberal trade theory. Thus, if liberal trade policy was to contribute to continued economic expansion, and if trade was to remain as it was originally envisaged by liberal theorists, essentially in the private rather than public domain, the transfer of certain industries to other countries was positively required.

The successive multilateral textile agreements thus represent a diplomatic attempt to resolve the contradiction by combining the principles of expansion and adjustment required by orthodox trade theory, and restraint required by the governments' domestic commitments. It could be argued, after all, that the MFA was created only as a temporary suspension of comparative advantage and that, in principle, the spirit of the MFA ultimately rests on this theory. Indeed its stated objectives are to expand trade, promote development, particularly of developing countries, and encourage structural adjustments in the importing countries. This is tantamount to saying developed countries should specialize to reap maximum benefits from trade.

The political explanation of why Third World countries are singled out for protection again goes back to the evolution of the post-war system. As we have noted, the commercial world was not to be divided permanently along developmental lines. However, the GATT had been established under the hegemony of the US and by states which were more or less on an equal footing. At the outset they had never anticipated the problems associated with emerging independent and industrializing countries. Indeed, the golden age of international liberalism had also been the age of the great European colonial empires which were substantially organized as extensions of the metropolitan economy, and therefore very largely fell outside the rules of the international market. As the colonies became independent states and demanded a greater voice in the organization of the global market, they also became an unbalancing factor in international economic relations. One could argue that the harder it became for the original member states of GATT to impose trade restrictions on one another, the greater was the temptation to seek a target elsewhere.

2 The contradictions of Swedish commercial policies

Having now examined the reasons how and why industrial states were able to conclude that there were no fundamental conflicts between liberal trade obligations and economic security, we will now consider how in practice these conflicts emerged and led to inconsistencies and self-defeating measures in the case of Sweden.

As we have seen, the changing political and economic realities of the post-1945 world have subjected a number of shocks to the eighteenth-century conception of the world as a cosmopolitan commercial society which, in a modified form, the framers of the GATT sought to revive. Modern industrial states have taken on social welfare commitments which go far beyond those of the original liberal constitution. While economic prosperity was able to mask the underlying contradictions, the economic recession of the 1970s has served to expose and dramatize them.

We have seen in Chapters 2 and 3 how these tensions between neutrality and liberal trade emerged in Sweden and how they were resolved through diplomatic compromises. Three developments in particular underlay both the tensions and the compromises through which the Swedish authorities attempted to resolve them. First, the prospect of total war represented the most obvious threat to Sweden's neutrality. In facing this threat, Sweden extended its inter-war policy which required building up both a strong military defence, and a strong economy in order to lend credibility to the government's determination to maintain its traditional policy. In the face of new kinds of threat which were not anticipated, however, the government also developed a new concept of total defence which included policies for civil and psychological defence as well as a broader economic defence policy than had operated between the wars.

Secondly, the formation of the EEC represented a threat to Swedish neutrality. This was because, although customs unions and free trade areas were compatible with the General Agreement, of which Sweden was a member, the implicit aims of the EEC to work towards political union excluded Sweden from the possibility of membership. Once EFTA was formed, and subsequent free trade agreements were signed with the EEC, Sweden appeared to have overcome this challenge as well. However, as we shall see, the 'solution' was an ironic one in the sense that Sweden's efforts to broaden and facilitate relations with Europe resulted in an interdependence which has ultimately proved to be much more damaging to Sweden's economic 'security' as traditionally defined, that is, the maintenance of a capability for self-sufficiency in the event of war, than the apparent threat of Third World imports.

Finally, the major contradictions in Sweden's policies are illustrated most dramatically in its relations with the Third World. On the one hand, these relations were originally considered to be important for both economic reasons, deriving from the need for export markets and raw materials, and for political reasons, deriving from the sympathetic relationship between Sweden's non-alliance and the non-aligned movement. On the other hand, it has been the perceived threat of Third World penetration of Sweden's market, particularly in the textile sector, that has exposed the conflict between the demands for economic liberalism and those of economic security.

Whether or not one assumes that liberal trade theory and its institutional order are currently unassailable, it seems quite clear that Sweden's responses to the Third World challenge in the context of the Multi-Fibre Arrangement are ignoring the real issues of economic security. The Swedes argue that they cannot allow the production of textiles and clothing to fall below a certain prescribed minimum 'viable' level for reasons of economic security. Their concern is that in case of war or international crisis Sweden, as a neutral country, may be isolated by a blockade and be unable to provide the civilian population with the basic needs that were previously supplied from abroad. In the case of clothing, the import penetration ratio was, in 1985, approximately 87 per cent, whereas the goal of government policy is for 30 per cent of consumption to be covered by domestic production. Various production subsidies have been provided but the main instrument relied upon appears to be trade protection. Thus, by negotiating a special 'Nordic' clause into the MFA in 1973, Sweden secured for itself the right to impose protective quotas against developing countries' exports of textiles and clothing which went beyond those of other importing industrialized countries, and economic nationalism thereby became increasingly equated with economic security. However, the main evidence that Sweden appears to be sidestepping the relevant issue is that, according to its own criteria for economic security in clothing, the policy has been unsuccessful and the problem remains unresolved. Before we turn to a discussion of the problem of economic security *per se* it will be useful to examine the particular weaknesses of Sweden's policy at a practical level. The logic of the minimum viable production policy in the textiles and clothing sectors seems to be questionable in four principal respects: it can be argued that it employs inappropriate methods; is aimed at the wrong target; is based on unclear motives; and is internally inconsistent.

(i) Methods

The inability of trade protection against one set of countries to give more than temporary shelter to domestic production has been frequently demonstrated in the specialist literature. In addition to the fact that trade protection cannot indefinitely make up for poor productivity, marketing or management, it has been shown that Swedish producers would gain from trade protection only to the extent that the price level, hence demand, in all of Europe would change. Given Sweden's small size, however, a change in EEC trade policy would affect Sweden's production and employment much more than if Sweden itself were to alter its policy.[3]

Sweden's trade restrictions against one group of countries, namely the LDCs, have had two further paradoxical consequences. First, they have encouraged imports from other areas, particularly Europe. The reason for this is that the price-raising effect of tariffs and quotas invites competition from similarly priced imports from certain unrestricted sources. Secondly, the protection provides an incentive to the restricted countries to maximize their profit from each unit exported and hence leads them to abandon low-cost items in favour of those which although still cheaper than the Swedish product are potentially in direct competition with it.

(ii) Target

For all the above reasons it is also evident that Sweden's security policy is aimed at the wrong target. Singling out

---

[3] Carl Hamilton, 'Kejsarens nya Kläder i tekopolitiken', *Skandinaviska Enskilda Banken Quarterly Review*, no. 1 (1985).

Third World producers is particularly illogical from a security point of view if over 60 per cent of the clothing imports originate in developed countries. After all, although their share of Sweden's imports has increased over the past two decades they have only recently emerged as major producers and exporters; the restrictions on their exports to Sweden cannot prevent other countries from increasing their exports. If Swedish goods do not satisfy consumer demand for whatever reason, then buyers will look elsewhere. Viewed from this perspective, production in Sweden may decline anyway and Sweden's self-sufficiency in textiles and clothing will be no more 'secure' than if the restrictions had never been imposed. The problem of security arises primarily in the context of Sweden's free trade agreements with the rest of Europe rather than with the developing countries.

This point is worth expanding for it is here that the major contradiction emerges. If the 'real' economic threat to Sweden's security derives from interdependence the problem lies with the country's relations with Europe, not the Third World. Sweden's commercial pattern has followed the general trade pattern of other industrialized countries. This pattern is characterized by the increasing exchange of manufactures for other manufactures and a faster growth of trade with other industrialized countries than with developing areas. In this light Sweden's final 'entry' into the free trade area of Europe—that is its membership of EFTA and trade agreement with the EEC—was seen as an undisputedly favourable development since it was believed to have opened up possibilities for greater specialization and profit maximization. Sweden has consequently become increasingly interdependent with the West yet unable to take countervailing action as a result of the free trade agreements and the possibility of retaliation. Moreover Sweden's vulnerability in the textiles and clothing sectors has been intensified because of the competitiveness of other industrialized countries and has very little to do with LDC competition. According to a study by Ohlsson textiles and clothing began to lose market shares well before 1960 and before LDCs appeared as sizeable suppliers to the world market. In fact Sweden's net export ratio was found to be less favourable in such traditional LDC industries than in all other industry groups.[4] Thus, the only viable solution to Sweden's declining production would be to improve competitiveness.

(iii) *Motives*

The third way in which Sweden's security policy has been inappropriate is in terms of its motivations. Although the official justification for the minimum viable production clause and its implementation is the need for economic security, narrowly defined, the apparent reason has more to do with sectional pressure than with economic analysis. Ever since the textile and clothing sectors began to decline rapidly, the unions have argued for government support for production and employment. Originally they did so within the context of the industrial, regional, and labour market policies which evolved under the post-war Social Democratic governments (Chapter 5). However, these social welfare policies were designed and first implemented seriously when the economy was still growing rapidly and unemployment had not yet reached the disturbing levels that are prevalent today. Nevertheless, various forms of subsidies were provided to cover the social and economic disruptions associated with market disturbances and as these grew in size and scope, so too did the workers' and industry's expectations. In the textile and clothing sectors alone, up to 80m. kr. (approximately $1 million at the 1984 exchange rate) have been allocated to various programmes on an annual basis. But as the sector continued its downward spiral and Third World imports increased in the 1970s they became the easiest target for blame. Industrial and labour groups began to call for import protection as a means of saving these sectors from extinction. From the view of government too there were advantages in import restrictions because of their less visible drain on the domestic budget. Thus, it appears that the employment issue has been the overriding element in Sweden's textile and clothing policy.

(iv) *Internal consistency*

Two further reasons which weaken the credibility of the

---

[4] Lennart Ohlsson, 'Sweden's specialization in typical LDC industries and its recent industrial intervention policies', Stockholm School of Economics (1980).

security argument are the discrepancy between policies for the textile sector and those for the clothing sector, and the question of economic defence priorities. While the import dependence on textile raw materials and fabrics is higher than that for clothing, the restrictions Sweden imposes in the MFA cover only clothing and other made-up goods. If security is the actual motivation then it would seem that a continuous inflow of textile raw materials is expected during a blockade but not of finished clothing. This seems contrary to common sense. This conclusion is supported by the fact that there is a conflict on this issue between ÖEF and the government. ÖEF decides on the level of subsidies which should go to a particular sector on the assumption that a certain level of production must be maintained for security purposes—and on this basis textile raw materials and fabrics already account for 47 per cent of the budget (1984)—while the government has insisted on protecting clothing at the border in response to political pressure to maintain employment levels.

With regard to priorities, there is a similar conflict between ÖEF and the government. ÖEF is concerned that economic security in clothing should be balanced against security in other sectors. The government, on the other hand, has insisted that there be a three-year supply capacity in clothing compared with only a one-year supply of oil. In the view of ÖEF, moreover, the over-emphasis on clothing is diverting both attention and resources from other more critical sectors such as electronic equipment and petrochemicals.[5]

One may conclude that Sweden's protection in clothing not only cannot effectively address the problems for which it was intended, but also falls most heavily on developing countries, penalizing them for producing at lower costs and thereby potentially undermining the special ties between Sweden and the Third World.

3 Economic security and the contemporary trading order

What finally can be said about the concept of economic security in an international commercial environment which is characterized, on the one hand, by a high degree of

---

[5] Interview with Director of ÖEF, Gunnar Nordbeck.

interdependence and specialization, and, on the other, by the state's accepting, at least in the West, responsibilities for social security and welfare in addition to those of providing physical defence? It seems certain that there is no unambiguous or theoretically 'correct' way of resolving the tension between economic liberalism and national defence. The examination of the Swedish case in this study, however, suggests four tentative conclusions, which may at least help to demarcate the boundaries of the problem.

(i) *National resilience and contingency planning*

First, it seems possible that an economic defence policy such as Sweden operates may contribute to the country's ability to cope with unforseen contingencies despite the contradictions and inconsistencies that, as we have seen, the policy involves. This conclusion can arguably be inferred from the well-known resilience of national crises in the face of political adversity, despite the complexity of the modern international division of labour. Thus it has often been observed that one reason why sanctions are so ineffective in forcing compliance from the target state is that they have the perverse effect of consolidating their community in its determination to resist coercion. Generally speaking, the resilience which is born of 'siege' mentalities of this type is generated spontaneously, that is, in the absence of any comprehensive contingency planning for the future. The Swedish commitment to neutrality, however, has led the government to elaborate a strategy of total defence in the anticipation of a future international crisis. It is at least arguable that some inconsistency, misdirection, and waste may be a price worth paying for maintaining an attitude of independence and self-reliance in the community. On this view the subjective perception of the authorities that they must maintain a productive capacity in what are deemed essential commodities such as textiles and clothing may be more important than the 'objective' ability to do so. No one can tell what the objective circumstances which they will have to face in a crisis will be: what is important is that they should have the will to face them.

(ii) *The disintegrating consensus on strategic goods*

If it is important to avoid the conclusion that complex inter-dependence has completely undermined the ability of modern states to maintain their independent existence, it must be admitted that it has rendered the task of contingency planning, in particular for neutral states, much more complicated than it was before. As we saw in Chapter 2 there was an attempt at the London Conference of 1909 to define and therefore protect neutral trade in time of war. But this attempt depended first on the prior agreement by prospective belligerents that war was itself part of the international system and hence subject to its rules, and second and more important, that it was possible to agree on a list of contraband, or in modern language, strategic goods, which should be exempted from the trade. Neither of these conditions any longer apply in this area; as in many other areas covered by the rules of war, the conventional distinction between belligerent and non-belligerent, or civil and military targets and uses, has broken down under the dual impact of technological innovation and the democratization of war. In these circumstances, a neutral government which decides on a policy of economic defence cannot assume that, except for a list of prohibited items, it will be able to trade as normal with states which are themselves involved in war. From this point of view, therefore, it is understandable that the Swedes should include so basic a commodity as textiles and clothing in their list of strategic goods, even though, as we have seen, their attempt to arrest the decline of the industry has been largely unsuccessful. The disintegration of even such a fragile consensus on the question of strategic goods as existed at the beginning of the century is arguably reflected in the wording of GATT's Article XXI, which makes no attempt to distinguish between goods which can and those which cannot be protected in the event of war or international crisis.

(iii) *Neutrality, economic integration, and the Western Alliance*

It has sometimes been argued, for example by Mancur Olson in the *Logic of Collective Action*,[6] that neutrals are able

---

[6] Mancur Olson, *The Logic of Collective Action* (Cambridge, Mass., 1971).

to free ride the Western system of security. This seems altogether too schematic an explanation, particularly given the level of resources which countries like Sweden and Switzerland in fact devote to their own independent defence systems. At the same time it is clear that Sweden's current problems with its economic defence policy partly arise from the fact that Sweden both belongs to the industrial world, sharing many of its problems, and stands outside it as a result of its political rather than its economic history. For the majority of industrial democracies the requirements of economic security are not openly in conflict with those of liberal trade. This is because, in a narrow sense, contingency planning, to the extent that it exists, is on an Alliance basis and, collectively, the Western Alliance dominates the international economy. The conflict is also masked because the debate about industrial policy harmonization takes place within EEC and OECD with little if any attention to its political or strategic implications.

Standing outside the Western Alliance and EEC, the Swedes have had to face a question which their counterparts elsewhere could avoid, that is, what kind of trade policy is dictated by the country's traditional policy of neutrality in international affairs? As we have seen, the attempt to pursue policies both of liberal trade and of national defence has led the Swedish authorities into contradiction. In other words, they have pursued integration with the rest of the industrial world, presumably on the assumption that there is no threat from Western Europe, while targeting Third World producers of textiles and clothing, from whom there is clearly no military threat either. One might have expected that an even-handed neutral policy would have led them to diversify their dependence, by increasing trade with the socialist bloc; but these states, like the Third World producers, have also had their exports restricted. Thus, while the Swedes do not receive their military security free of charge, the logic of their policies has led them to shift the cost of their integration in the Western industrial economy on to other parts of the system. If the unstated defence of their position is that the real threat is from the East, this still leaves unanswered the question as to why the Third World should shoulder a disproportionate share of the cost.

Furthermore, after embarking upon an extensive social welfare programme, the state has never ceased to increase its responsibilities and is unable to withdraw from its obligations. Although the tax system and wage solidarity policy have contributed significantly to the levelling of incomes and to minimizing inequalities at the domestic level it has become increasingly difficult to reconcile with competition at the international level; one of the main reasons why Sweden's production of clothing has declined so drastically is the wage structure, which is higher than that of many other countries. Since the special MVP clause is unable to protect Swedish production from European competition, then one can only concede that economic security includes the whole gamut of social welfare programmes and cannot be confined to contingency planning against the possibility of conventional war.

(iv) *Economic defence and social security*

Finally, this conclusion drawn from the Swedish experience discloses the more general failure of the industrial countries to come to terms with the international implications of the broader concept of security as it has developed in the post-war era.

It appears that despite a significant change in state/society relations, the international trade order has been unable to adapt and to cope with the increasing contradictions to which the state's new responsibilities have led. Article XIX was used abundantly in the early 1970s following a long period of infrequent use. Now states are circumventing its use, increasingly finding that it can no longer address contemporary circumstances. Similarly Article XXI is used on very rare occasions. On the other hand, the MFA appears to have developed as a result of the fact that no adequate means existed in the GATT to address problems related to adjustment and to unemployment.

There were, however, three major problems with the MFA which, in part, also explain its failure. First, it was designed only as a temporary deviation from GATT rules and not as a fundamental change of structure and, therefore, did not satisfactorily acknowledge GATT's inability to handle the evolving state/society balance.

Secondly, it was never made explicitly clear what the industrialized countries were protecting when they negotiated the MFA and what Sweden was protecting when it negotiated the MVP clause. Were they protecting employment or were they protecting production? Given that these aims would to some extent require opposing economic strategies, there is a built-in contradiction from the start. The ambiguity also lies in the uncertainty about which level of state or society the security is meant for, that is, whether it is the security of the individual or the group or the nation which is at stake. In the case of Sweden the official aim is to protect production but the objective voiced in most internal debates is the protection of employment. For industrialized countries generally the consequence of this ambiguity is that they can succeed in achieving neither of these aims, nor can the MFA redress the absence in the GATT of a means to effect a more just distribution of a state's wealth, particularly at a time of recession when certain groups are bound to suffer at the expense of others.

Finally, the MFA has been equally unsuccessful at effecting a more just distribution at the international level. Although its stated aims are to promote social and economic development of the developing countries, hence recognizing the special problems of this group of countries, it appears in practice to serve as a hindrance to their development by limiting their opportunities for increasing export earnings and thus escaping the poverty trap. But if the attempt to resolve the problem of overall security in the case of textiles under the MFA has failed it is not clear how it can best be handled within the existing trading system in this sector or indeed in any other. For some years there has been talk about the need to revise and include the possibility of selective action in Article XIX of the GATT which provides for emergency protection in the case of injury to an industry. The debate on this issue suggests that the broad shape of the problem is understood, even if it is not generally discussed in terms of security. The fact that this debate has not yet led to action suggests, however, that the problems to be overcome are still formidable.

Bibliography

ADLER-KARLSSON, GUNNAR, Western Economic Warfare 1947–67 (Stockholm, 1968).
—— Functional Socialism: Swedish Theory for Democratic Socialization (Stockholm, 1969).
AGGARWAL, VINOD, Liberal Protectionism: The International Politics of Organized Textile Trade (Berkeley, Calif., 1985).
ALLARD, S., 'Österrikisk och Svensk Neutralitet', Tiden, 54 (Dec. 1962).
ANDERSON, STANLEY, The Nordic Council (Stockholm, 1967).
ANDRÉN, NILS, 'Internationell Utveckling och Svensk Försvarsdoktrin', Försvar och Säkerhetspolitik (1978).
—— 'På Neutralitetens Smala Näsa', Svensk Tidskrift, no. 7 (1968).
—— FREYMOND, J. and WINTER, E. F., 'Neutralität, aktiver?', Schweizer Monatshefte, 49 (Apr. 1969).
—— and LANGQVIST, ÅKE, Svensk Utrikespolitik efter 1945 (Stockholm, 1965).
ARISTOTLE, The Works of Aristotle, Vol. 10, tr. Ernest Barker, The Politics of Aristotle (Oxford, 1946).
BALDWIN, ROBERT E., Non-Tariff Distortions of International Trade (Washington, DC, 1970).
BALL, GEORGE L., 'New Export Licensing Policies of the Department of Commerce', Foreign Commerce Weekly, vol. XXX, no. 10 (6 Mar. 1948).
BARDAN, BENJAMIN, 'The Cotton Textile Arrangement—1962–1972', Journal of World Trade Law, vol. 7, no. 1 (1973).
BARNES, IAN R., 'The Changing Nature of the Swedish Aid Relationship during the Social Democratic Period of Government', Cooperation and Conflict, XV (1980).
BAUER, ROBERT A. (ed.), The Interaction of Economics and Foreign Policy (Charlottesville, Va., 1975).
Beklädnadsarbetarnas förbund—90 års Jubileumskrift (Stockholm, 1978).
BERGSTEN, C. F., Managing International Economic Interdependence, Selected Papers of C.F.B., 1975–1976 (Lexington, Mass., 1977).
BERGQVIST, MATS, 'Trade and Security in the Nordic Area', Cooperation and Conflict, 4 (1969), 237.
—— 'Säkerhetspolitik och överstatliga Organisationer: ett neutralt lands problem', International Politics (Bergen), 4 (1975), 10–12.

234 Bibliography

BHAGWATI, J. N. and SRINIVASAN, T. N., 'Optimal Trade Policy and Compensation under Endogenous Uncertainty: The Phenomenon of Market Disruption', *Journal of International Economics*, 6 (1976).

BIRNBAUM, KARL E., *Swedish Foreign Policy* (Stockholm, 1962).

BLACK, J., 'Arguments for Tariffs', *Oxford Economic Papers*, vol. XI, no. 2 (1959).

BLACK, L., FALK, R. A., KNORR, K., and YOUNG, O., *Neutralization and World Politics* (Princeton, NJ, 1968).

BLACKHURST, RICHARD, MARIAN, NICOLAS, and TUMLIR, JAN, *Trade Liberalization, Protectionism and Interdependence*, GATT Studies in International Trade (Geneva, 1977).

BONJOUR, EDGAR, *Geschichte der schweizerischen Neutralität* (Basle, 1946).

BROWN, WILLIAM ADAMS, JR., *The United States and the Restoration of World Trade* (Washington, DC, 1950).

BURTON, JOHN W., *International Relations—A General Theory* (Cambridge, 1965).

—— *Non-alignment* (London, 1966).

CABLE, VINCENT, *An Evaluation of the Multifibre Arrangement and Negotiating Options*, Commonwealth Economic Papers No. 15, Commonwealth Secretariat (1981).

—— 'British Protectionism and LDC Imports', *ODI Review*, no. 2 (1977).

CAIN, PETER, 'Capitalism, War and Internationalism in the Thought of Richard Cobden', *British Journal of International Studies*, 5 (1979).

CARLGREN, W. M., *Svensk Utrikespolitik 1939–45* (Stockholm, 1973).

CARLSSON, BO, BERGHOLM, FREDRIK, and LINDBERG, THOMAS, *Industristödspolitiken och dess inverkan på Samhällsekonomin: Industrins Utredningsinstitut* (Stockholm, 1981).

CARR, E. H., *The Twenty Years Crisis* (London, 1939).

—— *Conditions of Peace* (London, 1942).

CHARD, J. S. and MACMILLAN, M. J., 'Sectoral Aids and Community Competition Policy—The Case of Textiles', *Journal of World Trade Law*, 13 (1979).

CHENERY, HOLLIS B., and TAYLOR, LANCE, 'Development Patterns: Among Countries and over Time', *The Review of Economics and Statistics*, Vol. L, no. 4 (1968).

CHOI, CHUNG and MARIAN, *The Multi-Fibre Arrangement in Theory and Practice* (London, 1985).

COBDEN, RICHARD, *The Political Writings of Richard Cobden* (London, 1868).

COOPER, RICHARD, *The Economics of Interdependence* (New York, 1968).

— 'Security and the Energy Crisis', *The Middle East and the International System*, Part II, Adelphi Paper No. 115 (1975).

CORBET, HUGH, and JACKSON, ROBERT (edd.), *In Search of a New World Economic Order* (London, 1974).

CORDEN, WILLIAM, *Trade Policy and Economic Welfare* (Oxford, 1974).

CURZON, GERARD, *Multilateral Commercial Diplomacy* (London, 1965).

CURZON VICTORIA, 'Surplus Capacity and What the Tokyo Round Failed to Settle', *World Economy* (Sept. 1979).

DAM, KENNETH, *The GATT: Law and International Economic Organization* (Chicago, 1970).

FISCHER, A. G. B., *Economic Self-Sufficiency*, Oxford Pamphlets on World Affairs, no. 4 (Oxford, 1939).

FLEISCHER, F., *The New Sweden: The Challenge of a Disciplined Democracy* (New York, 1967).

FOX, ANNETTE BAKER, 'The Small States of Western Europe in the United Nations', *International Organization* (Summer 1965).

— *The Power of Small States* (Chicago, 1959).

FRANK CHARLES F., JR., *Foreign Trade and Domestic Aid* (Washington, DC, 1977).

GALTUNG, JOHAN, 'Self-Reliance—Global Interdependence—Some Reflections on the NIEO', University of Oslo Paper 55 (1977).

GARDNER, RICHARD, *Sterling Dollar Diplomacy: The Origins and Prospects of Our International Economic Order* (New York, 1969).

GOUREVITCH, PETER *et al.*, *Unions and Economic Crisis: Britain, West Germany and Sweden* (London, 1984).

HAGER, WOLFGANG, *et al.*, *European Economic Issues*, Praeger Special Studies in International Economics and Development, Atlantic Institute Studies III (New York, 1977).

HÄGGLÖF, GUNNAR, 'A Test of Neutrality—Sweden in the Second World War', *International Affairs*, 36 (1960).

HAMILTON, CARL, *A New Approach to Estimation of the Effects of Non-Tariff Barriers to Trade on Prices, Employment and Imports: An Application to the Swedish Textile and Clothing Industry* (Stockholm, 1980).

— 'Keysarens nya Kläder i tekopolitiken', *Skandinaviska Enskilda Banken Quarterly Review*, no. 1 (1985).

HAMMARSKJÖLD, DAG, 'Sweden's International Credit Accommodation in 1944 and 1945', *Svenska Handelsbankens Index* (1945).

HAYEK, FRIEDRICH A., *The Road to Serfdom* (London, 1944).

— *New Studies in Philosophy, Politics, Economics and the History of Ideas* (London, 1978).

HECKSCHER, ELI, *Mercantilism* (London, 1935).

HEILPERIN, MICHAEL, *Studies in Economic Nationalism*, Graduate Institute of International Studies, series no. 35 (Geneva, 1960).

HELLEINER, G. K. *et al.*, *Protectionism or Structural Adjustment* (Paris, 1980).

HIGGINS, ALEXANDER PEARCE, *The Hague Peace Conference and other International Conferences Concerning the Laws and Usages of War* (Cambridge, 1909).

HIRSCHMAN, ALBERT O., *National Power and the Structure of Foreign Trade* (Berkeley, Calif., 1945).

HOLMSTRÖM, MIKAEL, and SIVERS, TOM VON, *USAs Exportkontroll: Tekniken som vapen* (Stockholm, 1985).

HOUTHAKKER, HENDRIK S., 'An International Comparison of Household Expenditure Patterns, Commemorating the Centenary of Engel's Law', *Econometrica* (1957).

—— 'The Influence of Prices and Income on Household Expenditures', *Bulletin of the International Institute of Statistics*, no. 2, vol. 36 (1960).

HUDEC, ROBERT, *The GATT Legal System and World Trade Diplomacy* (New York, 1975).

JACK, D. T., *Studies in Economic Warfare* (New York, 1941).

JACKSON, JOHN H., *World Trade and the Law of GATT* (Indianapolis, 1969).

JACOBSON, COX (ed.), *The Anatomy of Influence* (New Haven, Conn., 1973).

JESSUP, PHILIP, 'Neutrality—Its History, Economics and Law', in *Today and Tomorrow*, Vol. IV (New York, 1936).

JOHNSON, HARRY, *Aspects of the Theory of Tariffs* (Cambridge, 1972).

JOURDAIN, ANNE, 'Les Relations commerciales internationales textiles de la Communauté économique européenne', PhD thesis, University of Paris (1981).

KAJA, HELMUT, *Neutralität and europäische Integration*, Archiv des Völkerrechts, III. Band (1963).

KATZENSTEIN, PETER J., *Economic Dependency and Political Autonomy: The Small European States in the International Economy*, Cornell University, mimeo (1978).

—— *Between Power and Plenty* (Madison, Wis., 1978).

—— 'International Relations and Domestic Structures: Foreign Economic Policies of Advanced Industrial States', *International Organization*, vol. 30 (1976).

KEESING, DONALD and WOLF, MARTIN, *Textile Quotas against Developing Countries*, Thames Essay No. 23 (London, 1980).

—— 'Questions on International Trade in Textiles and Clothing', *The World Economy*, vol. 4, no. 1 (1981).

KEOHANE, ROBERT and NYE, JOSEPH, *Transnational Relations and World Politics* (Cambridge, Mass., 1970).
—— *Power and Interdependence* (Boston, Mass., 1977).
KEYNES, JOHN MAYNARD, 'National Self-Sufficiency', *Yale Review* (1933).
—— *General Theory of Employment, Interest and Money* (London, 1936).
KIERZKOWSKI, HENRYK, and SAMPSON, GARY, 'The Multi-Fibre Arrangement: The Approach and Setting to the Forthcoming Negotiations', *Aussenwirtschaft*, 36 (1981).
KINDLEBERGER, CHARLES P., *International Economics* (Homewood, Ill., 1978).
—— *The World in Depression, 1929–1939* (Berkeley Calif., 1973).
KLEBERG, OLOF, et al., *Är Svensk Neutralitet Möjlig?* (Stockholm, 1977).
KNORR, KLAUS, and TRAGER, FRANK, *Economic Issues and National Security*, National Security Education Programme (Lawrence, Kan., 1977).
KOBLIK, STEVEN (ed.), *Sweden's Development from Poverty to Affluence, 1750–1970* (Minneapolis, 1975).
KOCK, KARIN, *International Trade Policy and the GATT 1947–67* (Stockholm, 1969).
KRASNER, STEPHEN, *Defending the National Interest: Raw Materials Investment and U.S. Foreign Policy* (Princeton, NJ, 1978).
KRAUSS, MELVYN B., *The New Protectionism* (New York, 1978).
KRAVIS, IRVING, *Domestic Interests and International Obligations* (Westport, Conn., 1975).
KREUGER, ANNE, 'The Political Economy of the Rent-Seeking Society', *American Economic Review*, 64 (1974).
LAL, DEEPAK, *Resurrection of the Pauper Labour Argument* (London, 1981).
LINDBECK, ASSAR, *Swedish Economic Policy* (London, 1975).
LISEIN-NORMAN, M., 'Le Dépendance économique de la Suède à l'égard de l'Europe occidentale', *Revue Marché Commun.*, 177 (Sept. 1974).
LIST, FRIEDRICH, *Das nationale System der politischen Ökonomie* (Tübingen and Stuttgart, 1841).
LYON, PETER, *Neutralism* (Leicester, 1963).
MACCULLOCH, A., *Discourse on the Rise, Progress, Peculiar Objects and Importance of Political Economy* (Edinburgh, 1824).
—— *Principles of Political Economy* (Edinburgh, 1825).
MAIZELS, ALFRED, *Industrial Growth and World Trade: An Empirical Study of Trends in Production, Consumption and Trade in Manufactures from 1899 to 1959 with a Discussion of Probable Future Trends* (Cambridge, 1963).

MÅNSSON, OLLE, *Industriell beredskap om ekonomisk försvarsplanering inför andra världskriget* (Stockholm, 1976).

MARTIN, ANDREW, 'The Dynamics of Change in a Keynesian Political Economy: The Swedish Case and Its Implications', in Colin Crouch (ed.), *State and Economy in Contemporary Capitalism* (London, 1979).

MARTIN, LAWRENCE, *Neutralism and Nonalignment—The New States in World Affairs* (New York, 1962).

MATES, LEO, *Nonalignment, Theory and Current Research* (New York, 1972).

MAYALL, JAMES (ed.), *The Community of States* (London, 1982).

MAYER, WOLFGANG, 'The National Defense Tariff Argument Reconsidered', *Journal of International Economics*, 7 (1977).

MEDLICOTT, W. N., *The Economic Blockade*, I, and *Documents on German Foreign Policy*, VIII (London, 1952).

MERCIAI, PATRIZIO, 'Safeguard Measures in GATT', *Journal of World Trade Law* (Jan./Feb. 1981).

MILL, JAMES, *Commerce Defended. An Answer to the Arguments by which Mr. Spence, Mr. Cobbett and Others Have Attempted to Prove that Commerce is not a Source of National Wealth* (1807).

MUNN, THOMAS, *England's Treasure by Foreign Trade* (London, 1664: 2nd edn. 1669).

MYRDAL, ALVA, *Jämlikhet* (Stockholm, 1969).

MYRDAL, GUNNAR, 'Ett Misslyckande på Fyrtiotalet', unpublished memoirs (1980).

—— 'The Reconstruction of World Trade and Swedish Trade Policy', *Svenska Handelsbankens Index* (Stockholm, 1946).

NELSON, DOUGLAS, R., 'The Political Structure of the New Protectionism', World Bank Staff Working Paper No. 471 (July 1981).

OHLIN, BERTIL, *Utrikeshandel och Handelspolitik* (Stockholm, 1959).

OHLIN, GÖRAN, 'Adjustment Assistance in Sweden', in OECD, Development Centre, *Adjustment for Trade* (Paris, 1975).

OHLSSON, LENNERT, *Sweden's Specialization in Typical LDC Industries and Its Recent Intervention Policies* (Stockholm, 1980).

OLSON, MANCUR, *The Logic of Collective Action* (Cambridge, Mass., 1971).

ÖRVIK, NILS, *The Decline of Neutrality, 1914–1941* (London, 1971).

PETTERSSON, LENNART, *Det sårbara samhället* (Stockholm, 1977).

ROBBINS, LIONEL, *The Economic Basis of Class Conflict* (London, 1939).

—— 'Economic Readiness for War', *The Royal Engineers Journal* (June 1929).

ROBINSON, JOAN, *The New Mercantilism* (Cambridge, 1966).

ROLL, ERIC, *A History of Economic Thought* (London, 1938; 4th edn., 1973).

ROTHSTEIN, ROBERT L., 'Alignment, Neutrality, and Small Powers: 1945–1965', *International Organization*, vol. 20, no. 3 (1966).

RUGGIE, JOHN GERARD, 'International Regimes, Transactions, and Change: Embedded Liberalism in the Postwar Economic Order', *International Organization*, 36, 2 (Spring 1982).

SALIB, M., 'The GATT Multi-Fibre Arrangement and International Trade in Natural Fibre Textile Production', *COMITEXTIL*, *Bulletin*, 78/1 (1978).

SARNA, A., 'Safeguards against Market Disruption—The Canadian View', *Journal of World Trade Law*, vol. 10, no. 4 (1976).

SILBERNER, EDMUND, *The Problem of War in Nineteenth Century Economic Thought* (Princeton, NJ, 1946).

SMITH, ADAM, *The Wealth of Nations*, Cannon edn., Vol. 1 (London, 1930).

SRAFFA, P. (ed.), *The Works of David Ricardo* (London, 1951).

STONE, JULIUS, *Legal Controls of International Conflict* (New York, 1954).

SVENNILSON, INGVAR, *Perspektiv på Västeuropas Utveckling, 1955–75* (Stockholm, 1959).

Svenska Handelsbankens Index, 'Sweden and the Marshall Plan' (Stockholm, 1949).

TORRE, JOSÉ DE LA, 'Public Intervention Strategies in the European Clothing Industries', *Journal of World Trade Law*, vol. 15, no. 2 (1981).

TUCKER, ROBERT W., *The Law of War and Neutrality at Sea* (Washington, DC, 1957).

TUMLIR, JAN, 'Emergency Action against Sharp Increases in Imports', in Hugh Corbet and Robert Jackson (edd.), *In Search of a New World Economic Order* (London, 1979).

VASILYEV, P., 'USSR and Sweden (Development of Mutual Relations)', *International Affairs* (Moscow, 1976).

VERNON, RAYMOND, *Big Business and the State* (London, 1974).

WALLENSTEEN, IVAR, 'Återblick på 1946 års svensk-ryska kreditavtal', *Svenska Tidskrift*, vol. 40 (1953).

WHIDDEN, HOWARD P., *Preferences and Discriminations in International Trade*, Committee on International Economic Policy in Cooperation with the Carnegie Endowment for International Peace (1945).

WHITING, ALAN (ed.), *The Economics of Industrial Subsidies* (London, 1976).

WOLF, MARTIN, *Adjustment Policies and Problems in Developed Countries*, Staff Working Paper No. 349 (Washington, DC, 1979).

YOFFIE, D., *Power and Protectionism* (New York, 1983).

Index

Compiled by Jackie McDermott